A Sterling Collection

THE BEST OF THE JUNIOR LEAGUE OF MEMPHIS

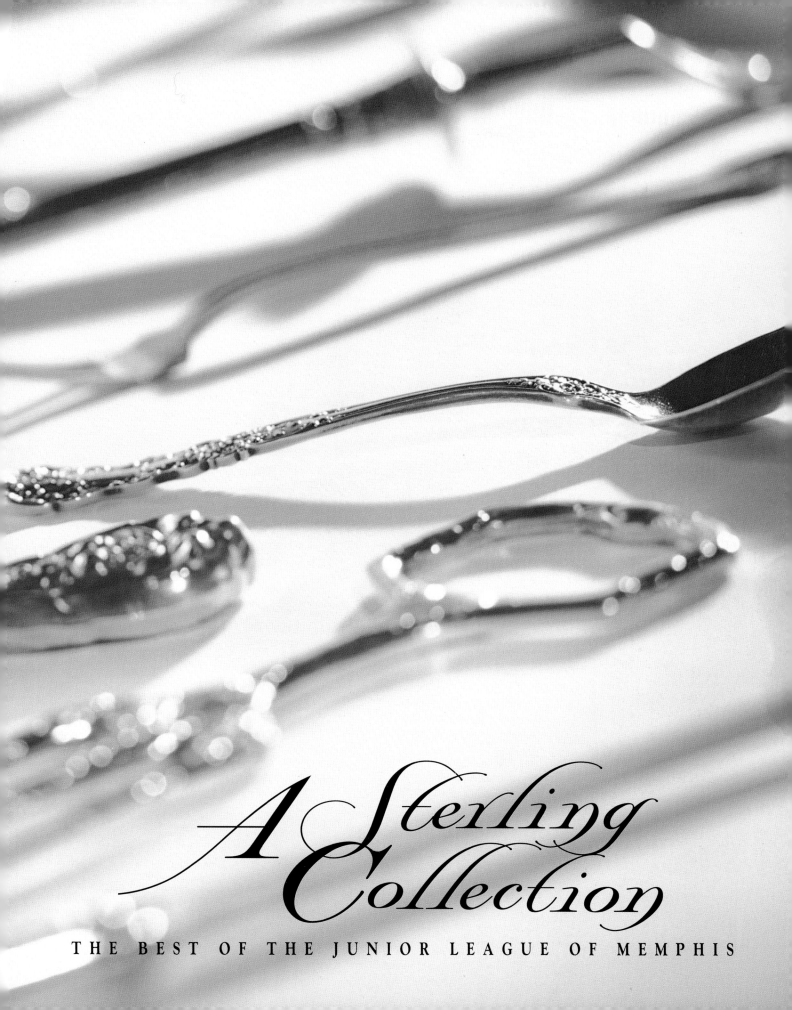

A Sterling Collection

THE BEST OF THE JUNIOR LEAGUE OF MEMPHIS

A Sterling Collection

CO-EDITORS: Gwynne Barton, Lili Jones
EDITORIAL COORDINATOR: Margaret Killebrew
SUSTAINING EDITOR: Helen Hays
PHOTOGRAPHER AND PHOTO STYLIST: Troy Glasgow

Cookbook Committee

Eileen Adams
Kim Blankenship
Anita Burkett
Cynthia Cross
Jennifer Danehy
Barbara Fitzgerald
Elaine Hare

Martha Hester
Julie Maroda
Laurel Mathews
Beth Ploch
Kitty Stimson
Evelyn Walker
Holly Walters

Throughout *A Sterling Collection*
our previous cookbooks will be denoted by the symbols
representing them shown on the guide below.

THE MEMPHIS
COOKBOOK

PARTY
POTPOURRI

A MAN'S TASTE

HEART & SOUL

A Sterling Collection
THE BEST OF THE JUNIOR LEAGUE OF MEMPHIS

Copyright © 2000 by
The Junior League of Memphis
3475 Central Avenue
Memphis, Tennessee 38111
901-452-2151

LIBRARY OF CONGRESS CATALOG NUMBER: 00-131127
ISBN: 0-9604222-5-0

Edited, Designed and Manufactured by
Favorite Recipes® Press
an imprint of

FRP

P.O. Box 305142, Nashville, Tennessee 37230
800-358-0560

ART DIRECTION: Steve Newman
BOOK DESIGN: Dave Malone and Pam Cole
PROJECT MANAGER: Linda A. Jones
EDITOR: Jane Hinshaw

Manufactured in the United States of America
First Printing: 2000   15,000 copies

"Heart & Soul" Copyright © 1938, 1956
Famous Music Corporation
AUTHORS: Frank Loesser and Hoagy Carmichael

Introduction

"Make new friends, but keep the old; one is silver and the other gold." And so it goes with cookbooks and recipes. Every cook has his or her favorite recipe. In fact, a cookbook will often open automatically to that specific page.

As we reviewed our collection of cookbooks, we found an abundance of marvelous recipes. There were a great number of favorites and many recipes that were "the best." In fact, there were so many sterling recipes that we thought it was time to bring these favorites together in a new collection, *A Sterling Collection: The Best of the Junior League of Memphis*.

The Junior League of Memphis has an extraordinary library of cookbooks, and these were our source of inspiration. Our first cookbook was published in 1952. It was titled, simply, *The Memphis Cookbook*. It is the second-oldest community cookbook still in print and has sold more than 274,000 copies. It is a fabulous collection of authentic southern recipes handed down through generations of good southern cooks, and offers a glimpse into the way the 50's generation cooked and entertained.

Party Potpourri is a direct descendant of *The Memphis Cookbook*. Printed in 1971, it was an instant success. Known as an outstanding entertainment guide, it included a mixture of menus, invitation ideas, party themes, and hostess hints that earned it an induction into the prestigious Southern Living Hall of Fame in 1993.

In 1980, the Junior League of Memphis produced a cookbook that was a little out of the ordinary. *A Man's Taste* is a book about men and cooking—what they do and how they feel in the kitchen. The recipes you would expect to find in a man's cookbook are here, of course, as they should be: barbecue sauces, grilled steaks, and wild game. But there is much more of the unexpected: delicate sauces, cold soups, salads, and even light pastries. It was another fine contribution to the distinguished cookbook-publishing tradition of the Junior League of Memphis.

Time marched forward and the 90's brought a new style of cooking and a more casual style of entertaining. *Heart and Soul* was published in 1992 to rave reviews and was promptly named the National Winner in the Tabasco Cookbook Awards—the equivalent to winning an Oscar in community cookbooks! *Heart and Soul* is an extraordinary cookbook. It is a first-class collection of recipes combined with heartwarming personal touches and a tour of the musical heart and soul that is the center of Memphis.

And now, as we enter a new millennium, we look back at these old friends. These old, gold, friends have paved the way for a new silver collection, *A Sterling Collection*. All of these recipes have been tried and tested and any resemblance between the recipes contained in this book and good things to eat and drink is purely intentional!

Projects founded and cofounded by the Junior League of Memphis

1939	Sight Conservation Program
1947	Speech and Hearing Center*
	Child Guidance Center
1952	Preschool Deaf Nursery
1953	Visiting Nurses Association*
1955	WKNO*
1959	Youth Museum*
1961	Memphis Arts Council*
1966	Community Day Care Association*
	Memphis Guide to Architectural Barriers
	for the Handicapped Handbook*
1971	Memphis House*
1972	Changing Exhibit Area
	Memphis Pink Palace Museum
1975	The Volunteer Center*
1977	Sunset Symphony/Memphis in May*
1978	Opera Memphis/Southern Opera Theater
	Memphis Association for Children with
	Learning Disabilities
1982	Community Board Institute*
1983	Visitors and Information Center*
1984	Senior Citizens' Craft Fair
1985	Parenting Center of Memphis*
1986	Adult Literacy Support Program*
	Martha's Manor
1987	Adolescent Pregnancy Clearinghouse*
1988	Church Health Center – Children's Dental
	Education*
1989	S.M.A.R.T. Summer Camp*
	All About Kids Show*
1990	Children's' Museum of Memphis – Playscape*
1991	Memphis Shelby County Board Bank*
	Junior League of Memphis Community
	Resource Center
1992	*Heart and Soul* Cookbook
1995	Hope House Daycare Centers

*Founded in association with other organizations

The Junior League of Memphis also maintains the Community Assistance Fund for emergency grants and the Sight Conservation Fund, a group that provides eyeglasses for Memphis City schoolchildren who are unable to afford them.

Mission Statement

The Junior League of Memphis is an organization of women committed to promoting voluntarism, developing the potential of women, and improving communities through the effective action and leadership of trained volunteers. Its purpose is exclusively educational and charitable.

More About the JLM

Since its formation in 1922, the spirit and dedication of the Junior League of Memphis has been positively and powerfully affecting our community. As one of the 295 members of American Junior Leagues, International, the membership is comprised of women of all races, religions, and national origins who demonstrate an interest and commitment to voluntarism. Dedicated to the belief that volunteer service is an essential part of responsible citizenship, the Junior League of Memphis sets itself apart as an organization by training its volunteers for effective participation in the community.

With its finger on the pulse of the community, the Junior League of Memphis continually researches the changing needs of the women and children of Memphis. Proposed ideas and/or projects are reviewed annually and are evaluated on the basis of current impact areas and the volunteers and funding required by the proposing organization. Final selections are made when the membership matches the needs of the community with its available resources.

To date, the compassion and dedication of the Junior League of Memphis has resulted in several million dollars of donations and untold millions of volunteer hours to the community.

Contents

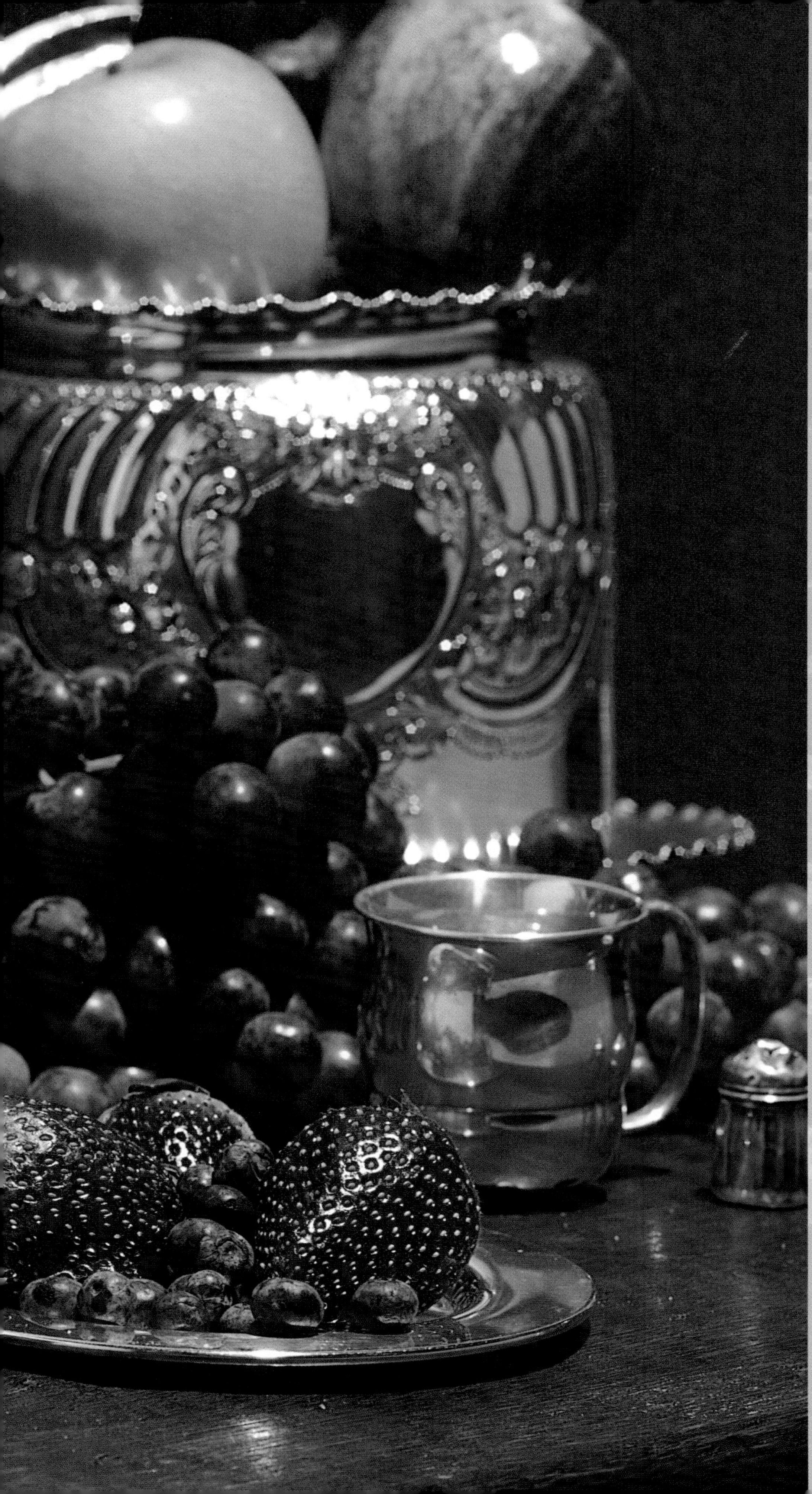

BRILLIANT BEGINNINGS

appetizers · beverages

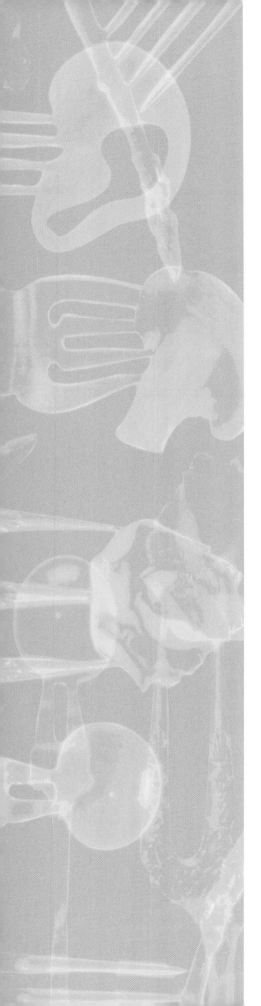

Cocktail Hamburgers

Hamburgers

3 POUNDS LEAN GROUND
    CHUCK
2 EGGS, LIGHTLY BEATEN
1/2 CUP GRATED ONION
1 GREEN BELL PEPPER,
    FINELY CHOPPED
1 TEASPOON SAGE
2 TEASPOONS SALT
1/4 TEASPOON SEASONED
    PEPPER

Hamburger Sauce

1 1/2 CUPS PACKED BROWN
    SUGAR
2 CUPS KETCHUP
2 TEASPOONS NUTMEG
3 TABLESPOONS DRY
    MUSTARD

For the burgers, combine the ground chuck, eggs, onion, bell pepper, sage, salt and pepper in a bowl; mix well with hands. Shape into 1-inch balls and press to flatten. Place in a broiler pan and broil until brown.

For the sauce, combine the brown sugar, ketchup, nutmeg and dry mustard in a saucepan. Simmer for 10 minutes. Add the burgers and cook until heated through.

Serve in a chafing dish with miniature cocktail buns. This is also great for a children's party.

Serves sixteen

Cocktail Meatballs

1 1/2 POUNDS GROUND
    CHUCK
SALT AND PEPPER
    TO TASTE
VEGETABLE OIL FOR
    BROWNING
1 (12-OUNCE) BOTTLE
    CHILI SAUCE
1 (12-OUNCE) JAR RED
    CURRANT JELLY

Season the ground chuck with salt and pepper and shape into 1-inch balls. Brown in a small amount of oil in a skillet; drain. Combine the chili sauce and jelly in a saucepan. Cook until the jelly melts, stirring to mix well. Add the meatballs. Simmer until the sauce thickens. Spoon into a chafing dish to serve.

Sausage may be substituted for the ground chuck. The meatballs may be made in advance and frozen until needed.

Makes forty to forty-five

Spicy Chicken On Pita Wedges

1 WHOLE MEDIUM CHICKEN
   BREAST
1/2 CUP WATER
LEMON PEPPER TO TASTE
12 OUNCES CREAM
   CHEESE, SOFTENED
1 1/2 CUPS (6 OUNCES)
   SHREDDED CHEDDAR
   CHEESE OR MONTEREY
   JACK CHEESE
1/4 CUP SOUR CREAM
1/4 CUP CHOPPED RED
   ONION
3 GREEN ONIONS, SLICED
1 TO 3 TABLESPOONS
   CHOPPED PICKLED
   JALAPEÑO PEPPERS
2 GARLIC CLOVES,
   MINCED
1 TEASPOON GROUND
   CUMIN
1 TEASPOON CHILI
   POWDER
1/2 TEASPOON GROUND
   CORIANDER
SALT AND PEPPER
   TO TASTE
4 PITA ROUNDS

Garnish

SLICED BLACK OLIVES
SLICED GREEN ONIONS
SHREDDED CHEDDAR
   CHEESE OR MONTEREY
   JACK CHEESE

Combine the chicken with the water and lemon pepper in a heavy 2-quart saucepan. Bring to a boil and reduce the heat. Cook, covered, until the chicken is tender; drain and cool. Chop the cooled chicken into small pieces, discarding the skin and bones.

Combine the chicken, cream cheese, Cheddar cheese, sour cream, onion, green onions, jalapeño peppers, garlic, cumin, chili powder, coriander, salt and pepper in a large bowl; mix well.

Split the pita rounds horizontally and place cut side up on a work surface. Spread with the chicken mixture. Cut each round into 8 wedges with a sharp pizza cutter and place the pita rounds on a nonstick baking sheet.

Bake at 375 degrees for 5 to 7 minutes or until the chicken mixture is bubbly.

Garnish with olives, green onions and cheese. Serve immediately.

The chicken mixture freezes well, making this a great fix-ahead hors d'oeuvre. Thaw in the refrigerator, spread the mixture on the pita rounds and bake at serving time.

Makes sixty-four

appetizers · beverages

Sausage Stroganoff

1 GARLIC CLOVE,
    CUT INTO HALVES
2 POUNDS BULK COUNTRY
    SAUSAGE
3 TABLESPOONS FLOUR
2 CUPS MILK
2 LARGE ONIONS,
    CHOPPED
1 (16-OUNCE) CAN
    MUSHROOMS
1/4 CUP (1/2 STICK) BUTTER
2 TEASPOONS SOY SAUCE
2 TABLESPOONS
    WORCESTERSHIRE
    SAUCE
PAPRIKA, SALT AND
    PEPPER TO TASTE
2 CUPS SOUR CREAM

Rub a large skillet with the cut sides of the garlic and heat the skillet. Add the sausage and sauté until brown and crumbly; drain. Sprinkle with the flour. Add the milk and simmer until slightly thickened, stirring constantly.

Sauté the onions and mushrooms in the butter in a skillet. Add to the sausage mixture. Add the soy sauce, Worcestershire sauce, paprika, salt and pepper and mix well. Cook until bubbly. Stir in the sour cream.

Serve in a chafing dish as a dip or spoon onto biscuits or pastry shells.

The mixture can be made in advance and frozen, omitting the sour cream. Reheat and add the sour cream to serve. Spoon over rice to serve 6 as a main dish.

Serves twelve

Crab-Stuffed Cocktail Tomatoes

8 OUNCES COOKED
    CRAB MEAT
1/2 CUP FINELY CHOPPED
    CELERY
1/4 CUP GRATED ONION
SALT AND PEPPER
    TO TASTE
MAYONNAISE
40 CHERRY TOMATOES

Garnish

PARSLEY SPRIGS

Pick over the crab meat, discarding any bits of shell. Combine with the celery, onion, salt and pepper in a bowl and mix well. Add enough mayonnaise to bind. Cut the tops from the cherry tomatoes; remove and discard the pulp. Spoon or pipe the crab meat mixture into the tomatoes. Arrange on a serving tray and garnish with parsley.

You may substitute tuna salad, chicken salad or seasoned cream cheese for the crab meat mixture.

Makes forty

CRAB MEAT JUSTINE

4 TOAST SQUARES
1 CUP FRESH LUMP
  CRAB MEAT
1/4 CUP (1/2 STICK) BUTTER,
  MELTED
2 TABLESPOONS SHERRY
1/2 TABLESPOON LEMON
  JUICE
TABASCO SAUCE
  TO TASTE
1 1/2 CUPS HOLLANDAISE
  SAUCE

 Arrange the toast squares in individual baking dishes. Combine the crab meat, butter, sherry, lemon juice and Tabasco sauce in a saucepan. Cook until heated through, stirring constantly. Spoon onto the toast squares and top with the hollandaise sauce. Place on a rack in a broiler pan. Broil until light brown. Serve immediately.

Serves four

SHRIMP REMOULADE

1/2 CUP VINEGAR
1 CUP OLIVE OIL
6 TABLESPOONS CREOLE
  MUSTARD
10 SPRIGS OF FRESH
  PARSLEY
1/4 CUP (ABOUT 3 OUNCES)
  ANCHOVY PASTE
1 TABLESPOON
  HORSERADISH
2 BUNCHES SHALLOTS
6 SMALL RIBS CELERY,
  CHOPPED
4 OR 5 DROPS OF TABASCO
  SAUCE
1 TEASPOON PAPRIKA
1 LARGE HEAD LETTUCE,
  SHREDDED
3 POUNDS PEELED COOKED
  SHRIMP, CHILLED

Process the vinegar and olive oil in a blender until smooth. Add the Creole mustard, parsley, anchovy paste, horseradish, shallots, celery, Tabasco sauce and paprika and process until smooth. Chill in an airtight container for 8 hours or longer.

Place the lettuce on serving plates and arrange the shrimp on the lettuce. Spoon the sauce over the top.

This will also serve 6 as a main course for a light supper or luncheon.

Serves ten

Anyone over the age of thirty will fondly remember Justine's as the finest and most elegant restaurant in Memphis. It was "the" place to celebrate an anniversary, birthday, or other special occasion. Countless young couples became engaged in the main dining room under a chandelier once owned by one of Napoleon's generals. Justine's was the ultimate in every respect; it won't be forgotten.

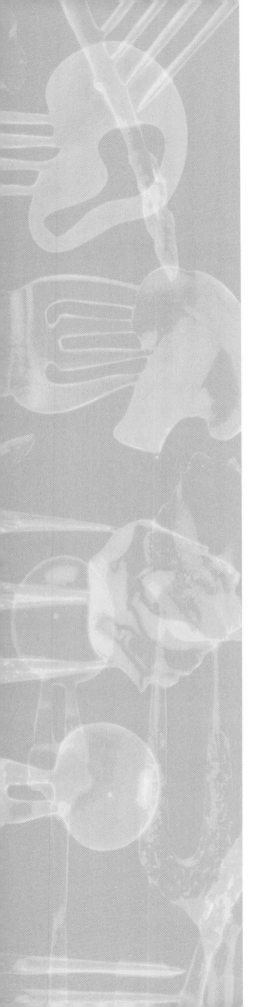

PICKLED SHRIMP

3 POUNDS PEELED COOKED
   SHRIMP
2 SMALL ONIONS, THINLY
   SLICED INTO RINGS
2 GARLIC CLOVES,
   CRUSHED
6 TABLESPOONS WINE
   VINEGAR
1/2 CUP WINE
1/2 CUP OLIVE OIL
2 TEASPOONS DRY
   MUSTARD
3 BAY LEAVES
2 TEASPOONS SALT
1 TABLESPOON WHOLE
   PEPPERCORNS

Combine the shrimp, onions and garlic in a bowl. Add the vinegar, wine, olive oil, dry mustard, bay leaves, salt and peppercorns and mix well. Marinate, covered, in the refrigerator for 8 hours or longer. Discard the bay leaves before serving.

Serve any leftovers in a chef's salad the next day.

Serves sixteen

SUNBURST ARTICHOKE

1 LARGE FRESH ARTICHOKE
1 CUP MAYONNAISE
1 TEASPOON
   WORCESTERSHIRE
   SAUCE
2 TEASPOONS DRY
   MUSTARD
3 HARD-COOKED EGGS,
   CUT INTO WEDGES
1 BUNCH PARSLEY

Cook the artichoke in water to cover in a saucepan for 30 minutes; drain. Chill in the refrigerator. Pull off the leaves and trim off the pointed ends.

Combine the mayonnaise, Worcestershire sauce and dry mustard in a bowl and mix until smooth. Spoon onto the base ends of the artichoke leaves and top each with an egg wedge. Arrange in a sunburst pattern on a serving tray. Place the parsley in the center of the tray.

You may substitute Curry Dip Britton (page 26) and a tiny cooked shrimp for the mayonnaise mixture.

Serves eight

Asparagus Foldovers

3 (16-OUNCE) CANS GREEN
    ASPARAGUS SPEARS
3 LOAVES SANDWICH
    BREAD
BUTTER
GRATED PARMESAN
    CHEESE

Drain the asparagus and place on paper towels to absorb any excess moisture. Trim the crusts from the bread and roll each slice flat between waxed paper. Spread with softened butter and sprinkle with cheese. Place 1 asparagus spear on the corner of each bread slice and roll to enclose the asparagus; secure with wooden picks.

Arrange on a baking sheet; brush with melted butter and sprinkle with additional cheese. Bake at 400 degrees for 10 to 12 minutes or until golden brown and heated through. Serve immediately.

You may prepare the rolls a day in advance and chill until time to bake. This recipe also works well with blanched fresh asparagus.

Makes six dozen

Bacon-Wrapped Water Chestnuts

2 (10-OUNCE) CANS WATER
    CHESTNUTS
1 (5-OUNCE) BOTTLE SOY
    SAUCE
SUGAR
1 POUND BACON SLICES,
    CUT CROSSWISE INTO
    HALVES

Drain the water chestnuts and combine with the soy sauce in a bowl. Marinate for 3 hours or longer, stirring frequently. Drain the water chestnuts and roll in sugar, coating well. Wrap each water chestnut in $1/2$ slice bacon and secure with a wooden pick; do not stretch the bacon.

Arrange on a baking sheet. Bake at 400 degrees for 15 to 20 minutes or until the bacon is partially crisp. Serve hot.

You may prepare these in advance and bake at serving time. You may substitute chicken livers for the water chestnuts.

Makes three dozen

Fried Dill Pickles

A number of years ago, a notable cook in Hollywood, Mississippi, concocted a fried dill pickle on a whim. He tinkered with the seasonings and batter ingredients until he got it just right. It has since become a favorite of folks throughout the mid-South. Unfortunately his Hollywood Plantation Cafe got in the way of casino progress, and the original pickle is no longer available.

FRIED DILL PICKLES

1/2 CUP FLOUR
1/4 CUP BEER
3 DASHES OF TABASCO
   SAUCE
1 TABLESPOON PAPRIKA
2 TEASPOONS GARLIC
   SALT
1 TEASPOON SALT
1 TABLESPOON CAYENNE
   PEPPER
1 TABLESPOON BLACK
   PEPPER
VEGETABLE OIL FOR
   DEEP-FRYING
5 DILL PICKLES, SLICED
   1/8 INCH THICK

Combine the flour, beer, Tabasco sauce, paprika, garlic salt, salt, cayenne pepper and black pepper in a bowl and mix well.

Heat the oil to 375 degrees in a deep fryer or electric skillet. Dip the pickle slices into the batter and fry in the heated oil for 4 minutes or until the pickles float to the surface of the oil; drain well.

Serves ten

GARLIC PICKLES

25 LARGE SOUR PICKLES,
   SLICED 1/4 INCH THICK
5 POUNDS SUGAR
1 PACKAGE PICKLING
   SPICE
5 GARLIC CLOVES
2 CUPS TARRAGON
   VINEGAR
1 CUP OLIVE OIL OR
   VEGETABLE OIL

Layer the pickle slices in a crock, sprinkling each layer with the sugar and pickling spice. Add the garlic. Let stand for 3 days, stirring occasionally with a wooden spoon. Add the vinegar and oil, mixing well. Let stand for 10 days longer. Spoon into jars and seal.

Makes ten to twelve pints

Mushrooms Stuffed With Spinach

12 LARGE MUSHROOMS
1 GARLIC CLOVE
3 TABLESPOONS BUTTER
1 (10-OUNCE) PACKAGE
   FROZEN CHOPPED
   SPINACH
3 TABLESPOONS
   MAYONNAISE
3 TABLESPOONS GRATED
   PARMESAN CHEESE
JUICE OF 1 LEMON
1/2 TEASPOON
   WORCESTERSHIRE SAUCE
TABASCO SAUCE TO TASTE
1 TEASPOON SEASONED
   SALT

Remove the stems from the mushrooms. Wipe the mushroom caps with a damp cloth. Sauté the garlic in the butter in a skillet. Dip the mushroom caps into the butter and arrange rounded side down in a buttered shallow baking dish.

Cook the spinach using the package directions; drain. Add the mayonnaise, cheese, lemon juice, Worcestershire sauce, Tabasco sauce and seasoned salt; mix well.

Spoon the spinach mixture into the mushroom caps. Bake at 350 degrees for 20 minutes or until heated through.

Serves six

Mamma Mia Crostini

1 MEDIUM EGGPLANT,
   PEELED, CHOPPED
1 TEASPOON SALT
3 TABLESPOONS CHOPPED
   FRESH BASIL
1 TABLESPOON MINCED
   GARLIC
1/4 CUP OLIVE OIL
PEPPER TO TASTE
1 BAGUETTE, SLICED 1/4
   INCH THICK
1/2 CUP PREPARED PESTO
1 (7-OUNCE) JAR ROASTED
   RED BELL PEPPERS, THINLY
   SLICED
1 CUP (4 OUNCES)
   SHREDDED PROVOLONE
   CHEESE
1/2 CUP (2 OUNCES)
   CRUMBLED FETA CHEESE

Spread the eggplant on paper towels and sprinkle with the salt. Let stand for 30 to 45 minutes. Pat firmly to remove the excess moisture. Sauté the eggplant, basil and garlic in the olive oil in a 10-inch skillet over medium heat for 10 minutes or until the eggplant is tender and beginning to brown. Season with pepper.

Spread the bread slices with the pesto and top with 2 teaspoons of the eggplant mixture. Arrange 2 slices of roasted bell pepper in an X over the tops and sprinkle with the cheeses.

Place on a baking sheet. Broil for 4 minutes or until the cheeses melt. Serve immediately. You may use 1 tablespoon crushed dried basil instead of the fresh basil.

Makes thirty

Lily Sandwiches

18 SLICES WHITE BREAD
1/4 CUP (1/2 STICK) BUTTER, SOFTENED
1 (51/2-OUNCE) CAN BONELESS CHICKEN
1/2 CUP FINELY CHOPPED CELERY
1 TEASPOON GRATED ONION
1/4 TEASPOON DRIED TARRAGON LEAVES
1/4 CUP MAYONNAISE
1/4 TEASPOON SALT
1/8 TEASPOON PEPPER
CHOPPED PARSLEY
18 THIN (1-INCH-LONG) CARROT STICKS

 Trim the bread and roll to flatten; cut into 2 1/2-inch squares. Spread with the butter. Shape into lilies by rolling in cornucopia fashion, overlapping 2 adjacent sides and securing with wooden picks.

Drain and chop the chicken. Combine with the celery, onion, tarragon, mayonnaise, salt and pepper in a bowl and mix well. Spoon into the bread lilies. Arrange close together on a tray and cover with plastic wrap. Chill for 1 hour or longer.

Remove the wooden picks and sprinkle with parsley. Insert 1 carrot stick into each lily for the stamen.

You may substitute flour tortillas for the bread.

Makes eighteen

Parsley And Bacon Sandwich Roll-Ups

2 BUNCHES PARSLEY OR WATERCRESS, CHOPPED
WORCESTERSHIRE SAUCE TO TASTE
1 POUND BACON, CRISP-FRIED, CRUMBLED
MAYONNAISE
GARLIC POWDER TO TASTE
BUTTER, SOFTENED
1 LOAF FRESH SANDWICH BREAD
SLICED CHERRY TOMATOES

Combine the parsley, Worcestershire sauce and bacon with enough mayonnaise to make of spreading consistency in a bowl and mix well. Blend garlic powder with butter in a bowl.

Trim the crusts from the bread and roll lightly to flatten. Spread with the garlic butter and then with the parsley mixture. Roll the bread to enclose the filling. Wrap in waxed paper and freeze until firm.

Cut each roll into 4 slices and arrange with the cut side down on a serving plate. Top each with a cherry tomato slice. Roll-ups will thaw quickly.

You may also spread this on melba toast rounds or use to fill sandwiches and cut into finger shapes or triangles.

Makes nine dozen

Black Bean Pinwheels Olé

¾ CUP COOKED BLACK
    BEANS
3 OUNCES CREAM
    CHEESE, SOFTENED
2 TEASPOONS FINELY
    CHOPPED JALAPEÑO
    PEPPER
8 (6-INCH) FLOUR
    TORTILLAS
1 CUP (4 OUNCES)
    SHREDDED CHEDDAR
    CHEESE
½ MEDIUM RED BELL
    PEPPER, FINELY CHOPPED
4 GREEN ONIONS, SLICED

Garnish

SALSA OR GUACAMOLE

Mash ½ cup of the beans in a medium bowl. Add the remaining ¼ cup beans, cream cheese and jalapeño pepper and mix well.

Spread the bean mixture on the tortillas. Sprinkle with the cheese, red bell pepper and green onions. Roll the tortillas to enclose the filling and wrap with plastic wrap.

Chill in the refrigerator for 2 to 8 hours. Slice ½ to ¾ inch thick and place cut side up on a serving platter. Garnish with salsa or guacamole.

To reduce the fat content, substitute Neufchâtel cheese for the cream cheese and use low-fat Cheddar cheese.

Makes fifty-six

Watercress Sandwiches

18 SLICES FRESH WHITE
    BREAD
2 TABLESPOONS BUTTER,
    SOFTENED
3 OUNCES CREAM CHEESE,
    SOFTENED
1 TEASPOON LEMON JUICE
⅓ CUP SOUR CREAM
1 TEASPOON MINCED
    CHIVES
WORCESTERSHIRE SAUCE
    TO TASTE
SALT TO TASTE
1 CUP LIGHTLY PACKED
    MINCED WATERCRESS

Garnish

SPRIGS OF WATERCRESS

Trim the crusts from the bread and roll to flatten. Spread with the butter. Combine the cream cheese, lemon juice, sour cream, chives, Worcestershire sauce and salt in a bowl and mix well. Stir in the minced watercress. Spread on the bread slices. Roll the bread to enclose the filling and arrange seam side down in a shallow dish.

Chill, covered, for 1 hour or longer. Slice each roll into halves. Arrange cut side down on a serving tray and insert a sprig of watercress into each piece for garnish. Arrange additional sprigs of watercress around the tray.

Makes thirty-six

Decorative Ideas

For *Frosted Grapes*, separate the grapes into small clusters and wash and dry well. Brush with lightly beaten egg whites and roll in sugar. Place on a wire rack and let stand for 1 hour to dry.

For *Decorative Serving Containers*, scoop out acorn squash, cabbage, lettuce, pumpkins, or bell peppers and fill with dips and spreads.

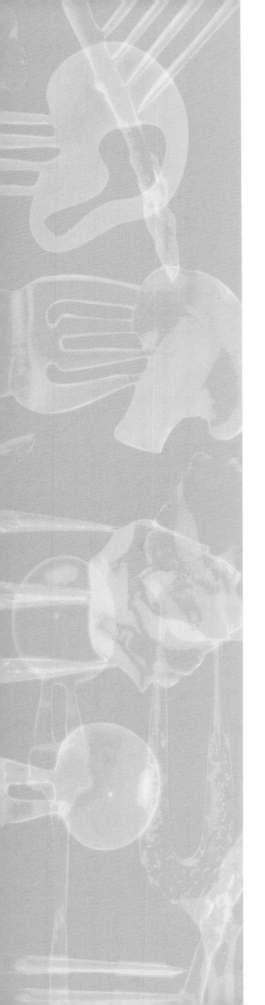

Bleu Cheese Wafers

2 CUPS (8 OUNCES)
   CRUMBLED BLEU
   CHEESE
1 CUP (2 STICKS) BUTTER
   OR MARGARINE
1¹/2 CUPS FLOUR
1 TEASPOON DRY
   MUSTARD
¹/4 TEASPOON SALT
1 EGG, LIGHTLY BEATEN
1 TEASPOON WATER
1 CUP CHOPPED PECANS

Combine the bleu cheese and butter in a food processor container or mixing bowl; process or mix until smooth. Add the flour, dry mustard and salt and mix well.

Divide into 2 equal portions and shape each into a roll 1¹/2 inches in diameter. Brush with a mixture of the egg and water and roll in the pecans, pressing the pecans gently to coat well. Wrap in waxed paper and chill for 4 to 24 hours.

Cut into ¹/4-inch slices and place on an ungreased baking sheet. Bake at 400 degrees for 10 minutes or until light brown. Cool on a wire rack and store in an airtight container.

The rolls may be frozen for several weeks. Thaw in the refrigerator before slicing and baking.

Makes four dozen

Cheese Straws

2 CUPS SIFTED FLOUR
1 TEASPOON SALT
¹/2 TEASPOON RED PEPPER
¹/2 CUP (1 STICK) BUTTER,
   SOFTENED
4 CUPS (16 OUNCES)
   SHREDDED SHARP
   CHEDDAR CHEESE

Sift the flour, salt and red pepper together. Beat the butter in a mixing bowl until light. Add the dry ingredients and mix well. Stir in the cheese.

Spoon into a cookie press and pipe into straws on a greased baking sheet. Bake at 400 degrees for 10 minutes. Cool on a wire rack.

You may also roll the dough on a floured surface and cut into strips or cut with a round cutter and top with a nut.

Makes three dozen

CRUMBLY CHEESE CRACKERS

1 CUP (2 STICKS)
   MARGARINE, SOFTENED
2 CUPS FLOUR
RED PEPPER TO TASTE
2 CUPS CRISP RICE CEREAL
2 CUPS (8 OUNCES)
   SHREDDED SHARP
   CHEDDAR CHEESE

Beat the margarine in a mixing bowl until light. Add the flour and red pepper and mix until smooth. Add the cereal and cheese and mix well. Shape into small balls and place on a baking sheet; press with a fork to flatten slightly. Bake at 375 degrees for 10 to 12 minutes or until golden brown. Cool on a wire rack and store in an airtight container.

Makes fifty

CURRIED CREAM CHEESE AND CHUTNEY SPREAD

8 OUNCES CREAM CHEESE,
   SOFTENED
2 TABLESPOONS CREAM
SEVERAL DROPS OF
   GARLIC JUICE
1 TEASPOON
   WORCESTERSHIRE
   SAUCE
TABASCO SAUCE
   TO TASTE
1 TEASPOON CURRY
   POWDER
SALT TO TASTE
1/4 CUP FINELY CHOPPED
   CHUTNEY

Beat the cream cheese with the cream in a mixing bowl until smooth. Add the garlic juice, Worcestershire sauce, Tabasco sauce, curry powder and salt and mix well. Stir in the chutney. Spread on crackers or spoon into a serving bowl or mold and serve with crackers.

Serves six

GOAT CHEESE TORTA

16 OUNCES CREAM CHEESE,
    SOFTENED
7 TO 8 OUNCES MILD
    GOAT CHEESE
2 GARLIC CLOVES, MINCED
4 TEASPOONS CHOPPED
    FRESH OREGANO
1/8 TEASPOON FRESHLY
    GROUND PEPPER
1/4 CUP PREPARED PESTO
1/2 CUP OIL-PACK
    SUN-DRIED TOMATOES

Garnish

RESERVED SUN-DRIED
    TOMATO STRIPS
1 TO 2 TABLESPOONS
    SLIVERED ALMONDS,
    TOASTED
SPRIG OF FRESH OREGANO
    OR PARSLEY

Combine the cream cheese, goat cheese, garlic, oregano and pepper in a food processor container or large mixing bowl. Process or beat until smooth. Spread 1/3 of the mixture in a 1-quart loaf pan or soufflé pan lined with plastic wrap. Spread the pesto evenly over the top. Spread 1/3 of the remaining cream cheese mixture over the pesto.

Drain the sun-dried tomatoes; cut 1 tomato into thin strips and reserve for garnish. Chop the remaining sun-dried tomatoes. Spread evenly over the layers in the pan and top with the remaining cream cheese mixture. Cover with plastic wrap and press lightly to compress the layers. Chill for several hours.

Invert the torta onto a serving plate and remove the plastic wrap. Garnish with the reserved sun-dried tomato strips, toasted almonds and oregano sprig. Serve with stone-ground wheat crackers or thin baguette slices.

Serves twelve to sixteen

WALNUT-GLAZED BRIE

2/3 CUP FINELY CHOPPED
    WALNUTS
1/4 CUP COFFEE LIQUEUR
3 TABLESPOONS BROWN
    SUGAR
1/2 TEASPOON VANILLA
    EXTRACT
1 (14-OUNCE) ROUND BRIE
    CHEESE

Spread the walnuts in a pie plate or in an 8×8-inch baking pan. Toast at 350 degrees for 10 to 12 minutes or until light brown, stirring occasionally. Remove from the oven and stir in the liqueur, brown sugar and vanilla.

Reduce the oven temperature to 325 degrees. Remove the top rind of the cheese and place the cheese round in a shallow baking dish. Spread the walnut mixture over the top. Bake for 8 to 10 minutes or until the cheese is heated through and soft. Serve immediately with crackers and pear slices.

Serves twelve to fifteen

PALACE CHEESECAKE

6 STONE-GROUND WHEAT
   CRACKERS, CRUSHED
16 OUNCES CREAM CHEESE,
   SOFTENED
1 EGG
SALT TO TASTE
10 OIL-PACK SUN-DRIED
   TOMATOES, DRAINED
1 CUP PREPARED PESTO
3/4 CUP SOUR CREAM
1 TEASPOON FLOUR

Garnish

EDIBLE FLOWER PETALS
CHIVES

Sprinkle the cracker crumbs over the bottom of a buttered 7-inch springform pan. Beat the cream cheese in a mixing bowl until light. Add the egg and salt and beat at low speed just until mixed. Chop the sun-dried tomatoes in a food processor. Add the pesto and process until smooth.

Layer half the cream cheese mixture, sun-dried tomato mixture and remaining cream cheese mixture evenly in the prepared pan. Bake at 325 degrees for 35 minutes.

Mix the sour cream and flour in a small bowl. Spread over the cheesecake. Bake for 5 minutes longer. Cool on a wire rack and chill, covered, for 4 to 24 hours. Place on a bed of baby lettuce leaves and remove the side of the pan. Garnish with edible flower petals and chives.

Serves twenty-four

HOT ONION SOUFFLÉ

12 TO 16 OUNCES (3 TO
   4 CUPS) FROZEN
   CHOPPED ONIONS,
   THAWED
24 OUNCES CREAM
   CHEESE, SOFTENED
2 CUPS (8 OUNCES) GRATED
   PARMESAN CHEESE
1/2 CUP MAYONNAISE

Press the onions with paper towels to remove the excess moisture. Combine with the cream cheese, Parmesan cheese and mayonnaise in a bowl and mix well. Spoon into a shallow 2-quart soufflé dish. Bake at 425 degrees for 15 minutes or until golden brown. Serve with corn chips or assorted crackers.

Makes six cups

Piggly Wiggly Playground

In the heart of Memphis is a little jewel called Chickasaw Gardens. Once the estate of Clarence Saunders, grocery magnate, it was the backyard of his "Pink Palace," now a fine museum. Today, handsome residences surround the picturesque lake in the center of the Gardens, and many Memphians gather there to spend happy hours chatting on the bank, playing with frisky dogs, people-watching, and picnicking. Many a family photograph has been posed in front of the beautiful old magnolias, and it is certain that countless family stories began here with a marriage proposal offered in this perfectly romantic setting.

CREAMED SHRIMP AND ARTICHOKE BOTTOMS

4½ TABLESPOONS BUTTER
4½ TABLESPOONS FLOUR
½ CUP MILK
¾ CUP HEAVY CREAM
SALT AND FRESHLY
    GROUND PEPPER
    TO TASTE
¼ CUP DRY VERMOUTH
    OR OTHER WHITE WINE
1 TABLESPOON
    WORCESTERSHIRE
    SAUCE
1½ POUNDS SHRIMP,
    COOKED, PEELED,
    DEVEINED
2 (20-OUNCE) CANS
    ARTICHOKE BOTTOMS,
    DRAINED, CHOPPED
¼ CUP (1 OUNCE) GRATED
    PARMESAN CHEESE

Melt the butter in a saucepan and stir in the flour. Whisk in the milk and cream gradually. Cook until thickened, whisking constantly. Season with salt and pepper. Stir in the vermouth and Worcestershire sauce. Add the shrimp and artichoke bottoms. Cook until heated through. Spoon into a chafing dish and sprinkle with the Parmesan cheese. Serve with buttered toast rounds.

You may add Gruyère cheese to the sauce, substitute sliced artichoke hearts for the artichoke bottoms and/or substitute chopped cooked chicken for the shrimp. Serve over hot cooked pasta for an entrée.

Serves fifty

SMOKED CATFISH PÂTÉ

1 POUND CATFISH FILLETS
¾ CUP WATER
2 TABLESPOONS
    VERMOUTH
16 OUNCES CREAM
    CHEESE, SOFTENED
2 TABLESPOONS FRESH
    LEMON JUICE
1 GARLIC CLOVE, MINCED
½ TEASPOON LIQUID
    SMOKE
1 TEASPOON PAPRIKA
SALT AND PEPPER
    TO TASTE

Combine the catfish fillets with the water and vermouth in a deep 12-inch skillet and cook until the fish flakes easily with a fork; drain. Combine with the cream cheese, lemon juice, garlic, liquid smoke, paprika, salt and pepper in a food processor container and process until smooth. Spoon into a serving bowl and chill, covered, for 2 to 48 hours. Serve with assorted crackers or garlic toast rounds.

Makes four cups

HERBED MUSHROOM PÂTÉ

12 LARGE MUSHROOMS,
   ABOUT 1 POUND

1 GARLIC CLOVE, MINCED

2 TABLESPOONS BUTTER
   OR MARGARINE

8 OUNCES CREAM CHEESE,
   SOFTENED

3 TABLESPOONS DRY
   SHERRY

1 TABLESPOON CHOPPED
   FRESH TARRAGON

1 TABLESPOON CHOPPED
   FRESH MARJORAM

1 TABLESPOON CHOPPED
   FRESH THYME

1/2 TEASPOON CHOPPED
   FRESH ROSEMARY

1/2 TEASPOON SALT

1 TEASPOON LEMON PEPPER

1 TEASPOON PEPPER

Garnish

SPRIGS OF FRESH HERBS

MUSHROOM SLICES

Sauté the mushrooms and garlic in the butter in a 12-inch skillet for 5 minutes or until the liquid evaporates. Cool to room temperature. Combine with the cream cheese, sherry, tarragon, marjoram, thyme, rosemary, salt, lemon pepper and pepper in a food processor container and process until smooth.

Spoon into a generously oiled 2 1/2- to 3-cup mold. Chill, covered, for 8 hours or longer. Unmold onto a serving plate and garnish with fresh herbs and fresh mushroom slices. Serve with bagel chips or crackers.

The flavors improve if the pâté is made a day or two before serving.

Makes two and one-half cups

CUCUMBER DIP

1 CUP GRATED UNPEELED
   CUCUMBER

16 OUNCES CREAM CHEESE,
   SOFTENED

2 TABLESPOONS GRATED
   ONION

1 TABLESPOON
   WORCESTERSHIRE
   SAUCE

3 TABLESPOONS
   MAYONNAISE

2 TABLESPOONS LEMON
   JUICE

MSG, SALT AND PEPPER
   TO TASTE

Spread the cucumber on a paper towel and let stand for several minutes. Press to remove the excess moisture. Combine with the cream cheese, onion, Worcestershire sauce, mayonnaise, lemon juice, MSG, salt and pepper in a blender container. Process until smooth. Spoon into a serving bowl and chill in the refrigerator. Serve chilled with vegetables or crackers.

Makes three cups

Handling Mushrooms

The delicate mushroom deserves special attention when it comes to choosing, storing, and cleaning. Try to purchase mushrooms within a day or two of using them, especially if you plan to serve them uncooked. Look for firm, dry mushrooms free of spots or bruises.

Keep mushrooms in the refrigerator in a paper bag or open container loosely covered with a slightly moistened paper towel.

Wait to clean the mushrooms until you are ready to use them. Though cleaning mushrooms is very important, too much water can make them soggy. Most cultivated button mushrooms are clean enough that a tender wiping with a moist paper towel is all they need.

Curry Dip Britton

1 CUP MAYONNAISE

3 TABLESPOONS KETCHUP

1/2 TEASPOON TABASCO
SAUCE

1 TABLESPOON
WORCESTERSHIRE
SAUCE

2 TABLESPOONS GRATED
ONION

1 TABLESPOON CURRY
POWDER

SALT TO TASTE

Combine the mayonnaise, ketchup, Tabasco sauce, Worcestershire sauce, onion, curry powder and salt in a bowl and mix well. Chill, covered, for up to several days to blend the flavors. Serve with cauliflower florets or shrimp.

Serves eight

Dill Dip In A Rye Loaf

1 1/3 CUPS MAYONNAISE

1 1/3 CUPS SOUR CREAM

2 TABLESPOONS DRIED
ONION FLAKES

2 TABLESPOONS DRIED
PARSLEY FLAKES

2 TEASPOONS (HEAPING)
DILLWEED

KRAZY JANE'S MIXED-UP
SALT TO TASTE

2 TEASPOONS GARLIC
SALT OR SEASONED SALT

1 ROUND (10-INCH) LOAF
RYE BREAD

Combine the mayonnaise, sour cream, onion flakes, parsley flakes, dillweed, mixed-up salt and garlic salt in a bowl and mix well. Chill, covered, for 24 hours.

Slice off the top 1/4 of the bread and remove the interior, reserving the bread shell and the top. Tear the bread removed into bite-size pieces. Fill the shell with the dill dip and place on a platter. Lean the bread top against the loaf and arrange the bread pieces around the loaf.

When the bread bowl is empty you may cut it into pieces to serve as well. You may also serve the dip with fresh vegetables.

Serves twelve

DIXIE CAVIAR

4 CUPS FROZEN OR CANNED
    BLACK-EYED PEAS
1 (16-OUNCE) CAN WHITE
    HOMINY, DRAINED
    (OPTIONAL)
2 MEDIUM TOMATOES,
    CHOPPED
1 CUP CHOPPED GREEN
    BELL PEPPER
1/2 CUP CHOPPED ONION
4 GREEN ONIONS, SLICED
1 OR 2 JALAPEÑO PEPPERS,
    SEEDED, CHOPPED
1 OR 2 GARLIC CLOVES,
    MINCED
1 CUP ITALIAN SALAD
    DRESSING

Garnish

1/4 CUP SOUR CREAM OR
    PLAIN YOGURT
CHOPPED FRESH CILANTRO

Cook frozen black-eyed peas using the package directions and drain; rinse and drain canned black-eyed peas. Combine with the hominy, tomatoes, bell pepper, onion, green onions, jalapeño peppers, garlic and salad dressing in a large bowl and mix well. Chill, covered, for 1 to 2 days.

Drain the black-eyed pea mixture, reserving the liquid. Pulse the mixture in a food processor just until coarsely chopped; do not purée. Combine with enough of the reserved liquid to make of the desired consistency. Spoon into a serving bowl and garnish with sour cream and cilantro. Serve chilled with tortilla chips or crackers.

You may also serve this as a salad in tomato cups or on a bed of lettuce.

Makes ten cups

CHUTNIED SHRIMP DIP

3 TABLESPOONS SLICED
    ALMONDS
3 TABLESPOONS COARSELY
    SHREDDED COCONUT
8 OUNCES CREAM CHEESE,
    SOFTENED
3 TABLESPOONS SOUR
    CREAM
1 1/2 TEASPOONS CURRY
    POWDER
1/2 CUP SLICED GREEN
    ONIONS
1/2 CUP GOLDEN RAISINS
6 OUNCES SMALL SHRIMP,
    COOKED, PEELED
1 (8-OUNCE) JAR PREPARED
    CHUTNEY

Sprinkle the almonds and coconut into a shallow baking pan. Toast at 350 degrees for 5 to 10 minutes or until light golden brown, stirring once.

Combine the cream cheese, sour cream and curry powder in a medium bowl and mix until smooth. Mix in the green onions and raisins. Add the shrimp and mix gently. Shape into a ball and place on a serving plate. Spoon the chutney over the top and sprinkle with the toasted almonds and coconut.

Makes four cups

Les Carlos' Shrimp And Crawfish

1½ CUPS (3 STICKS) UNSALTED BUTTER

2 TABLESPOONS CREOLE SEASONING

1 POUND FRESH OR THAWED FROZEN PEELED CRAWFISH TAILS

1 POUND FRESH OR THAWED FROZEN PEELED SHRIMP

1 CUP FINELY CHOPPED ONION

1 CUP FINELY CHOPPED CELERY

1 CUP FINELY CHOPPED GREEN BELL PEPPER

½ CUP FINELY CHOPPED RED BELL PEPPER

6 TABLESPOONS CHOPPED FRESH BASIL, OR 2 TABLESPOONS CRUSHED DRIED BASIL

3 TABLESPOONS CHOPPED FRESH THYME, OR 1 TABLESPOON CRUSHED DRIED THYME

3 TABLESPOONS MINCED GARLIC

¼ CUP FLOUR

2 TABLESPOONS WORCESTERSHIRE SAUCE

3 TABLESPOONS TOMATO PASTE

2 CUPS SLICED GREEN ONIONS

HOT PEPPER SAUCE TO TASTE

Heat ½ cup of the butter in a 12-inch skillet and add 2 teaspoons of the Creole seasoning and crawfish. Sauté over high heat for 3 to 4 minutes, stirring occasionally to scrape up the seasoning from the skillet. Remove to a large bowl with a slotted spoon.

Heat ½ cup of the remaining butter in the skillet and add 2 teaspoons of the remaining Creole seasoning and the shrimp. Sauté over high heat for 4 minutes, stirring occasionally to scrape up the seasoning from the skillet. Remove to the bowl with the crawfish with a slotted spoon.

Heat the remaining ½ cup butter in the skillet and stir in the remaining 2 teaspoons Creole seasoning. Add the onion, celery and bell peppers. Sauté for 5 minutes, stirring constantly. Reduce the heat and add the basil, thyme and garlic. Sauté for 5 minutes.

Combine the flour, Worcestershire sauce and tomato paste in a small bowl. Add to the vegetable mixture in the skillet. Return the shrimp and crawfish to the skillet and mix well. Cook over medium heat for 5 minutes, stirring constantly. Stir in the green onions. Cook for 5 minutes longer, stirring constantly. Season with pepper sauce. Serve hot with thin garlic toasts.

Makes eight cups

GUACAMOLE

3 RIPE AVOCADOS

2 TOMATOES, PEELED, SEEDED, FINELY CHOPPED

2 GREEN ONIONS WITH TOPS, FINELY CHOPPED

1/2 GARLIC CLOVE, MINCED

3 TABLESPOONS OLIVE OIL

MAYONNAISE

LEMON JUICE, CUMIN, CHILI POWDER, SALT AND RED PEPPER TO TASTE

Garnish

FRESH LIME WEDGES

Mash the avocados in a bowl. Add the tomatoes, green onions, garlic and olive oil and mix well. Add enough mayonnaise to make of the desired consistency. Add the lemon juice, cumin, chili powder, salt and red pepper and mix well. Spoon into a serving bowl or a salt-rimmed margarita glass and garnish with lime wedges. Serve with tortilla chips.

Serves ten to twelve

TAMALE DIP

2 (20-OUNCE) CANS TAMALES

1 MEDIUM ONION, CHOPPED

VEGETABLE OIL

1 (28-OUNCE) CAN TOMATOES

1 (14-OUNCE) CAN TOMATO SAUCE

1 GARLIC CLOVE, MINCED

1 1/2 TABLESPOONS CHILI SAUCE

1 (5-OUNCE) CAN BLACK OLIVES, DRAINED, CHOPPED

TABASCO SAUCE TO TASTE

CHILI POWDER, SALT AND PEPPER TO TASTE

1 CUP (4 OUNCES) SHREDDED CHEDDAR CHEESE

Remove the tamales from the cans, reserving the sauce from the cans; chop the tamales. Sauté the onion in a small amount of oil in a saucepan until tender. Add the tamales, reserved sauce, tomatoes, tomato sauce, garlic, chili sauce, olives, Tabasco sauce, chili powder, salt and pepper and mix well. Simmer until heated through and of the desired consistency. Spoon into a chafing dish and sprinkle with the cheese. Serve with corn chips or breadsticks.

Serves twenty-five to thirty

Swiss Cheese Fondue

Shred 2 pounds of Gruyère cheese and combine with 12 ounces warmed white wine in a fondue pot or chafing dish over a high flame. Heat until the cheese melts and bubbles, stirring to mix well. Stir in a mixture of 1 teaspoon flour and 1 tablespoon warm water. Add 3 ounces warmed kirsch or brandy. Serve hot with cubed French bread, apples or pears.

Spinach Dip

1 (10-OUNCE) PACKAGE
   FROZEN CHOPPED
   SPINACH, THAWED
3 GREEN ONIONS WITH
   TOPS, THINLY SLICED
1/4 TEASPOON ONION SALT
1/4 TEASPOON CELERY SALT
1/4 TEASPOON GARLIC SALT
1/2 TEASPOON SEASONED
   PEPPER
1/4 TO 1/2 CUP MAYONNAISE

Press the spinach to remove the excess moisture. Combine with the green onions, onion salt, celery salt, garlic salt and pepper in a bowl and mix well. Add enough mayonnaise to make of the desired consistency. Serve with fresh vegetables and/or chips.

Serves eight

Baked Mexican Spinach Dip

3 MEDIUM TOMATOES
1 (10-OUNCE) PACKAGE
   FROZEN CHOPPED
   SPINACH, THAWED
4 OUNCES CREAM CHEESE
1 CUP CHOPPED ONION
2 TABLESPOONS
   VEGETABLE OIL
2 TO 4 TABLESPOONS
   CHOPPED JALAPEÑO
   PEPPERS
2 1/2 CUPS (10 OUNCES)
   SHREDDED MONTEREY
   JACK CHEESE
1 CUP LIGHT CREAM
1/2 CUP SLICED BLACK
   OLIVES
1 TABLESPOON RED WINE
   VINEGAR
SALT AND PEPPER TO TASTE

Peel, seed and chop the tomatoes. Press the spinach to remove the excess moisture. Cut the cream cheese into 1/2-inch cubes. Sauté the onion in the oil in a 10-inch skillet until tender. Add the jalapeño peppers and 2/3 of the tomatoes and sauté for 2 minutes longer. Combine with the spinach, 2 cups of the Monterey Jack cheese, cream cheese, cream, olives, vinegar, salt and pepper in a bowl and mix well.

Spoon into a 1 1/2-quart baking dish. Bake at 400 degrees for 35 minutes or until bubbly and heated through. Garnish with the remaining tomatoes and remaining 1/2 cup cheese. Serve with tortilla chips.

Makes six and one-half cups

FRONT PORCH TEA

2 CUPS WATER

1 CUP SUGAR

2 CUPS BOILING WATER

2 (FAMILY-SIZE) TEA BAGS

8 CUPS WATER

1 (12-OUNCE) CAN FROZEN
LEMONADE
CONCENTRATE, THAWED

1 TABLESPOON VANILLA
EXTRACT

1 TABLESPOON ALMOND
EXTRACT

Garnish

SLICED FRESH PEACHES

Combine 2 cups water with the sugar in a 1-quart saucepan and cook until the sugar dissolves, stirring frequently. Pour 2 cups boiling water over the tea bags in a 4-quart pitcher and let stand for 5 minutes; discard the tea bags.

Add the sugar syrup, 8 cups water, lemonade concentrate and flavorings to the pitcher and mix well. Serve over ice. Garnish the servings with fresh peach slices.

Serves fourteen

INSTANT SPICED TEA

1 (7-OUNCE) JAR ORANGE
DRINK MIX

3/4 CUP LEMON-FLAVOR
INSTANT TEA GRANULES

1 1/2 CUPS SUGAR

1 1/2 TEASPOONS GROUND
CLOVES

1 1/2 TEASPOONS GROUND
CINNAMON

Combine the orange drink mix, instant tea granules, sugar, cloves and cinnamon in a bowl and mix well. Store in an airtight container.

To serve, dissolve 2 teaspoons of the mixture in a cup of boiling water for each cup.

Serves sixty

Clarence Moody

For many years Clarence Moody has brewed a punch at Christmastime that has come to be known as Clarence Moody's Holiday Punch. It is similar to the old English wassail. He has mailed the recipe to people in every state in the union and many in foreign countries. He also makes a Holiday Scent, not intended for consumption. To make the scent, combine 1 quart each of pineapple juice, apple cider and water. Add 4 pieces gingerroot, three 3-inch cinnamon sticks, 16 whole cloves, 1 teaspoon allspice and 1 to 2 teaspoons pickling spice in a large saucepan. Simmer during the holiday season to give the house a wonderful festive aroma.

BOILED CUSTARD

2 CUPS MILK
3 EGG YOLKS OR 2 EGGS
1/4 CUP SUGAR
SALT TO TASTE
1/2 TEASPOON VANILLA
 EXTRACT

Bring the milk just to a simmer in a double boiler. Beat the egg yolks lightly in a bowl and add the sugar and salt; mix well. Stir a small amount of the hot milk into the egg mixture; stir the egg mixture into the hot milk. Cook until the custard thickens and coats the spoon, stirring constantly; custard will be thin. Cool and stir in the vanilla.

For a thicker custard, add a mixture of 2 tablespoons cornstarch dissolved in a small amount of milk. If the custard separates or lumps, place the pan in a larger pan of cold water at once and beat with a rotary beater until smooth.

Serves two

CLARENCE MOODY'S HOLIDAY PUNCH

3 PIECES GINGERROOT
1 (3-INCH) CINNAMON
 STICK
8 WHOLE CLOVES
3 OR 4 CARDAMOM SEEDS
1 GALLON APPLE CIDER
1 QUART PINEAPPLE JUICE
6 LEMONS, PEELED, SLICED
6 SMALL ORANGES, PEELED,
 SLICED
1/2 TEASPOON SALT
RUM TO TASTE

Combine the ginger, cinnamon, cloves and cardamom seeds in a fine-mesh cheesecloth bag. Combine with the apple cider, pineapple juice, lemon slices and orange slices in a stockpot. Bring to a low simmer and simmer for 15 minutes, stirring constantly. Stir in the salt. Remove the spice bag and stir in the rum. Serve hot.

This is similar to the old English wassail.

Serves forty to fifty

POPLAR PUNCH

1 (6-OUNCE) CAN FROZEN
    ORANGE JUICE
    CONCENTRATE, THAWED
1 (6-OUNCE) CAN FROZEN
    LEMONADE
    CONCENTRATE, THAWED
1 QUART CRANBERRY JUICE
    COCKTAIL
1 QUART GINGER ALE OR
    CHAMPAGNE, CHILLED

Garnish

1 ORANGE, THINLY SLICED

Combine the orange juice concentrate, lemonade concentrate and cranberry juice cocktail in a pitcher and mix well. Chill, covered, until serving time. Stir in the ginger ale and serve immediately, garnished with orange slices.

Serves twelve

HOMEMADE KAHLÚA

1½ CUPS INSTANT COFFEE
    GRANULES
3 CUPS BOILING WATER
6 CUPS SUGAR
1 VANILLA BEAN
1 FIFTH OF VODKA

Dissolve the coffee granules in the boiling water in a heatproof bowl. Add the sugar and vanilla bean, stirring to dissolve the sugar. Let stand until cool. Add the vodka. Pour into a 1-gallon container and seal. Let stand for 30 days. Serve as a liqueur or dessert sauce.

Makes seven cups

POINSETTIA

3 CUPS CHAMPAGNE,
  CHILLED
3 CUPS CRANBERRY JUICE
  COCKTAIL, CHILLED
1/2 CUP ORANGE LIQUEUR

Garnish

FRESH CRANBERRIES

Combine the Champagne, cranberry juice cocktail and orange liqueur in a 2-quart pitcher and mix gently. Serve in Champagne glasses. Garnish the servings with cranberries.

Serves eight

LA FONDA SANGRIA

4 LEMONS, SLICED
4 NAVEL ORANGES, SLICED
6 TABLESPOONS WATER
1 CUP PLUS
  2 TABLESPOONS SUGAR
3 CUPS CRACKED ICE
2 CUPS RED OR WHITE
  WINE, CHILLED
2 CUPS CLUB SODA,
  CHILLED

Garnish

LEMON AND ORANGE
  SLICES

Cut the lemon and orange slices into halves. Place half the slices in each of two 2-quart pitchers. Combine the water and sugar in a small saucepan and cook over medium heat until the mixture boils and the sugar dissolves, stirring constantly. Let cool.

Pour half the mixture into each pitcher. Add 1 1/2 cups ice, 1 cup wine and 1 cup soda water to each pitcher; stir with a wooden spoon. Serve in 14- to 16-ounce glasses. Garnish with additional fruit slices.

Serves six

How To Cook A Husband

*Lifestyles and customs have changed since this was first published
in* The Memphis Cookbook *in 1952, but some things remain the same.*

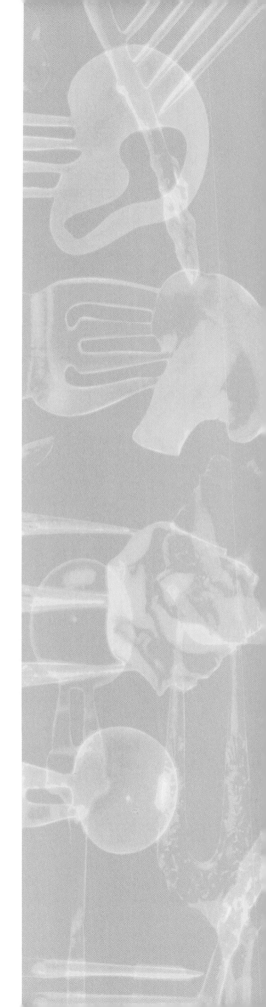

A good many husbands are utterly spoiled by mismanagement in cooking and so are not tender and good. Some women keep them constantly in hot water; others let them freeze by their carelessness and indifference. Some keep them in a stew with irritating ways and words. Some wives keep them pickled, while others waste them shamefully. It cannot be supposed that any husband will be tender and good when so managed, but they are really delicious when prepared properly.

In selecting a husband, you should not be guided by the silvery appearance as in buying a mackerel; nor by the golden tint as if you wanted a salmon. Do not go to the market for him, as the best ones are always brought to the door. Be sure to select him yourself as tastes differ. It is far better to have none unless you will patiently learn how to cook him.

Of course, a preserving kettle of the finest porcelain is best, but if you have nothing better than an earthenware pipkin, it will do—with care. Like crabs and lobsters, husbands are cooked alive. They sometimes fly out of the kettle and so become burned and crusty on the edges, so it is wise to secure him in the kettle with a strong silken cord called Comfort, as the one called Duty is apt to be weak. Make a clear, steady flame of love, warmth and cheerfulness. Set him as near this as seems to agree with him.

If he sputters, do not be anxious, for some husbands do this until they are quite done. Add a little sugar in the form of what confectioners call kisses, but use no pepper or vinegar on any account. Season to taste with spices, good humor and gaiety preferred, but seasoning must always be used with great discretion and caution. Avoid sharpness in testing him for tenderness. Stir him gently, lest he lie too flat and close to the kettle and so become useless. You cannot fail to know when he is done. If so treated, you will find him very digestible, agreeing with you perfectly; and he will keep as long as you choose unless you become careless and allow the home fires to grow cold. Thus prepared, he will serve a lifetime of Happiness.

Cold Orange Tomato Soup

For a great first course on a hot summer night or a ladies' luncheon, combine 2 cups tomato juice, 2 cups orange juice, 1/2 cup white wine and the juice of 1 lemon in a bowl. Add 1 teaspoon sugar, 1 1/2 teaspoons salt and cayenne pepper to taste. Chill, covered, until serving time. Sprinkle the servings with chopped parsley and serve cold.

Black Bean Soup

1 POUND DRIED BLACK
   BEANS
1/2 TEASPOON BAKING
   SODA
2 QUARTS WATER
3 ONIONS, CHOPPED
1/2 GREEN BELL PEPPER,
   CHOPPED
3 GARLIC CLOVES,
   CHOPPED
4 SLICES BACON, CHOPPED
1 TABLESPOON VINEGAR
2 BAY LEAVES
1/4 CUP OLIVE OIL
SALT AND PEPPER
   TO TASTE

Combine the beans and baking soda with water to cover in a bowl and let stand for 8 hours or longer. Drain and rinse the beans and combine with 2 quarts water in a saucepan. Bring to a simmer.

Sauté the onions, bell pepper, garlic, bacon, vinegar and bay leaves in the olive oil in a skillet until golden brown. Add to the beans and simmer until cooked through.

Press the mixture through a sieve. Return to the saucepan and season with salt and pepper. Cook until heated through.

To improve the flavor, let the soup stand for several hours and reheat to serve.

Serves six to eight as a first course or four as a main dish

Comforting Chicken Noodle Soup

8 CUPS CHICKEN BROTH
1 CUP CHOPPED ONION
1 CUP CHOPPED CELERY
1 CUP CHOPPED CARROTS
1 GARLIC CLOVE, MINCED
2 TO 3 CUPS CHOPPED
   COOKED CHICKEN
2 MEDIUM TOMATOES,
   PEELED, CHOPPED
1/2 CUP UNCOOKED BROAD
   EGG NOODLES
1 TEASPOON CHOPPED
   FRESH BASIL
1/2 TEASPOON CHOPPED
   FRESH THYME
1/4 TO 1/2 TEASPOON PEPPER

Garnish

1 TO 2 TABLESPOONS
   CHOPPED FRESH PARSLEY

Combine the chicken broth, onion, celery, carrots and garlic in a 6-quart saucepan and mix well. Bring to a boil and reduce the heat. Simmer for 20 minutes.

Add the chicken, tomatoes, noodles, fresh basil and thyme. Season with the pepper. Simmer for 8 minutes or until the noodles are tender. Garnish servings with parsley. For Homemade Chicken Broth, see sidebar, page 46.

Serves eight

SOUTHERN CORN CHOWDER

8 TO 10 MEDIUM EARS OF
   FRESH CORN
1 POUND BACON
1 LARGE ONION,
   THINLY SLICED
4 CUPS CHICKEN BROTH
1 MEDIUM POTATO,
   CHOPPED
1 OR 2 CARROTS,
   SHREDDED
1/4 CUP FLOUR
1 1/2 CUPS MILK
1 1/2 CUPS LIGHT CREAM
   OR MILK
1 TABLESPOON LEMON
   JUICE
HOT PEPPER SAUCE
   TO TASTE
SALT AND PEPPER
   TO TASTE

Garnish

FRESH BAY LEAVES

Cut the tops of the corn kernels from the ears with a sharp knife. Scrape the pulp from the ears with the dull edge of the knife. Cook the bacon in a heavy 6-quart saucepan until crisp; drain, reserving the drippings. Crumble the bacon.

Sauté the onion in 3 tablespoons of the reserved drippings until tender; drain. Add the corn, chicken broth, potato and carrots to the onion in the saucepan and bring to a boil. Boil for 10 minutes or until the potato is tender.

Add enough of the remaining reserved drippings to a 10-inch skillet to measure 1/4 inch. Stir in the flour. Cook over medium-low heat for 10 minutes or until the mixture is light brown.

Add the milk and cream to the vegetables in the saucepan. Cook until heated through. Stir in the lemon juice, hot pepper sauce, salt and pepper. Whisk in the flour mixture. Stir in the bacon. Simmer until thickened, stirring constantly. Garnish servings with fresh bay leaves.

You may add instant potato flakes 2 tablespoons at a time if necessary to thicken the soup to the desired consistency. May substitute one 16-ounce package frozen whole kernel corn for the corn.

Serve eight to ten

EASY MUSHROOM SOUP

1 CUP CHOPPED
   MUSHROOMS
2 ONIONS, CHOPPED
VEGETABLE OIL
2 CUPS CHICKEN BROTH
SALT AND PEPPER
   TO TASTE
1 CUP CREAM
1 HARD-COOKED EGG,
   SHREDDED

Sauté the mushrooms and onions in a small amount of oil in a skillet. Bring the chicken broth to a simmer in a saucepan and season with salt and pepper. Add the mushroom mixture. Heat the cream in a small saucepan and add to the soup. Cook until heated through. Stir in the egg just before serving.

Serves four

Swiss Onion Soup

6 MEDIUM ONIONS, THINLY
  SLICED INTO RINGS
1/4 CUP (1/2 STICK) BUTTER
  OR MARGARINE
2 VEGETABLE BOUILLON
  CUBES
2 1/2 CUPS WATER
8 CUPS RICH BEEF
  BOUILLON
1 TEASPOON DRY SHERRY
2 TEASPOONS GRATED
  PARMESAN CHEESE
2 TEASPOONS GRATED
  ROMANO CHEESE
8 CUPS (2 POUNDS)
  SHREDDED SWISS
  CHEESE
10 TOAST SQUARES

Sauté the onions in the butter in a heavy saucepan over low heat until tender. Dissolve the vegetable bouillon cubes in the water and add to the saucepan. Add the beef bouillon. Simmer for 30 minutes.

Add the sherry, Parmesan cheese, Romano cheese and 6 cups of the Swiss cheese and cook just until the cheeses melt, stirring to mix well.

Ladle into ovenproof soup bowls. Place the toast squares on the surface and sprinkle with the remaining 2 cups Swiss cheese. Broil until the cheese is light brown.

You may substitute 3 cans of condensed beef consommé diluted with 3 cans of water for the beef bouillon. Do not add salt to this recipe.

Serves ten

Sherried Crab Bisque

2 CUPS COOKED
  CRAB MEAT
1 CUP SHERRY
2 (10-OUNCE) CANS
  PEA SOUP
2 (10-OUNCE) CANS
  TOMATO SOUP
3 CUPS LIGHT CREAM
1/4 CUP CHOPPED PARSLEY
CURRY POWDER, SALT AND
  PEPPER TO TASTE

Combine the crab meat with the sherry in a bowl and marinate in the refrigerator for 1 hour. Combine the pea soup, tomato soup and cream in a double boiler and mix well. Bring just to a simmer, stirring occasionally. Stir in the crab meat with the sherry, parsley, curry powder, salt and pepper. Serve hot.

Serves eight

*L*OBSTER *B*ISQUE

1 ONION, SLICED

1 LEEK, CHOPPED

1 CARROT, SLICED

1 RIB CELERY, CHOPPED

2 TABLESPOONS BUTTER

1/2 TEASPOON THYME

1 BAY LEAF

1 TEASPOON SALT

2 CUPS WHITE WINE OR
    HOT WATER

1/4 CUP COGNAC

CHOPPED MEAT OF
    2 SMALL LOBSTERS

1 CUP COOKED RICE

2 TABLESPOONS BUTTER,
    MELTED

3 TABLESPOONS CREAM

2 EGG YOLKS, BEATEN

1/4 CUP COGNAC

Sauté the onion, leek, carrot and celery in 2 tablespoons butter in a 2-quart saucepan for 3 minutes or until light brown. Add the thyme, bay leaf and salt. Cook for 5 minutes, stirring occasionally. Add the wine and 1/4 cup Cognac. Simmer for 15 minutes.

Process the soup in batches in a food processor. Return to the saucepan and add the lobster and rice. Simmer for 45 minutes or until thickened to the desired consistency.

Combine the melted butter, cream, egg yolks and 1/4 cup Cognac in a bowl and mix well. Add to the soup and simmer just until heated through, stirring constantly; do not boil.

Serves four

*S*HRIMP *S*OUP

1 1/2 POUNDS UNCOOKED
    SHRIMP

SALT TO TASTE

3 OR 4 PEPPERCORNS

1 SMALL ONION, FINELY
    CHOPPED

1/2 CUP (1 STICK) BUTTER

PEPPER TO TASTE

3 CUPS HOT MILK

1 CUP HEAVY CREAM

1/3 CUP SHERRY

Combine the shrimp with the salt and peppercorns in water to cover in a saucepan and simmer for 15 minutes; drain, reserving the cooking liquid and discarding the peppercorns. Peel, devein and chop the shrimp. Combine with the reserved cooking liquid in a bowl.

Sauté the onion in the butter in a saucepan; do not brown. Combine with the shrimp and reserved liquid in a double boiler. Add the pepper. Cook over hot water for 5 minutes. Add the milk gradually. Cook for several minutes. Add the cream gradually and salt to taste. Stir in the sherry. Cook just until heated through; do not boil. Serve with oyster crackers.

Serves six to eight

VICHYSSOISE

4 LEEK BULBS, OR 6 GREEN
   ONIONS, SLICED
1 MEDIUM ONION, SLICED
2 TABLESPOONS BUTTER
5 MEDIUM POTATOES,
   PEELED, CHOPPED
4 CUPS CHICKEN BROTH
1 TABLESPOON SALT
2 CUPS MILK
2 CUPS LIGHT CREAM
1 CUP HEAVY CREAM

Garnish

CHOPPED CHIVES OR
   PARSLEY SPRIGS

Sauté the leeks and onion in the butter in a large saucepan until golden brown. Add the potatoes, chicken broth and salt. Cook for 35 to 40 minutes or until the potatoes are very tender. Process the mixture in batches in a food processor and return to the saucepan. Stir in the milk and light cream and adjust the seasoning. Bring to a boil.

Pour into a bowl and chill, covered, in the refrigerator. Stir in the heavy cream. Serve cold, garnished with chives or parsley.

Serves eight

LIGHTSIDE POTATO SOUP

4 TO 6 LARGE BAKING
   POTATOES
1/2 CUP SHREDDED OR
   SLICED CARROTS
6 CUPS CHICKEN BROTH
1 1/2 CUPS CHOPPED CELERY
1 CUP MINCED ONION
2 TABLESPOONS
   VEGETABLE OIL
1 1/2 CUPS SKIM MILK
2 TABLESPOONS LOW-FAT
   SOUR CREAM
2 TABLESPOONS REDUCED-
   CALORIE MARGARINE
1 TABLESPOON WHITE WINE
   WORCESTERSHIRE SAUCE
2 TO 3 TABLESPOONS FRESH
   LEMON JUICE
HOT PEPPER SAUCE, SALT
   AND PEPPER TO TASTE

Garnish

DILLWEED

Peel and chop the potatoes. Combine the potatoes and carrots with 4 cups of the chicken broth in a heavy 6-quart saucepan. Cook for 15 to 20 minutes or until the vegetables are tender; drain. Remove half the vegetables to a bowl and mash. Return to the saucepan.

Sauté the celery and onion in the oil in a 10-inch skillet until tender. Add to the potato mixture in the saucepan. Stir in remaining 2 cups chicken broth, skim milk, sour cream, margarine, Worcestershire sauce, lemon juice, hot pepper sauce, salt and pepper. Simmer for 10 minutes. Serve hot or cold, garnished with dillweed.

You may add instant potato flakes 1 tablespoon at a time if needed to thicken the soup to the desired consistency.

Serves four to six

Hearty Vegetable Soup

BEEF STEW MEAT, CUBED

LEFTOVER ROAST BEEF OR
  STEAK, CUBED

2 ENVELOPES ONION
  SOUP MIX

3 QUARTS WATER

1 (16-OUNCE) CAN TOMATO
  SAUCE

1 (16-OUNCE) CAN
  CHOPPED TOMATOES

1^1/$_2$ TEASPOONS MARJORAM

1^1/$_2$ TEASPOONS BASIL

1^1/$_2$ TEASPOONS PARSLEY
  FLAKES

1 TEASPOON GARLIC
  POWDER

2 BAY LEAVES

1 TABLESPOON SALT

1^1/$_2$ TEASPOONS PEPPER

1 (16-OUNCE) PACKAGE
  FROZEN MIXED
  VEGETABLES

1 (10-OUNCE) PACKAGE
  FROZEN SLICED OKRA

Garnish

GRATED PARMESAN CHEESE

Combine the stew meat, roast beef, soup mix and water in a large saucepan and cook for 25 to 30 minutes.

Add the tomato sauce, undrained tomatoes, marjoram, basil, parsley flakes, garlic powder, bay leaves, salt and pepper. Cook for 15 minutes.

Add the frozen vegetables and okra. Cook for 2 to 2^1/$_2$ hours or until of the desired consistency; remove and discard the bay leaves. Garnish servings with Parmesan cheese.

Serves twelve

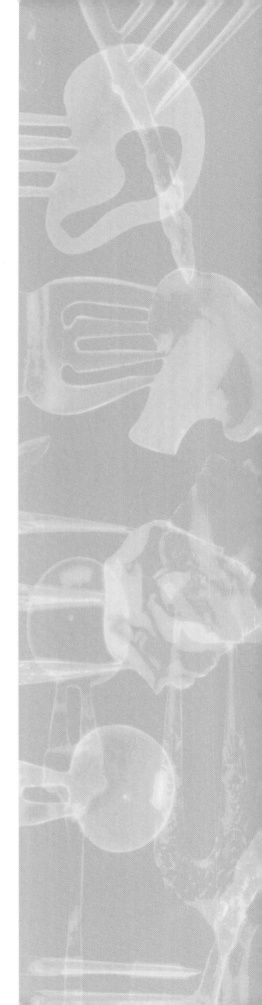

Ten Cents a Bowl

There was a spot on "old" Beale Street run by Sunbeam Mitchell. Here all of the musicians around, including the notable B.B. King, could eat cheap and get a big bowl of the best chili in town.

B.B. remembers, "If you had 15 cents at that time, you could eat well; a nickel's worth of crackers and a dime's worth of chili!" "Lucille's Chili," named for B.B.'s famed guitar, is patterned after this memorable feast.

LUCILLE'S CHILI

2 POUNDS GROUND CHUCK
1 CUP CHOPPED ONION
3/4 CUP CHOPPED GREEN
   BELL PEPPER
1 GARLIC CLOVE, MINCED
1 (16-OUNCE) CAN WHOLE
   TOMATOES, CHOPPED
1 (10-OUNCE) CAN
   CHOPPED TOMATOES
   WITH GREEN CHILES
1 (16-OUNCE) CAN KIDNEY
   BEANS, DRAINED
2 (8-OUNCE) CANS TOMATO
   SAUCE
1 JALAPEÑO CHILE, SEEDED,
   CHOPPED
1 TABLESPOON CHILI
   POWDER
1 TABLESPOON CHOPPED
   FRESH OREGANO
1 1/2 TEASPOONS CHOPPED
   FRESH BASIL
2 TEASPOONS GROUND
   CUMIN
1 1/2 TEASPOONS SALT
1/4 TEASPOON PEPPER

Garnish

CHOPPED ONION
SOUR CREAM
SHREDDED CHEDDAR
   CHEESE

Brown the ground chuck with the onion, bell pepper and garlic in a heavy 4-quart saucepan, stirring until the ground chuck is crumbly; drain.

Add the undrained tomatoes, undrained tomatoes with green chiles, kidney beans, tomato sauce, jalapeño chile, chili powder, oregano, basil, cumin, salt and pepper. Cook over medium heat for 10 minutes. Reduce the heat and simmer, covered, for 1 hour. Serve with onion, sour cream and cheese for garnish.

You may substitute 1 teaspoon crushed dried oregano for the fresh oregano and 1/2 teaspoon crushed dried basil for the fresh basil.

Serves eight

CREOLE GUMBO

1/4 CUP FLOUR

1/4 CUP BACON DRIPPINGS

5 GARLIC CLOVES

4 MEDIUM YELLOW ONIONS

2 LARGE GREEN BELL
   PEPPERS

1 (16-OUNCE) CAN
   TOMATOES

1 (6-OUNCE) CAN TOMATO
   PASTE

2 POUNDS FRESH OKRA,
   SLICED

8 CUPS CHICKEN STOCK

8 OUNCES BABY LIMA
   BEANS

KERNELS FROM 2 OR
   3 FRESH EARS OF CORN

1 TEASPOON TABASCO
   SAUCE

1 1/2 TABLESPOONS KITCHEN
   BOUQUET

1 1/2 TABLESPOONS
   MARJORAM

3 OR 4 BAY LEAVES

SALT TO TASTE

3 POUNDS UNCOOKED
   PEELED SHRIMP

1 PINT OYSTERS

1 POUND CRAB MEAT

1 POUND (OR MORE) FISH,
   CUT INTO 1/2-INCH PIECES

CHOPPED COOKED CHICKEN
   (OPTIONAL)

2 TABLESPOONS GUMBO
   FILÉ

Stir the flour into the bacon drippings in a heavy saucepan. Cook until the mixture is medium brown.

Crush or finely chop the garlic. Chop the onions and bell peppers. Add the garlic, onions and bell peppers to the flour mixture in the saucepan. Cook until the onions are tender, stirring constantly. Add the undrained tomatoes, tomato paste and okra. Cook for 10 minutes, stirring constantly.

Add the chicken stock, lima beans, corn, Tabasco sauce, Kitchen Bouquet, marjoram, bay leaves and salt. Simmer for several hours or until of the desired consistency, adding additional chicken stock if necessary.

Increase the heat and add the shrimp, undrained oysters, crab meat, fish and chicken. Cook just until the seafood is tender; remove and discard the bay leaves. Stir in the filé and adjust the seasonings. Serve over rice.

Serves twelve

Sausage And Duck Gumbo

2 POUNDS SMOKED
    SAUSAGE
8 MEDIUM WILD OR
    DOMESTIC DUCKS
3 CELERY RIBS
1 CUP CHOPPED ONION
^{1}/$_3$ CUP CHOPPED FRESH
    PARSLEY
1 BAY LEAF
6 QUARTS (OR MORE)
    WATER
^{1}/$_2$ CUP VEGETABLE OIL
1 CUP FLOUR
2 CUPS CHOPPED ONION
2 CUPS CHOPPED CELERY
2 CUPS CHOPPED GREEN
    BELL PEPPER
2 (10-OUNCE) PACKAGES
    FROZEN SLICED OKRA,
    THAWED
1 TABLESPOON
    WORCESTERSHIRE
    SAUCE
^{1}/$_2$ TEASPOON CRUSHED
    DRIED THYME
2 TEASPOONS BLACK
    PEPPER
HOT PEPPER SAUCE
    TO TASTE
GROUND RED PEPPER
    TO TASTE
HOT COOKED RICE

Cook the sausage in a 10-inch skillet until light brown on all sides. Remove and cut into bite-size pieces. Combine the ducks, celery ribs, 1 cup onion, parsley and bay leaf in a 16-quart stockpot. Add 6 quarts water or enough to cover completely. Bring to a boil and reduce the heat.

Simmer, covered, for 1^1/$_2$ hours or until the ducks are tender. Remove the ducks and strain the cooking liquid, reserving 4 cups; discard the vegetables and herbs. Cut the ducks into bite-size pieces, discarding the skin and bones.

Heat the oil in the same stockpot and stir in the flour. Cook for 15 minutes or until the mixture is a dark reddish brown, stirring constantly. Add 2 cups onion, chopped celery, bell pepper, okra, Worcestershire sauce, thyme and black pepper. Cook until the vegetables are tender, stirring constantly.

Add the reserved duck broth, duck meat and sausage. Bring to a boil and reduce the heat. Simmer for 3 hours. Season with hot pepper sauce and red pepper. Serve over hot cooked rice.

Serves twenty

Avocado Mousse

1 (3-OUNCE) PACKAGE LIME
GELATIN
1 CUP BOILING WATER
2 CUPS AVOCADO PURÉE
JUICE OF 1 LEMON
3 TABLESPOONS GRATED
ONION
1/2 CUP MAYONNAISE
3/4 CUP SOUR CREAM
1 TABLESPOON FINELY
CHOPPED PARSLEY
1/4 TEASPOON
WORCESTERSHIRE SAUCE
TABASCO SAUCE TO TASTE
1 TEASPOON (SCANT) SALT

Garnish

FRESH FRUITS, SUCH AS
GREEN GRAPES,
STRAWBERRIES AND/OR
PINEAPPLE SPEARS

Dissolve the gelatin in the boiling water in a bowl. Let stand until cool. Combine the avocado, lemon juice, onion, mayonnaise, sour cream, parsley, Worcestershire sauce, Tabasco sauce and salt in a bowl. Add to the gelatin and mix well.

Spoon into an oiled 1 1/2-quart mold. Chill until firm. Unmold onto a bed of salad greens and garnish with fresh fruit.

For variety, mold in a ring and fill the center with chicken or shrimp salad or a mixture of mayonnaise, chopped pecans and grated orange zest and garnish with citrus fruits.

Serves eight to ten

Frosty Summer Salad

2 CUPS SOUR CREAM
3/4 CUP SUGAR
1/8 TEASPOON SALT
2 BANANAS
LEMON JUICE
1 (20-OUNCE) CAN
CRUSHED PINEAPPLE,
DRAINED
1/4 CUP PITTED DARK
SWEET CHERRIES OR
MARASCHINO CHERRIES,
CUT INTO HALVES
1/4 CUP CHOPPED NUTS

Combine the sour cream, sugar and salt in a bowl and mix well. Slice the bananas into a bowl and sprinkle with lemon juice. Add the pineapple, cherries and nuts to the bananas. Add the fruit to the sour cream mixture and mix gently. Spoon into foil-lined muffin cups. Freeze, covered, until firm. Remove the foil liners to serve.

Serves sixteen

ORANGE AND CRANBERRY SALAD

2 (3-OUNCE) PACKAGES
　　LEMON GELATIN
2 CUPS BOILING WATER
2 CUPS COLD WATER
3 LARGE UNPEELED
　　SEEDLESS ORANGES
3 CUPS FRESH
　　CRANBERRIES
1 CUP SUGAR

Garnish

MAYONNAISE

Dissolve the gelatin in the boiling water in a bowl. Stir in the cold water. Process the oranges and cranberries in the food processor until finely chopped. Add the sugar and mix well. Add to the gelatin and mix well. Spoon into a greased ring mold or individual molds and chill until firm. Unmold onto lettuce leaves and garnish with mayonnaise.

Serves six to eight

CITRUS SALAD MOLD

2 (11-OUNCE) CANS
　　MANDARIN ORANGES
1 (16-OUNCE) CAN
　　CRUSHED PINEAPPLE
2 (3-OUNCE) PACKAGES
　　ORANGE GELATIN
1 (6-OUNCE) CAN FROZEN
　　ORANGE JUICE
　　CONCENTRATE,
　　THAWED

Drain the oranges and pineapple, reserving the syrup. Add enough water to the reserved syrup to measure $3^{1}/2$ cups. Pour 2 cups of the liquid into a saucepan and bring to a boil. Remove from the heat and add the gelatin; stir to dissolve completely. Stir in the remaining $1^{1}/2$ cups liquid. Chill until slightly thickened.

Add the oranges, pineapple and orange juice concentrate. Chill until firm. Unmold onto a bed of fresh lettuce or spinach.

Serves eight

HENNY PENNY PASTA SALAD

Salad

8 OUNCES UNCOOKED
ROTINI

1 1/2 POUNDS BROCCOLI

4 CHICKEN BREASTS,
COOKED, CHOPPED

1/2 CUP CHOPPED RED OR
GREEN BELL PEPPER

1/4 CUP SLICED BLACK
OLIVES

1 TABLESPOON SLICED
GREEN ONIONS

Creamy Tarragon Dressing

1/2 CUP SOUR CREAM

1/4 CUP MAYONNAISE OR
MAYONNAISE-TYPE
SALAD DRESSING

3 TABLESPOONS WHITE
WINE VINEGAR

2 TABLESPOONS HEAVY
CREAM

1 1/2 TEASPOONS SUGAR

1 TEASPOON CRUSHED
DRIED TARRAGON

1 TEASPOON SALT

1/4 TEASPOON PEPPER

For the salad, cook the pasta using the package directions; rinse under cold water and drain. Cut the broccoli into florets and combine with a small amount of water in a saucepan. Cook for 3 to 5 minutes or until tender-crisp; drain. Combine the pasta, broccoli, chicken, bell pepper, black olives and green onions in a large bowl and toss lightly.

For the dressing, combine the sour cream, mayonnaise, vinegar, heavy cream, sugar, tarragon, salt and pepper in a small bowl and mix well. Pour over the salad and toss lightly. Chill, covered, until serving time.

You may substitute cooked peeled shrimp for the chopped cooked chicken.

Serves four

Artichoke And Rice Salad

2 (6-OUNCE) PACKAGES
   CHICKEN-FLAVOR
   RICE MIX
³/₄ CUP CHOPPED GREEN
   OR RED BELL PEPPER
16 PIMENTO-STUFFED
   GREEN OLIVES, SLICED
¹/₂ CUP SLICED GREEN
   ONIONS
2 (6-OUNCE) JARS
   MARINATED ARTICHOKE
   HEARTS
¹/₂ CUP MAYONNAISE
1 TEASPOON CURRY
   POWDER

Cook the rice using the package directions and omitting the butter. Spoon into a large bowl and cool to room temperature. Add the bell pepper, olives and green onions; mix lightly. Drain the artichokes, reserving the liquid. Slice the artichokes and add to the rice mixture.

Combine the reserved liquid with the mayonnaise and curry powder in a bowl and mix well. Pour over the rice mixture and toss to mix well. Chill, covered, until serving time.

Serves twelve

Curried Chicken Salad

Curry Mayonnaise

¹/₂ CUP MAYONNAISE
1 TABLESPOON CHOPPED
   GINGERROOT
   PRESERVED IN SYRUP
1 TEASPOON GRATED
   ONION
2 TEASPOONS CURRY
   POWDER
¹/₂ TEASPOON SALT
¹/₂ CUP WHIPPING CREAM

Salad

3 CUPS CHOPPED COOKED
   CHICKEN
¹/₄ CUP OIL AND VINEGAR
   SALAD DRESSING
2 CUPS (1-INCH) CHUNKS
   FRESH PINEAPPLE
1¹/₂ CUPS CHOPPED PEELED
   APPLES
1¹/₂ CUPS SEEDLESS GRAPES
¹/₄ CUP CHUTNEY
¹/₄ CUP CHOPPED GREEN
   BELL PEPPER

For the mayonnaise, combine the mayonnaise, gingerroot, onion, curry powder and salt in a bowl and mix well. Beat the whipping cream in a bowl until soft peaks form. Fold into the mayonnaise mixture. Chill, covered, in the refrigerator.

For the salad, combine the chicken and salad dressing in a bowl and toss to mix well. Chill, covered, for 2 hours or longer.

Add the pineapple, apples, grapes, chutney and bell pepper to the chicken and mix well. Fold in the curry mayonnaise. Chill, covered, for 2 hours or longer. Mound on a bed of lettuce to serve.

You may substitute chopped cooked turkey for the chicken and one drained 16-ounce can pineapple chunks for the fresh pineapple.

Serves six to eight

Gringo Chicken Salad

Gringo Dressing

1/2 CUP MAYONNAISE OR
  MAYONNAISE-TYPE
  SALAD DRESSING
1/2 CUP LOW-FAT SOUR
  CREAM
1 TEASPOON CHILI
  POWDER
1/2 TEASPOON GROUND
  CUMIN
1/4 TEASPOON CRUSHED
  DRIED BASIL
SALT AND PEPPER TO TASTE

Salad

4 CUPS CHOPPED COOKED
  CHICKEN
2 CUPS (8 OUNCES)
  SHREDDED SHARP
  CHEDDAR CHEESE
1 (16-OUNCE) CAN KIDNEY
  BEANS, DRAINED
1/2 CUP CHOPPED ONION
1/2 CUP SLICED BLACK
  OLIVES
1/2 CUP CHOPPED RED OR
  GREEN BELL PEPPER
SHREDDED LETTUCE
2 MEDIUM AVOCADOS,
  PEELED, SLICED
2 MEDIUM TOMATOES,
  CHOPPED
CORN CHIPS

For the dressing, combine the mayonnaise, sour cream, chili powder, cumin, basil, salt and pepper in a small bowl and mix well.

For the salad, combine the chicken, cheese, kidney beans, onion, black olives and bell pepper in a medium bowl and mix well. Add the gringo dressing and toss lightly. Chill, covered, in the refrigerator until serving time.

Spoon onto a bed of shredded lettuce. Top with the avocados, tomatoes and corn chips.

Serves six to eight

Croutons

For *Cheese Croutons*, combine 1 tablespoon melted butter with 1 tablespoon grated Parmesan cheese in a bowl. Add 1 cup 1/2-inch bread cubes and toss lightly. Spread on a baking sheet and toast at 350 degrees for 5 minutes or until golden brown.

For *Garlic Croutons*, cut bread with crust into small cubes and spread on a baking sheet. Toast at 200 degrees until dry and golden brown, stirring frequently. Sauté 1 garlic clove in butter in a skillet. Remove the garlic and add the bread cubes; toss to coat well. Store in an airtight container in the refrigerator. Reheat to serve.

BROCCOLI WITH A TWIST

Sweet-and-Sour Mayonnaise

1 1/2 CUPS MAYONNAISE OR
   MAYONNAISE-TYPE
   SALAD DRESSING
3/4 CUP SUGAR
2 TABLESPOONS CIDER
   VINEGAR
1 TABLESPOON LEMON
   JUICE

Salad

5 CUPS BROCCOLI FLORETS
1/2 CUP RAISINS
1/2 CUP CHOPPED PECANS,
   TOASTED
1/2 CUP CHOPPED RED
   ONION
12 SLICES BACON, CRISP-
   FRIED, CRUMBLED

For the mayonnaise, combine the mayonnaise, sugar, vinegar and lemon juice in a small bowl and mix well. Chill, covered, for 2 hours or longer.

For the salad, combine the broccoli, raisins, pecans, onion and bacon in a large bowl and mix well. Add the sweet-and-sour mayonnaise and toss lightly. Serve immediately or chill, covered, until serving time.

Serves six

CAESAR SALAD

Mock Caesar Dressing

3/4 CUP OLIVE OIL
1/4 CUP WINE VINEGAR
2 TEASPOONS LEMON
   JUICE
2 TEASPOONS
   WORCESTERSHIRE
   SAUCE
1 1/2 GARLIC CLOVES,
   MINCED
1 TABLESPOON GRATED
   PARMESAN CHEESE

Salad

6 CUPS TORN MIXED
   SALAD GREENS
1 CUP CROUTONS (AT LEFT)
SALT AND PEPPER TO TASTE

For the dressing, combine the olive oil, vinegar, lemon juice, Worcestershire sauce, garlic and cheese in a bowl and mix well.

For the salad, combine the salad greens with the croutons in a bowl. Season with salt and pepper. Add the mock Caesar dressing and toss lightly to coat evenly. Serve immediately.

Serves six

Country Coleslaw

1/2 HEAD CABBAGE,
   SHREDDED
1 ONION, SHREDDED
2 CARROTS, SHREDDED
1/4 CUP MAYONNAISE
3 TABLESPOONS VINEGAR
1 TEASPOON SUGAR
SALT AND PEPPER TO TASTE

Combine the cabbage, onion and carrots in a large bowl and mix well. Mix the mayonnaise, vinegar, sugar, salt and pepper in a bowl. Add to the cabbage mixture and toss to coat well. Chill, covered, for several hours before serving.

Serves eight

Summer Corn Salad

Salad

4 CUPS FRESH CORN
   KERNELS
1 CUCUMBER, PEELED,
   CHOPPED
1 LARGE TOMATO, SEEDED,
   CHOPPED
1 PURPLE ONION, CHOPPED
1/2 CUP CHOPPED GREEN
   BELL PEPPER

Sour Cream Dressing

1/2 CUP SOUR CREAM
3 TABLESPOONS
   MAYONNAISE OR
   MAYONNAISE-TYPE
   SALAD DRESSING
2 TABLESPOONS WHITE
   WINE VINEGAR
1/2 TEASPOON DRY
   MUSTARD
1/2 TEASPOON CELERY SEEDS
1 TEASPOON SALT
1/2 TEASPOON PEPPER

Garnish

SHREDDED SALAD GREENS
CHOPPED RED BELL PEPPER

For the salad, combine the corn with a small amount of water in a 2-quart saucepan. Cook, covered, for 5 to 7 minutes or until tender-crisp; drain and cool to room temperature. Combine with the cucumber, tomato, onion and bell pepper in a large bowl and mix well.

For the dressing, combine the sour cream, mayonnaise, vinegar, dry mustard, celery seeds, salt and pepper in a bowl and mix well. Spread over the corn mixture, sealing to the edge of the bowl. Chill, covered, for 8 hours or longer.

Toss the salad lightly to serve. Garnish with shredded lettuce and red bell pepper.

You may substitute two 10-ounce packages frozen whole kernel corn for the fresh corn.

Serves twelve

GAZPACHO ASPIC

Aspic

2 ENVELOPES UNFLAVORED
GELATIN
3 CUPS TOMATO JUICE
1/4 CUP WINE VINEGAR
1 GARLIC CLOVE,
CRUSHED
2 TEASPOONS SALT
CAYENNE PEPPER
TO TASTE
1/4 TEASPOON BLACK
PEPPER
2 LARGE TOMATOES,
CHOPPED, DRAINED
1/2 CUP FINELY CHOPPED
ONION
3/4 CUP FINELY CHOPPED
GREEN BELL PEPPER
3/4 CUP CHOPPED
CUCUMBER, DRAINED
1/4 CUP FINELY CHOPPED
PIMENTOES

Aspic Dressing

1/2 CUP SOUR CREAM
1/3 CUP MAYONNAISE
1/2 TEASPOON SALT

Garnish

HOT PEPPERS
DILLED OKRA

For the aspic, soften the gelatin in 1 cup of the tomato juice in a saucepan. Bring to a simmer, stirring to dissolve the gelatin. Add the remaining 2 cups tomato juice, vinegar, garlic, salt, cayenne pepper and black pepper and mix well. Chill, covered, until partially set.

Add the tomatoes, onion, bell pepper, cucumber and pimentoes and mix well. Spoon into a 6-cup mold and chill, covered, until set. Unmold onto a lettuce-lined serving plate.

For the dressing, mix the sour cream, mayonnaise and salt in a bowl. Spread over the salad. Garnish with hot peppers and dilled okra.

Serves eight

Potato Salad

6 MEDIUM POTATOES
1 CUP ITALIAN OR ONION
  SALAD DRESSING
1 ONION, FINELY CHOPPED
2 HARD-COOKED EGGS,
  CHOPPED
1/2 CUP CHOPPED CELERY
1 CUP MAYONNAISE
2 TEASPOONS PREPARED
  MUSTARD
1/2 TEASPOON CELERY SEEDS
SALT, SEASONED SALT AND
  PEPPER TO TASTE

Garnish

LETTUCE
CHOPPED TOMATOES
CHOPPED HARD-COOKED
  EGGS

Cook the potatoes in boiling water in a saucepan until tender; drain. Let cool and chop the potatoes into bite-size pieces. Combine the potatoes with the salad dressing in a bowl and mix gently. Marinate, covered, in the refrigerator for several hours.

Add the onion, eggs, celery, mayonnaise, mustard, celery seeds, salt, seasoned salt and pepper and mix gently. Chill, covered, until serving time. Garnish with lettuce, tomatoes and additional hard-cooked eggs.

Serves six to eight

Salade Parmesan

3 TABLESPOONS GRATED
  PARMESAN CHEESE
1/4 CUP OLIVE OIL
2 TABLESPOONS FRESH
  LEMON JUICE
2 GARLIC CLOVES, MINCED
1 TEASPOON DRY MUSTARD
SALT TO TASTE
1/2 TEASPOON CRACKED
  PEPPER
10 TO 12 CUPS TORN
  SALAD GREENS
2 TABLESPOONS GRATED
  PARMESAN CHEESE

Combine 3 tablespoons Parmesan cheese, olive oil, lemon juice, garlic, dry mustard, salt and pepper in a large salad bowl and mix well.

Place the torn salad greens on top of the olive oil mixture. Let stand without mixing until serving time. Toss to coat well and sprinkle with 2 tablespoons Parmesan cheese. Serve immediately.

You may sprinkle the salad with croutons, crumbled goat cheese, walnut pieces and/or balsamic vinegar.

Serves eight to ten

Spinach And Mandarin Orange Salad

12 SLICES BACON
1½ POUNDS FRESH
    SPINACH LEAVES
1 (11-OUNCE) CAN
    MANDARIN ORANGES,
    DRAINED
ARTICHOKE HEARTS
FRENCH DRESSING
    (PAGE 57)

Cook the bacon in a skillet until crisp; crumble. Tear the spinach into bite-size pieces. Combine the bacon, spinach and oranges in a bowl and mix lightly. Add artichoke hearts and toss to mix. Add the French dressing and toss lightly.

You may substitute hearts of palm or pineapple chunks for the artichoke hearts.

Serves six to eight

Yellow Squash Salad

2 POUNDS YELLOW
    SQUASH
SALT TO TASTE
2 TO 3 HEADS BIBB
    LETTUCE, TORN
½ CUP OIL AND VINEGAR
    SALAD DRESSING
½ CUP SOUR CREAM
½ CUP MAYONNAISE

Garnish

DILLSEED

Parboil the whole squash in salted water in a saucepan until tender-crisp; do not overcook. Drain the squash and chill in the refrigerator. Slice and season with salt.

Toss the lettuce with the salad dressing in a salad bowl. Spoon onto salad plates and arrange the squash over the top. Mix the sour cream with the mayonnaise in a small bowl. Spoon over the squash. Garnish with dillseeds.

Serves eight

Vinaigrette Your Way

½ CUP WINE VINEGAR,
CIDER VINEGAR OR
MALT VINEGAR

¾ TEASPOON SALT

¼ TEASPOON WHITE
PEPPER

1½ CUPS OLIVE OIL OR
SALAD OIL

Combine the vinegar, salt and white pepper in a bowl and mix well with a fork. Add the olive oil and beat until thickened.

Makes two cups

Variations

For *Bellevue Vinaigrette*, add ¾ cup sour cream and 2 tablespoons finely chopped chives. Serve on citrus salads.

For *Caper Vinaigrette*, add 4 teaspoons drained chopped capers, ½ teaspoon anchovy paste, 2 grated large garlic cloves, ¼ cup chopped hard-cooked egg yolk and several drops of Tabasco sauce. Serve on green salads or fish salads.

For *Chutney Vinaigrette*, substitute lemon juice for half of the vinegar and add ½ to 2 cups chutney.

For *Cottage Cheese Vinaigrette*, add 6 tablespoons cottage cheese and 2 tablespoons each chopped sweet pickle and parsley or watercress. Serve on tomato salads.

For *Curry Vinaigrette*, add 2 teaspoons curry powder and 2 tablespoons finely chopped shallots. Serve on green salads.

For *Grenadine Vinaigrette*, add ¼ cup grenadine, 2 teaspoons each grated orange zest and lemon zest. Add Tabasco sauce to taste. Serve on fruit salads.

For *Horseradish Vinaigrette*, add 6 tablespoons drained horseradish, 4 teaspoons paprika, and several drops of Tabasco sauce. Serve on meat salads.

For *Hot Vinaigrette*, bring the basic vinaigrette to a simmer and add 4 chopped hard-cooked eggs, 2 tablespoons each finely chopped parsley and green celery leaves, 1 teaspoon Worcestershire sauce and 2 teaspoons dry mustard. Beat until smooth and serve on asparagus, broccoli, cauliflower or hot potato salad.

For *Martinique Vinaigrette*, add 4 teaspoons each finely chopped parsley, green bell pepper, shallots and chervil. Serve on mixed vegetable salads and greens.

For *Mushroom Vinaigrette*, add ½ cup thinly sliced fresh mushrooms. Serve on green salads.

For *Sherry Vinaigrette*, add ½ cup sherry, 2 teaspoons chopped chervil and ¼teaspoon sugar. Serve on fruit salads.

For *Vinaigrette Deluxe*, add 2 teaspoons each finely chopped green olives, drained capers, chives, parsley, gherkins and 1 finely chopped hard-cooked egg yolk. Serve on green salads.

French Dressing

Combine ¾ cup vegetable oil, ¼ cup vinegar, the juice of 1 lemon, 1 chopped garlic clove, ½ teaspoon Mrs. Dash seasoning or MSG, ½ teaspoon salt and ¼ teaspoon pepper in a bowl and mix well. Serve on spinach salads or other green salads.

Biscuits

2 CUPS SIFTED FLOUR
2 TEASPOONS BAKING
  POWDER
1/4 TEASPOON BAKING
  SODA
1/4 TEASPOON SALT
1/4 CUP SHORTENING
1/2 CUP BUTTERMILK

Sift the flour, baking powder, baking soda and salt into a bowl. Cut or work the shortening into the dry ingredients until the mixture resembles coarse crumbs. Add the buttermilk and mix to form a soft dough.

Knead very lightly on a floured surface or just until the dough can be rolled. Roll 1/2 inch thick and cut with a floured biscuit cutter. Place on a baking sheet and prick the tops with a fork. Bake at 450 degrees for 8 minutes.

To make a substitute for the buttermilk, combine 1/2 cup of milk with 1 1/2 teaspoons lemon juice or vinegar and let stand for 20 minutes.

Makes sixteen

Baby Butterball Biscuits

1 CUP (2 STICKS) BUTTER
  OR MARGARINE
2 CUPS SELF-RISING FLOUR
1 CUP SOUR CREAM

Cut the butter into the flour in a bowl. Add the sour cream and mix well. Drop by heaping teaspoonfuls onto an ungreased baking sheet. Bake for 20 minutes or until firm to the touch; biscuits will not be brown.

Makes two and one-half dozen

DEVIL IN DISGUISE CORN BREAD

1 TABLESPOON
   SHORTENING
1¹/2 CUPS SELF-RISING
   CORNMEAL
1 CUP YELLOW CREAM-
   STYLE CORN
1 CUP (4 OUNCES)
   SHREDDED SHARP
   CHEDDAR CHEESE
¹/2 CUP CHOPPED ONION
2 TO 4 JALAPEÑO PEPPERS,
   SEEDED, CHOPPED
1 CUP BUTTERMILK
¹/2 CUP VEGETABLE OIL
2 EGGS, BEATEN

Place the shortening in a 10-inch cast-iron skillet or other ovenproof skillet. Heat in a 400-degree oven until the shortening melts.

Combine the cornmeal, corn, cheese, onion, and jalapeño peppers in a medium bowl. Add the buttermilk, oil and eggs and mix just until moistened.

Pour the batter into the hot skillet. Bake at 400 degrees for 35 to 40 minutes or until golden brown. Serve warm.

You may spoon the batter into 12 muffin cups, filling cups ²/3 full. Bake at 400 degrees for 18 to 20 minutes or until golden brown.

Serves eight

SPOON BREAD

2 CUPS MILK
1 CUP WATER
1 CUP CORNMEAL
1 TEASPOON SALT
¹/4 CUP (¹/2 STICK) BUTTER
   OR MARGARINE,
   MELTED
3 EGGS, BEATEN

Combine the milk and water in a saucepan and bring just to a simmer. Stir in the cornmeal and salt. Cook until thickened, stirring constantly; remove from the heat. Fold in the butter and eggs.

Spoon into a greased 2-quart baking dish. Bake at 350 degrees for 1 hour. Serve immediately.

Serves six

Popovers

Mix 1 cup flour and a pinch of salt in a bowl. Beat 3 eggs in a medium bowl until light. Add 1 cup milk and beat until smooth. Add to the flour mixture gradually and mix for 1 or 2 minutes. Pour into 6 greased heated muffin cups or individual ramekins. Bake at 450 degrees for 30 minutes. Remove from the muffin cups or ramekins immediately and serve warm with a mixture of strawberry preserves and butter.

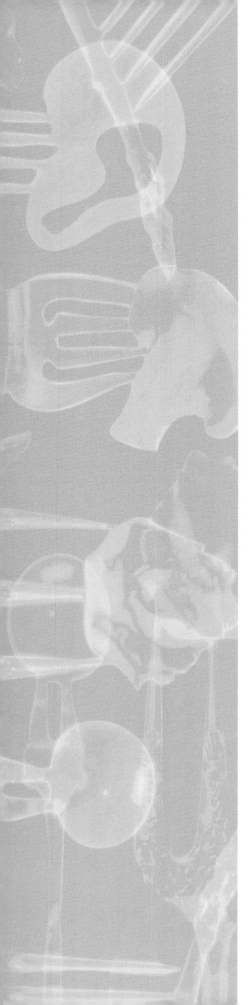

Turn-But-Once Pancakes

2¹/₂ CUPS SIFTED FLOUR
1 TABLESPOON BAKING
   POWDER
2 TEASPOONS BAKING
   SODA
1 TABLESPOON SUGAR
1 TEASPOON SALT
2 CUPS BUTTERMILK
3 EGG YOLKS
1 CUP SOUR CREAM
¹/₄ CUP (¹/₂ STICK) BUTTER,
   MELTED
3 EGG WHITES

Sift the flour, baking powder, baking soda, sugar and salt together. Combine the buttermilk and egg yolks in a mixing bowl and beat until smooth. Stir in the sour cream and melted butter. Add the dry ingredients and stir just until moistened. Beat the egg whites until stiff peaks form. Fold into the batter.

Ladle the batter onto a heated griddle and cook until bubbles appear on the top. Turn and cook until golden brown.

You may add additional buttermilk if the batter appears too thick.

Makes two dozen

Grandma's Bran Muffins

1 (15-OUNCE) PACKAGE
   RAISIN BRAN CEREAL
5 CUPS FLOUR
3 CUPS SUGAR
5 TEASPOONS BAKING
   SODA
1 TEASPOON CINNAMON
1 TEASPOON NUTMEG
1 TEASPOON CLOVES
2 TEASPOONS SALT
4 EGGS, BEATEN
4 CUPS BUTTERMILK
1 CUP VEGETABLE OIL
2 TEASPOONS VANILLA
   EXTRACT
1 CUP CHOPPED NUTS
   (OPTIONAL)

Mix the cereal, flour, sugar, baking soda, cinnamon, nutmeg, cloves and salt in a large bowl. Combine the eggs, buttermilk, oil and vanilla in a medium mixing bowl and beat until smooth. Add to the cereal mixture and mix just until moistened. Stir in the nuts.

Spoon the mixture into greased or paper-lined muffin cups, filling ²/₃ full. Bake at 400 degrees for 15 minutes or until light brown.

You may store the batter in an airtight container in the refrigerator for up to 4 days and bake the muffins as needed.

Makes forty

LEMON MUFFINS

2 CUPS FLOUR

2 TEASPOONS BAKING
POWDER

1 TEASPOON SALT

1 CUP (2 STICKS) BUTTER
OR SHORTENING,
SOFTENED

1 CUP SUGAR

4 EGG YOLKS

1/2 CUP LEMON JUICE

4 EGG WHITES

2 TEASPOONS GRATED
LEMON ZEST

Sift the flour, baking powder and salt together. Cream the butter and sugar in a mixing bowl until light and fluffy. Beat in the egg yolks. Add the lemon juice alternately with the dry ingredients, mixing just until moistened after each addition. Beat the eggs whites until stiff peaks form. Fold into the batter with the lemon zest.

Spoon into buttered muffin cups, filling 3/4 full. Bake at 375 degrees for 20 minutes.

You may freeze the muffins. They are good split and toasted for breakfast.

Makes two dozen

GLAZED MUFFIN CAKES

Muffins

3 1/2 CUPS SIFTED FLOUR

2 TEASPOONS BAKING
POWDER

1 CUP (2 STICKS) BUTTER,
SOFTENED

2 CUPS SUGAR

3 EGGS

1 CUP MILK

Fruit Glaze

1/4 CUP LEMON JUICE

1/4 CUP ORANGE JUICE

1/4 CUP PINEAPPLE JUICE

2 TABLESPOONS BUTTER

2 1/4 CUPS CONFECTIONERS'
SUGAR

For the muffins, sift the flour and baking powder into a bowl. Cream the butter and sugar in a mixing bowl until light and fluffy. Beat in the eggs. Add the dry ingredients 1/3 at a time alternately with the milk, ending with the flour and mixing just until moistened after each addition.

Spoon into greased muffin cups, filling 2/3 full. Bake at 350 degrees for 20 to 25 minutes or until golden brown.

For the glaze, combine the lemon juice, orange juice, pineapple juice and butter in a saucepan and heat until bubbly. Add the confectioners' sugar and mix well. Spoon over the warm muffins.

The batter can also be baked in miniature muffin cups, making 100 small muffins. The glaze is also good spooned over warm sponge cake, pound cake or white cake.

Makes thirty

Sally Lunn Muffins

2 CUPS FLOUR
4 TEASPOONS BAKING
   POWDER
1/4 TEASPOON SALT
1/2 CUP (1 STICK) BUTTER,
   SOFTENED
1/4 CUP SUGAR
1 CUP MILK
1 EGG, BEATEN

Sift the flour, baking powder and salt together. Cream the butter and sugar in a mixing bowl until light and fluffy. Add the dry ingredients alternately with the milk, mixing well after each addition. Stir in the egg.

Spoon into greased muffin cups. Bake at 375 degrees for 25 minutes. Serve hot.

Makes one dozen

Orange Blossom Muffins

Spice Topping

4 TEASPOONS FLOUR
1/4 CUP SUGAR
1/2 TEASPOON CINNAMON
1/4 TEASPOON NUTMEG
3 TABLESPOONS BUTTER
   OR MARGARINE

Muffins

2 CUPS BUTTERMILK
   BAKING MIX
1/4 CUP SUGAR
1 EGG
1/2 CUP ORANGE JUICE
2 TABLESPOONS VEGETABLE
   OIL OR MELTED
   SHORTENING
1/2 CUP ORANGE
   MARMALADE
1/2 CUP CHOPPED PECANS

For the topping, combine the flour, sugar, cinnamon and nutmeg in a medium bowl and mix well. Cut in the butter until the mixture resembles coarse crumbs.

For the muffins, combine the buttermilk baking mix and sugar in a large bowl and mix well; make a well in the center. Beat the egg, orange juice and oil in a small bowl until smooth. Pour into the well and mix just until moistened. Stir in the marmalade and pecans.

Spoon the batter into greased or paper-lined muffin cups, filling 2/3 full. Sprinkle with the topping. Bake at 400 degrees for 20 minutes or until golden brown.

Makes one dozen

$\mathcal{A}$PRICOT $\mathcal{P}$ECAN $\mathcal{B}$READ

1¹/2 CUPS FLOUR

¹/4 TEASPOON BAKING
   POWDER

1 TEASPOON BAKING
   SODA

¹/2 TEASPOON CINNAMON

¹/2 TEASPOON GINGER

¹/2 TEASPOON ALLSPICE

¹/2 TEASPOON SALT

¹/2 CUP (1 STICK) BUTTER
   OR MARGARINE,
   SOFTENED

1 CUP PLUS 2 TABLESPOONS
   SUGAR

2 EGGS

1 CUP PURÉED PEELED FRESH
   OR CANNED APRICOTS

¹/3 CUP CHOPPED PECANS

Combine the flour, baking powder, baking soda, cinnamon, ginger, allspice and salt in a bowl and mix well.

Cream the butter and sugar in a mixing bowl until light and fluffy. Beat in the eggs and apricot purée. Add the dry ingredients and mix just until moistened. Stir in the pecans.

Spoon the batter into a greased 5×9-inch loaf pan. Bake at 325 degrees for 45 minutes or until a wooden pick inserted near the center comes out clean.

Cool in the pan for 10 minutes. Remove to a wire rack to cool completely.

Serves twelve

$\mathcal{B}$ANANA $\mathcal{N}$UT $\mathcal{B}$READ

2 CUPS FLOUR

1 TEASPOON BAKING
   SODA

3 VERY RIPE BANANAS

¹/2 CUP (1 STICK) BUTTER
   OR MARGARINE,
   SOFTENED

1 CUP SUGAR

2 EGGS

¹/2 CUP FINELY CHOPPED
   PECANS

Sift the flour and baking soda together. Beat the bananas in a mixing bowl until very smooth. Cream the butter and sugar in a mixing bowl until light and fluffy. Beat in the eggs. Add the dry ingredients and mix well. Stir in the pecans and bananas.

Spoon into a greased loaf pan. Bake at 350 degrees for 1 hour.

Serves eight

Marmalade Magic

For *Marmalade Muffins*, separate refrigerator biscuits and place 1 in each muffin cup. Press with your thumb to indent the centers. Place a pat of butter and 1 spoonful of orange marmalade in each indentation. Bake at 450 degrees for 12 to 15 minutes or until golden brown.

For *Marmalade Roll-Ups*, remove the crusts from thinly sliced bread and spread lightly with butter and orange marmalade. Roll up to enclose the filling and secure with wooden picks. Toast under the broiler and serve hot.

For *Hot Mustard*, combine one 12-ounce jar of orange marmalade, one 10-ounce jar of apple jelly, one 6-ounce jar of prepared mustard and 1 jar of cream-style horseradish in a mixing bowl and beat until smooth. Store in an airtight container in the refrigerator. Serve hot or cold.

ORANGE POPPY SEED BREAD

Bread

3 CUPS FLOUR

2 1/4 CUPS SUGAR

1 1/2 TEASPOONS BAKING
   POWDER

2 TABLESPOONS POPPY
   SEEDS

1/2 TEASPOON SALT

3 EGGS

1 1/2 CUPS MILK

1 CUP VEGETABLE OIL

2 TABLESPOONS FINELY
   SHREDDED ORANGE
   ZEST

1 TEASPOON VANILLA
   EXTRACT

1/2 TEASPOON ALMOND
   EXTRACT

Orange Glaze

3/4 CUP SIFTED
   CONFECTIONERS' SUGAR

1/4 CUP ORANGE JUICE

1/2 TEASPOON VANILLA
   EXTRACT

1/2 TEASPOON ALMOND
   EXTRACT

For the bread, mix the flour, sugar, baking powder, poppy seeds and salt in a large mixing bowl. Add the eggs, milk, oil, orange zest and flavorings and beat at medium speed for 2 minutes.

Spoon into 2 greased 4×8-inch loaf pans. Bake at 350 degrees for 1 hour or until a wooden pick inserted in the center comes out clean.

For the glaze, combine the confectioners' sugar, orange juice and flavorings in a medium bowl and mix well.

To glaze, pierce the bread with a long-tined fork and pour the glaze over the loaves. Cool in the pans for 10 minutes. Remove from the pans and cool on wire racks.

Makes two loaves

Photograph for muffins prepared from this recipe is on page 36.

PUMPKIN BREAD

3 1/2 CUPS FLOUR

1 TEASPOON BAKING
POWDER

2 TEASPOONS BAKING
SODA

1 TEASPOON NUTMEG

1 TEASPOON ALLSPICE

1 TEASPOON CINNAMON

1/2 TEASPOON CLOVES

2 TEASPOONS SALT

3 CUPS SUGAR

1 CUP VEGETABLE OIL

4 EGGS, BEATEN

1 (16-OUNCE) CAN PUMPKIN

2/3 CUP WATER

Sift the flour, baking powder, baking soda, nutmeg, allspice, cinnamon, cloves and salt into a medium bowl. Combine the sugar and oil in a mixing bowl and beat until smooth. Beat in the eggs and pumpkin. Add the dry ingredients alternately with the water, mixing well after each addition.

Spoon into 2 greased and floured 5×9-inch loaf pans. Bake at 350 degrees for 1 to 1 1/2 hours or until the loaves test done. Cool in the pans for 10 minutes. Remove from the pans to a wire rack to cool completely.

Makes two loaves

ZUCCHINI BREAD

3 EGGS

1 CUP VEGETABLE OIL

2 CUPS SUGAR

1/4 TEASPOON BAKING
POWDER

1 TEASPOON BAKING
SODA

2 TEASPOONS VANILLA
EXTRACT

1 TEASPOON CINNAMON

1 TEASPOON SALT

2 CUPS SHREDDED
ZUCCHINI

3 CUPS FLOUR

1/2 CUP CHOPPED WALNUTS

Combine the eggs and oil in a large bowl and beat until thick and pale yellow. Add the sugar, baking powder, baking soda, vanilla, cinnamon and salt and mix well. Stir in the zucchini. Add the flour and walnuts and mix just until moistened.

Spoon into 2 greased and floured 4×8-inch loaf pans. Bake at 350 degrees for 1 hour or until a wooden pick inserted in the center comes out clean. Cool in the pans for 10 minutes. Remove from the pans to a wire rack to cool completely.

Makes two loaves

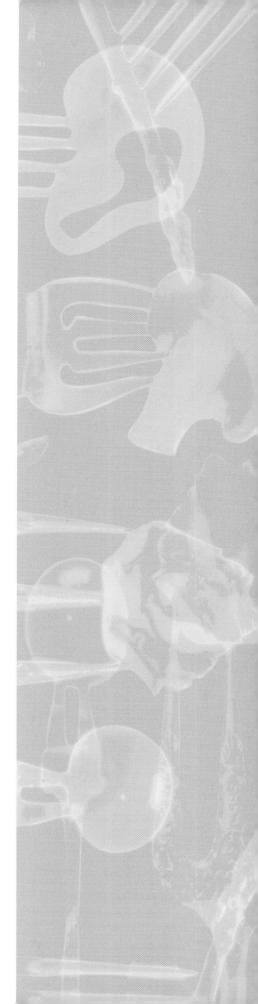

Beer Rolls

There was nothing quite like *A Man's Taste*, published in 1980, and from which many of the recipes in this book are taken. The recipes were created, tasted, and submitted by men with no editorial input from the Junior League. Beer Rolls is truly as tasty as it is entertaining in its original form:

Throw 2 cups baking mix and 1 tablespoon sugar in a pot of some kind and mix well. Take a 6-pack of beer out of the icebox and open 1 can. Pour half of it in a glass so it will warm to room temperature. You now have 5$^{1}/_{2}$ cans of cold beer. You might use some of this to pass the time while the 6 ounces warm up. When the right temperature, pour the warm beer in the pot and mix it up good. Drop the dough in a greased muffin pan. Bake in a 450-degree oven for about 10 minutes and eat.

1 ENVELOPE DRY YEAST
2 CUPS WARM (115- TO 120-DEGREE) WATER
$^{1}/_{2}$ CUP SUGAR
1 EGG, BEATEN
2 TEASPOONS SALT
$^{1}/_{2}$ CUP (1 STICK) BUTTER, MELTED
5 CUPS FLOUR
$^{1}/_{2}$ CUP (1 STICK) BUTTER, MELTED

Dissolve the yeast in the warm water. Combine the sugar, egg and salt in a large mixing bowl. Stir in the yeast mixture. Add $^{1}/_{2}$ cup butter and 3 cups of the flour and mix well. Mix in the remaining flour.

Place in an airtight container. Let rise for 1 to 2 hours or until doubled in bulk. Punch the dough down. Roll $^{1}/_{2}$ to $^{3}/_{4}$ inch thick on a floured surface. Cut with a floured 2$^{1}/_{2}$-inch cutter and dip in $^{1}/_{2}$ cup melted butter.

Arrange with sides nearly touching in 2 lightly greased 9×13-inch baking pans. Let rise, uncovered, for 1 to 2 hours or until nearly doubled in bulk. Bake at 350 degrees for 25 to 30 minutes or until golden brown.

The dough may be covered and placed in the refrigerator for up to 24 hours after the first rising and before shaping.

To freeze rolls, bake for only 15 minutes or just until light brown. Cool, wrap and freeze until needed. Thaw at room temperature for 15 minutes and bake at 350 degrees for 15 minutes or until golden brown.

Makes thirty

Monkey Bread

1 ENVELOPE DRY YEAST
1/2 CUP LUKEWARM WATER
2/3 CUP SUGAR
1 CUP MASHED COOKED
    POTATOES
1 TEASPOON SALT
2/3 CUP BUTTER
2/3 CUP MARGARINE
1 CUP MILK
6 CUPS SIFTED FLOUR
2 EGGS, BEATEN
MELTED BUTTER

Dissolve the yeast in the lukewarm water in a bowl. Combine the sugar, potatoes and salt in a mixing bowl and mix until smooth. Melt 2/3 cup butter and margarine with the milk in a saucepan over low heat. Add to the potato mixture and mix well. Add the yeast mixture and half the flour and mix well. Add the eggs to the remaining flour and mix until smooth. Add to the potato mixture and mix well.

Let rise in a warm place for 1 hour. Stir down the dough and place, covered, in the refrigerator until ready to bake.

Shape into small elongated rolls and dip into additional melted butter. Arrange in 2 layers in a buttered tube pan. Bake at 350 degrees for 30 to 40 minutes or until golden brown. Remove from the pan. Tear rolls apart rather than slicing to serve.

Serves eight to ten

Martha's Meant-To-Be Cheese Danish

Danish

2 (8-COUNT) CANS
    CRESCENT ROLLS
16 OUNCES CREAM
    CHEESE, SOFTENED
1 CUP SUGAR
1 EGG
1 TEASPOON VANILLA
    EXTRACT

Pecan Topping

1/2 CUP (1 STICK) BUTTER
    OR MARGARINE,
    MELTED
1/2 CUP SUGAR
1 TEASPOON CINNAMON
1 CUP CHOPPED PECANS

For the Danish, unroll 1 can of the rolls and press over the bottom of a greased 9×13-inch baking dish; press the perforations to seal, easing the dough slightly up the sides of the dish.

Combine the cream cheese, sugar, egg and vanilla in a mixing bowl and mix until smooth. Spread over the roll dough. Unroll the remaining can of rolls and arrange over the top, pinching the perforations and pressing the edges to seal.

For the topping, combine the butter, sugar, cinnamon and pecans in a bowl and mix well. Spread evenly over the top layer.

Bake at 350 degrees for 30 minutes or until golden brown. Cut into rectangles to serve.

Serves sixteen

Cinnamon Pecan Coffee Cake

Streusel

1/2 CUP SUGAR
1 TEASPOON BAKING
   COCOA
1 CUP CHOPPED PECANS
1/4 CUP MINCED RAISINS
1 TABLESPOON
   CINNAMON

Coffee Cake

3 CUPS FLOUR
1 TEASPOON BAKING
   SODA
1/4 TEASPOON SALT
1 CUP (2 STICKS) BUTTER,
   SOFTENED
1 1/2 CUPS SUGAR
4 EGG YOLKS
1 CUP BUTTERMILK
2 TEASPOONS BAKING
   POWDER
4 EGG WHITES
BUTTER

For the streusel, combine the sugar, baking cocoa, pecans, raisins and cinnamon in a bowl and mix well.

For the coffee cake, sift the flour, baking soda and salt together 6 times. Cream 1 cup butter and sugar in a mixing bowl until light and fluffy. Beat in the egg yolks 1 at a time, mixing well after each addition. Add the dry ingredients alternately with the buttermilk, adding the baking powder to the dry ingredients just before the last addition and mixing well. Beat the egg whites until stiff peaks form. Fold into the batter.

Alternate layers of the batter and streusel in a greased and floured tube or bundt pan, beginning with the batter and ending with the streusel. Dot with additional butter. Bake at 375 degrees for 1 hour. Cool in the pan for 10 minutes. Remove to a wire rack to cool completely. Store in an airtight container. Best served after 1 day, but keeps for up to 3 days.

Serves twelve

Poppy Seed And Ham Biscuits

2/3 CUP (1 1/3 STICKS)
   BUTTER OR
   MARGARINE, SOFTENED
1/4 CUP FINELY CHOPPED
   ONION
1 TABLESPOON POPPY
   SEEDS
2 1/2 TEASPOONS DIJON
   MUSTARD
4 1/2 DOZEN BISCUITS OR
   SMALL PARTY ROLLS
1 POUND SHAVED HAM

Combine the butter, onion, poppy seeds and mustard in a small bowl and mix well. Chill, covered, for 24 hours to blend the flavors.

Let the butter mixture stand at room temperature to soften. Split the biscuits into halves horizontally. Spread the bottom halves with the butter mixture and top with the ham. Replace the tops and arrange in a shallow baking pan. Bake, covered with foil, at 350 degrees for 10 minutes or until heated through.

You may use either country or honey-baked ham for the ham.

Makes four and one-half dozen

PEPPERONI BREAD

1 (16-OUNCE) LOAF
  FROZEN BREAD DOUGH,
  THAWED
2 GARLIC CLOVES, MINCED
2 TABLESPOONS BUTTER
  OR MARGARINE
5 OUNCES THINLY SLICED
  PEPPERONI
2 CUPS (8 OUNCES)
  SHREDDED MOZZARELLA
  CHEESE
1/4 TEASPOON CRUSHED
  DRIED BASIL
1/4 TEASPOON CRUSHED
  DRIED OREGANO

Roll the bread dough to a 10×16-inch rectangle on a lightly floured surface. Sauté the garlic in the butter in an 8-inch skillet over medium heat for 2 minutes. Remove the garlic with a slotted spoon and sprinkle over the dough, reserving the butter.

Arrange the pepperoni evenly over the dough, leaving a 2-inch margin on 1 long side and a 1-inch margin on the remaining sides. Sprinkle the cheese over the pepperoni.

Moisten the edges of the dough with water. Roll to enclose the filling, starting from 1 long side and rolling toward the side with the 2-inch margin. Press the seam to seal and turn under the ends. Place on an ungreased baking sheet; do not allow the dough to rise.

Stir the basil and oregano into the reserved butter in the skillet. Brush over the bread roll. Bake at 350 degrees for 20 to 30 minutes or until light brown. Cool slightly and cut into 1-inch slices. Serve warm or cooled.

Teenagers like this for an early morning start or to grab on the run any time of the day.

Serves twelve to fourteen

SAUSAGE-STUFFED FRENCH BREAD

1 POUND BULK HOT PORK
    OR ITALIAN SAUSAGE
1/2 CUP CHOPPED ONION
1/2 CUP CHOPPED GREEN
    BELL PEPPER
1/2 CUP CHOPPED CELERY
1 GARLIC CLOVE, MINCED
2 TABLESPOONS BUTTER
    OR MARGARINE
1 1/2 CUPS (6 OUNCES)
    SHREDDED CHEDDAR
    CHEESE
1 (16-OUNCE) LOAF
    UNSLICED FRENCH
    BREAD

Cook the sausage in a 10-inch skillet, stirring until brown and crumbly; remove with a slotted spoon to drain on paper towels. Drain and wipe the skillet. Sauté the onion, bell pepper, celery and garlic in the butter in the skillet until tender. Stir in the sausage and cheese.

Cut the bread into halves horizontally. Hollow out the bottom half and fill with the sausage mixture; replace the top. Wrap in foil and place on a baking sheet. Bake at 375 degrees for 20 to 25 minutes or until heated through. Cut into 2-inch slices to serve.

You may make the sausage mixture ahead of time and store, covered, in the freezer.

Serves six to eight

CHEESE STRATA

8 SLICES DRIED WHITE
    BREAD
SOFTENED BUTTER
1 1/2 POUNDS SHARP
    CHEDDAR CHEESE,
    SHREDDED
6 EGGS
2 1/2 CUPS HALF-AND-HALF
1 GREEN ONION, FINELY
    CHOPPED
1 TEASPOON (ROUNDED)
    BROWN SUGAR
1/2 TEASPOON
    WORCESTERSHIRE
    SAUCE
1/2 TEASPOON DRY
    MUSTARD
1/4 TEASPOON PAPRIKA
1/2 TEASPOON SALT
1/8 TEASPOON CAYENNE
    PEPPER
1/8 TEASPOON BLACK PEPPER

Trim the crusts from the bread and spread generously with butter. Cut the bread into 1/2-inch squares. Layer the buttered bread cubes and cheese 1/2 at a time in a buttered shallow 2-quart baking dish.

Beat the eggs in a mixing bowl. Add the half-and-half, green onion, brown sugar, Worcestershire sauce, dry mustard, paprika, salt, cayenne pepper and black pepper and mix well. Pour over the layers. Add additional half-and-half if necessary to cover the layers. Chill, covered with plastic wrap, for 8 hours or longer.

Let stand at room temperature for 30 minutes. Place the baking dish in a larger pan. Pour 1/2 inch cold water into the larger pan. Bake at 300 degrees for 1 hour. Turn off the oven. Let the strata stand in the oven for 20 minutes longer before serving.

Serves eight

HOLA MEMPHIS!

6 (6-INCH) TORTILLAS

1¹/₂ POUNDS LEAN MILD
    SAUSAGE

1 CUP CHOPPED ONION

1 GARLIC CLOVE, MINCED

1 TEASPOON CRUSHED
    DRIED OREGANO

1 TEASPOON GROUND
    CUMIN

¹/₂ TEASPOON SALT

1 TEASPOON GROUND
    RED PEPPER

2 CUPS (8 OUNCES)
    SHREDDED MONTEREY
    JACK CHEESE

8 EGGS

2¹/₂ CUPS MILK

1 (4-OUNCE) CAN CHOPPED
    GREEN CHILES, DRAINED

1 CUP SOUR CREAM

Garnish

CHOPPED TOMATOES

SLICED GREEN ONIONS

SHREDDED LETTUCE

SLICED BLACK OLIVES

SALSA

Line a lightly greased 9×13-inch baking dish with the tortillas, cutting to fit. Brown the sausage with the onion and garlic in a 10-inch skillet over medium heat, stirring until the sausage is crumbly; drain. Stir in the oregano, cumin, salt and red pepper.

Spoon into the prepared baking dish and sprinkle with the cheese.

Combine the eggs and milk in a large mixing bowl and beat until smooth. Stir in the green chiles. Pour over the cheese.

Bake at 350 degrees for 45 minutes or until a knife inserted near the center comes out clean. Let stand for 5 minutes. Spread with the sour cream. Garnish with tomatoes, onions, lettuce and olives. Serve with salsa.

You may make this a lighter dish by decreasing the cheese by as much as half.

Serves eight

Crepes

1 CUP COLD MILK
1 CUP COLD WATER
4 EGGS
1/2 TEASPOON SALT
2 CUPS SIFTED FLOUR
1/4 CUP (1/2 STICK) BUTTER,
   MELTED

Chicken Filling

24 MEDIUM FRESH
   MUSHROOMS, SLICED
6 TO 8 TABLESPOONS
   (3/4 TO 1 STICK) BUTTER
21/4 CUPS SHREDDED
   COOKED CHICKEN
6 HARD-COOKED EGGS,
   CHOPPED
1 CUP PLUS
   5 TABLESPOONS SOUR
   CREAM
1 TABLESPOON CHOPPED
   FRESH PARSLEY
3/4 CUP (3 OUNCES) GRATED
   PARMESAN CHEESE
SALT, RED PEPPER AND
   BLACK PEPPER TO TASTE

Garnish

SOUR CREAM
GRATED PARMESAN CHEESE
PARSLEY SPRIGS

For the crepes, combine the milk, water, eggs and salt in a blender container. Add the flour and butter. Process at high speed for 2 minutes; scrape the sides of the container. Process until smooth. Chill for 2 hours or longer.

Brush a 5-inch crepe pan or nonstick sauté pan with oil. Heat over medium-high heat. Ladle 3 to 4 tablespoons of the batter into the pan at a time and tilt to cover the bottom evenly. Cook for 1 minute to 1 minute and 20 seconds. Loosen crepe and turn to the other side. Cook until light brown. Stack between sheets of waxed paper.

For the filling, sauté the mushrooms in the butter in a skillet for 4 to 5 minutes or until tender. Combine with the chicken, eggs, sour cream, parsley, cheese, salt, red pepper and black pepper in a double boiler. Heat over hot water until the mixture is heated through.

To assemble, place the crepes with the more evenly brown side down on a work surface and spoon about 2 tablespoons of the chicken mixture onto each crepe. Roll to enclose the filling and arrange in a greased baking dish. Bake at 250 degrees until heated through. Garnish servings with a dollop of sour cream, Parmesan cheese and parsley sprigs.

You may make the crepes in advance and freeze them between layers of waxed paper in an airtight container until ready to fill and serve.

Serves twelve

CRAB MEAT CREPES

Crepe Sauce

4 CUPS MILK, CHICKEN
    STOCK, FISH STOCK OR
    MUSHROOM STOCK
6 TABLESPOONS (^{3}/$_4$ STICK)
    BUTTER
7^1/$_2$ TABLESPOONS FLOUR
SALT AND PEPPER
    TO TASTE
3 EGG YOLKS
^{3}/$_4$ CUP HEAVY CREAM

Crepes

4^1/$_2$ TABLESPOONS MINCED
    GREEN ONIONS
6 TABLESPOONS (^{3}/$_4$ STICK)
    BUTTER
3^3/$_4$ CUPS FRESH
    CRAB MEAT
^{3}/$_4$ CUP WHITE WINE OR
    SHERRY
SALT AND PEPPER
    TO TASTE
1 RECIPE CREPES (PAGE 72)
^{3}/$_4$ CUP (3 OUNCES)
    SHREDDED SWISS
    CHEESE

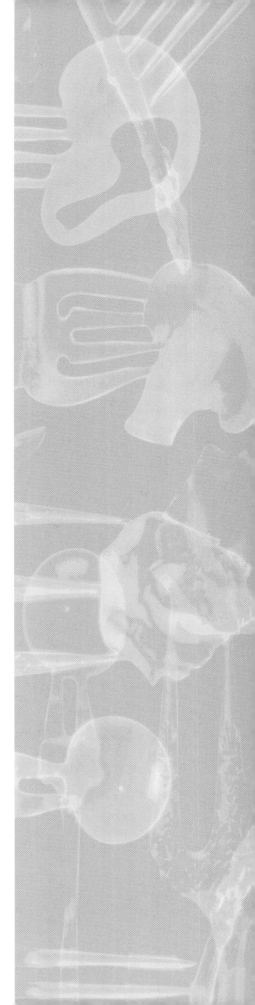

For the sauce, bring the milk just to a boil in a saucepan. Melt the butter in a double boiler. Stir in the flour and cook for 2 minutes, stirring constantly. Remove from the heat and whisk in the milk, salt and pepper. Cook for 1 minute longer, whisking constantly.

Beat the egg yolks with the cream in a bowl. Whisk a small amount of the hot sauce into the egg mixture; whisk the egg mixture into the hot sauce. Adjust the seasonings.

For the crepes, cook the green onions in the butter in a saucepan over low heat for 1 minute. Add the crab meat. Cook for 2 minutes. Add the wine. Simmer, covered, for 1 minute. Increase the temperature and boil, uncovered, until the liquid has nearly evaporated. Season with salt and pepper.

To assemble, combine the crab mixture with just enough of the sauce to moisten in a bowl. Spoon the crab mixture onto the crepes and roll to enclose the filling. Arrange in a single layer in a buttered baking dish. Spoon the remaining sauce over the top. Top with the cheese.

Bake at 350 degrees for 20 to 25 minutes or until heated through. Broil until golden brown.

The crepes may be filled a day in advance; store the filled crepes and remaining sauce separately, covered, in the refrigerator. Reheat the sauce in a double boiler and spoon over the crepes when time to bake and top with the cheese.

Serves twelve

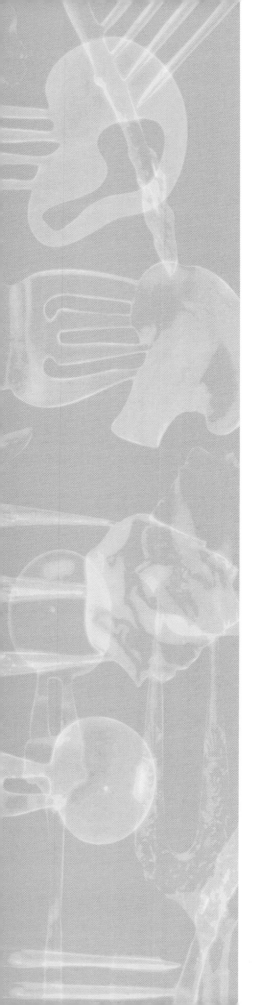

CHEESE SOUFFLÉ

3 TABLESPOONS BUTTER
3 TABLESPOONS FLOUR
SALT TO TASTE
1¹/₃ CUPS MILK
8 OUNCES (2 CUPS)
   CHEDDAR CHEESE,
   CHOPPED OR SHREDDED
3 LARGE OR 4 SMALL EGG
   YOLKS
1 OR 2 TEASPOONS
   BRANDY (OPTIONAL)
MUSTARD AND ONION
   SALT TO TASTE
3 LARGE OR 4 SMALL
   EGG WHITES

Melt the butter in a double boiler. Stir in the flour and salt. Cook for several minutes, stirring constantly. Stir in the milk gradually and reduce the heat. Add the cheese gradually. Cook until the mixture is thickened and smooth, stirring constantly. Stir a small amount of the hot mixture into the egg yolks; stir the egg yolks into the hot mixture. Cook for several minutes, stirring constantly. Add the brandy, mustard, onion salt and salt to taste and mix well. Cool for 20 minutes.

Beat the egg whites until stiff peaks form. Fold into the cheese mixture. Spoon into a soufflé dish and place in a large pan of water. Bake at 325 degrees for 1 hour or until puffed and golden brown.

Serves six

Variations

For *Chicken Soufflé*, substitute 2 cups minced cooked chicken for the cheese and marjoram, ²/₃ teaspoon curry powder and pepper for the seasonings. Serve with a mixture of cream of mushroom soup heated with chopped cooked bacon, parsley and mushrooms. Use the same recipe for Turkey or Ham Soufflé, substituting turkey or ham for the chicken.

For *Shrimp Soufflé*, substitute 2 cups cooked peeled shrimp for the cheese and fennel, celery salt, pepper and ¹/₂ teaspoon chopped parsley for the seasonings. Squeeze the juice of 1 lemon over the top before baking and serve with a heated mixture of 2 cups sour cream and ¹/₂ cup chopped seeded cucumber.

For *Fruit Soufflé*, use only 1 cup of milk and substitute 2 small jars of puréed baby food fruit for the cheese. Substitute 2 teaspoons sugar and a pinch each of cinnamon, nutmeg and salt for the seasonings. Serve with crushed fresh strawberries.

Eggs Benedict

1/2 TEASPOON SALT
1 TEASPOON VINEGAR
4 EGGS
2 ENGLISH MUFFINS,
    SPLIT, TOASTED
BUTTER
4 SLICES HAM OR
    CANADIAN BACON
BLENDER HOLLANDAISE
    SAUCE (BELOW)

Garnish
PAPRIKA

Combine the salt and vinegar with enough water to cover the eggs in a skillet. Bring to a boil and remove from the heat. Break 1 egg at a time into a cup and slip into the hot water. Let stand for 3 to 5 minutes or until the whites are firm. Remove with a slotted spoon and drain.

Spread the cut sides of the toasted muffins lightly with butter. Place 1 half on each serving plate. Top each with 1 slice of ham and a poached egg. Spoon Blender Hollandaise Sauce over the top. Garnish with paprika.

Serves four

Blender Hollandaise

1/2 CUP (1 STICK) BUTTER
3 EGG YOLKS
2 TABLESPOONS LEMON
    JUICE
1/4 TEASPOON SALT
CAYENNE PEPPER
    TO TASTE

Melt the butter in a small saucepan and heat until bubbly but not brown. Combine the egg yolks, lemon juice, salt and cayenne pepper in a blender container and process at low speed just until blended. Add the butter gradually, processing constantly until smooth.

Makes three-fourths cup

QUICHE LORRAINE

4 SLICES BACON
1/2 CUP CHOPPED COOKED
   HAM
1/2 CUP (2 OUNCES)
   CHOPPED SWISS CHEESE
1 UNBAKED (9-INCH) PIE
   SHELL
4 EGGS
1 CUP HALF-AND-HALF
1/4 TEASPOON NUTMEG
1/2 TEASPOON SALT
1/4 TEASPOON WHITE
   PEPPER

Cook the bacon in a skillet over medium heat until crisp; drain. Crumble the bacon. Layer the bacon, ham and cheese in the pie shell. Combine the eggs, half-and-half, nutmeg, salt and white pepper in a blender container and process until smooth. Pour over the layers.

Bake at 350 degrees for 45 minutes or until set. Serve hot.

Serves six

CHEESE GRITS

4 CUPS MILK
1/2 CUP (1 STICK) BUTTER
1 CUP UNCOOKED GRITS
1 TEASPOON SALT
1/2 TEASPOON WHITE
   PEPPER
1 CUP (4 OUNCES)
   SHREDDED GRUYÈRE
   CHEESE OR CHEDDAR
   CHEESE
1/3 CUP BUTTER
1/2 CUP (2 OUNCES) GRATED
   PARMESAN CHEESE

Bring the milk to a boil in a saucepan and add 1/2 cup butter. Stir in the grits. Cook for 5 minutes or until thickened to the consistency of oatmeal, stirring constantly. Remove from the heat and season with salt and white pepper. Beat until smooth. Add the Gruyère cheese and 1/3 cup butter; mix well.

Spoon into a greased 2-quart baking dish and sprinkle with the Parmesan cheese. Bake at 350 degrees for 1 hour.

The dish may be prepared the day before and baked at serving time.

Serves ten

Hot Sherried Fruit Compote

4 MEDIUM PEACHES,
    PEELED, CUT INTO
    HALVES
4 MEDIUM PEARS, PEELED,
    CUT INTO HALVES
10 MEDIUM APRICOTS,
    PEELED, CUT INTO
    HALVES
8 OUNCES FRESH
    PINEAPPLE, PEELED,
    CORED, SLICED
1/2 CUP (1 STICK) BUTTER
    OR MARGARINE
2 TABLESPOONS FLOUR
1/2 CUP CREAM SHERRY
3/4 CUP PACKED LIGHT
    BROWN SUGAR
1/4 CUP CHOPPED PECANS
1/2 CUP FLAKED COCONUT

Layer the peaches, pears, apricots and pineapple in a buttered 2-quart baking dish. Melt the butter in a 1-quart saucepan over medium heat. Stir in the flour 1 tablespoon at a time. Add the sherry and 1/2 cup of the brown sugar. Bring to a boil, stirring constantly. Pour over the fruit.

Sprinkle with the remaining 1/4 cup brown sugar, pecans and coconut. Let stand until cool. Chill, covered, for 8 hours or longer. Remove the cover and bake at 350 degrees for 30 minutes.

You may substitute drained 16-ounce cans of peach halves, pear halves and apricot halves and a drained 8-ounce can of sliced pineapple for the fresh fruit if preferred.

Serves eight to ten

Fresh Fruit In White Wine

4 PEACHES
3 PEARS
2 APPLES
2 BANANAS
1 PINT STRAWBERRIES
SUGAR TO TASTE
3/4 CUP WHITE WINE

Peel the peaches, pears, apples and bananas. Cut the peaches, pears, apples, bananas and strawberries into thin slices. Layer the fruit in a serving bowl, sprinkling each layer with sugar. Pour the wine over the layers and chill, covered, for 2 hours.

You may vary the fruit to suit individual tastes and the season.

Serves eight to ten

The Top Ten Gift Ideas

A *Sterling Collection* Cookbook

Heart & Soul Cookbook

The Memphis Cookbook

Cheese Straws, page 20

Homemade Kahlúa, page 33

Crumbly Cheese Crackers, page 21

Chocolate Sauce, page 157

Instant Spiced Tea, page 31

Chocolate-Dipped Spoons, page 179, with a package of gourmet coffee

Garlic Pickles, page 16

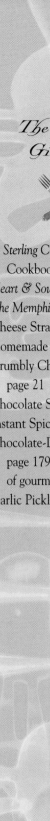

Congratulations
on the new baby!
♥, gran

entrées

KANSAS CITY BEEF BRISKET

1 (5-POUND) BEEF BRISKET
1 TABLESPOON MEAT
    TENDERIZER (OPTIONAL)
2 TO 4 TABLESPOONS
    LIQUID SMOKE
1 TEASPOON CELERY SALT
1 TEASPOON ONION SALT
1 TEASPOON GARLIC SALT
2 TEASPOONS SALT
1/2 TEASPOON PEPPER
1/4 CUP PACKED BROWN
    SUGAR
WORCESTERSHIRE SAUCE
    TO TASTE
1/2 TEASPOON NUTMEG
1 TEASPOON PAPRIKA

Sprinkle the beef brisket with the meat tenderizer, liquid smoke, celery salt, onion salt, garlic salt, salt and pepper. Wrap in foil and chill in the refrigerator for 8 hours or longer.

Open the foil and sprinkle the brisket with the brown sugar, Worcestershire sauce, nutmeg and paprika. Seal the foil well and place seam side up in a roasting pan.

Roast at 275 degrees for 5 hours. Cut diagonally into thin slices and serve with barbecue sauce and egg buns.

Serves twelve to fifteen

ESCOFFIER BEEF

1 (4-POUND) RUMP ROAST
    OR OTHER BEEF ROAST
NUTMEG, SALT AND
    PEPPER TO TASTE
RED WINE
2 POTATOES, PEELED,
    CHOPPED
2 CARROTS, SLICED
2 ONIONS, SLICED
2 OR 3 RIBS CELERY,
    FINELY CHOPPED
1 POUND (OR MORE)
    MUSHROOMS
1 GARLIC CLOVE, MINCED
BUTTER

Sprinkle the beef with the nutmeg, salt and pepper. Combine with enough wine to cover in a shallow dish. Marinate in the refrigerator for 5 hours. Drain, reserving the wine.

Sauté the potatoes, carrots, onions, celery, mushrooms and garlic in butter in a Dutch oven until light brown; remove with a slotted spoon. Add the beef to the drippings and sear on all sides; remove the beef. Return the vegetables to the Dutch oven and top with the beef. Add the reserved wine.

Roast at 325 degrees for 2 to 3 hours or until the beef is done to taste. Slice the roast and serve with the vegetables.

Serves eight

The Best Tenderloin Ever

1 CUP RUBY PORT
3/4 CUP SOY SAUCE
1/2 CUP OLIVE OIL
2 OR 3 GARLIC CLOVES,
    MINCED
1 BAY LEAF
HOT PEPPER SAUCE
    TO TASTE
1 TEASPOON FRESHLY
    GROUND PEPPER
1 (4- TO 6-POUND) BEEF
    TENDERLOIN
16 TO 20 SLICES BACON

Combine the wine, soy sauce, olive oil, garlic, bay leaf, hot pepper sauce and pepper in a bowl and mix well. Place the beef in a sealable plastic bag in a shallow dish. Add the marinade and seal the bag. Marinate in the refrigerator for 8 hours or longer, turning once or twice; drain.

Wrap the bacon slices around the beef, securing with wooden picks. Insert a meat thermometer into the thickest portion and place on a rack in a shallow roasting pan; tuck under the end. Roast at 450 degrees for 25 to 35 minutes or to 140 degrees on the meat thermometer for rare. Let stand for several minutes; cut into thin slices to serve.

Serves sixteen to twenty

Roasted Beef In Salt

1 (4-POUND) SIRLOIN TIP
    STEAK, 2 TO 2 1/2 INCHES
    THICK
SALT
HORSERADISH MOUSSE
    (THIS PAGE)

Place the beef in a roasting pan and cover with 1 inch of salt. Broil for 10 to 15 minutes or until crusty. Turn the beef and repeat the process, broiling until done to taste. Brush away the salt; the beef should be seared on the outside and pink inside. Cut into thin slices and serve hot or cold with Horseradish Mousse.

Serves twelve to sixteen

Horseradish Mousse

Soften 1 envelope unflavored gelatin in 1/4 cup cold water in a saucepan for 5 minutes. Heat until dissolved and whisk in 1/2 teaspoon dry mustard, 1/2 cup heavy cream and 1/2 cup sour cream. Stir in 3 ounces drained horseradish, 1/2 teaspoon lemon juice, 1 tablespoon chopped green onions, 1/4 teaspoon salt and 1 tablespoon cracked pepper. Pour into an oiled mold and chill for 6 hours or until firm. Unmold onto a serving plate. Serve with thinly sliced roast beef and prepared rolls for a cocktail party; guests can serve themselves and there is no hostess assembly required.

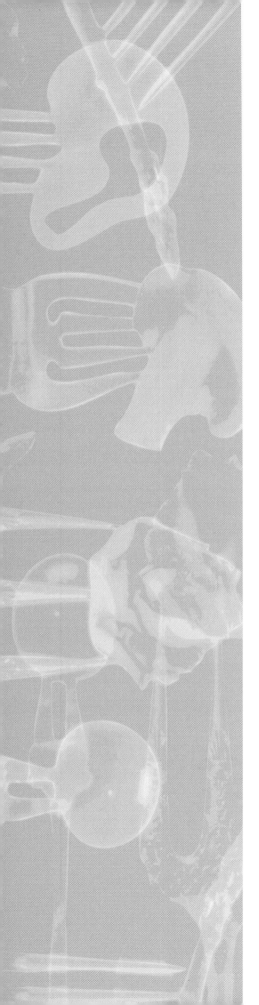

TOURNEDOS IN MADEIRA SAUCE

Tournedos

4 (1-INCH) BEEF FILLETS
BUTTER
4 ARTICHOKE BOTTOMS
4 SLICES FOIE GRAS

Madeira Sauce

1/2 TEASPOON POTATO
    FLOUR
3 TABLESPOONS WATER
1/4 CUP MADEIRA

Creamed Mushrooms

12 OUNCES FRESH
    MUSHROOMS, SLICED
LEMON JUICE
BUTTER
1/2 CUP HEAVY CREAM

For the tournedos, sauté the fillets in butter in a heavy skillet for 3 to 4 minutes on each side; remove to a plate. Sauté the artichoke bottoms in butter in the skillet. Place 1 fillet on each artichoke bottom and top with a slice of foie gras. Arrange around the outer edge of a serving plate.

For the sauce, stir the potato flour, water and wine into the beef drippings in the skillet. Simmer for 2 to 3 minutes. Strain into a bowl. Spoon over the beef.

For the creamed mushrooms, sprinkle the mushrooms with lemon juice. Sauté in butter in a skillet. Stir in the cream and cook until heated through. Spoon into the center of the serving plate.

Serves four

BEEF STROGANOFF

1 1/2 POUNDS BEEF FILLETS
    OR SIRLOIN
3 TABLESPOONS PREPARED
    MUSTARD
1 CUP THINLY SLICED
    ONION
BUTTER
1 (6-OUNCE) CAN TOMATO
    PASTE
1 (6-OUNCE) CAN WATER
1 TABLESPOON
    WORCESTERSHIRE SAUCE
1 TABLESPOON PAPRIKA
1 (8-OUNCE) CAN SLICED
    MUSHROOMS
1 CUP SOUR CREAM

Cut the beef into strips and spread with the mustard. Place in a shallow dish and marinate, covered, in the refrigerator for 1 hour. Sauté the onion in butter in a skillet. Add the beef and cook until brown. Add the tomato paste, water, Worcestershire sauce and paprika and mix well.

Simmer for 30 minutes or until the beef is tender. Add the mushrooms and sour cream and mix well. Cook just until heated through; do not boil. Serve over hot rice or noodles.

Serves four to six

Boeuf A La Bourguignonne

6 SLICES BACON, CUT INTO
    1/2-INCH PIECES

3 POUNDS (11/2-INCH) BEEF
    CHUCK CUBES

1 LARGE CARROT, SLICED

1 MEDIUM ONION, SLICED

3 TABLESPOONS FLOUR

1 TEASPOON SALT

1/4 TEASPOON PEPPER

2 (10-OUNCE) CANS
    CONDENSED BEEF
    BROTH

2 CUPS RED BURGUNDY

1 TABLESPOON TOMATO
    PASTE

2 GARLIC CLOVES,
    MINCED

1/2 TEASPOON DRIED
    THYME

1 BAY LEAF

1 POUND SMALL
    MUSHROOMS OR
    QUARTERED LARGE
    MUSHROOMS

2 TABLESPOONS
    VEGETABLE OIL

3 TABLESPOONS BUTTER

18 TO 24 TINY WHOLE
    ONIONS, ABOUT
    1 POUND

1/4 CUP FLOUR

2 TABLESPOONS BUTTER,
    SOFTENED

Cook the bacon in a heavy saucepan until crisp; remove the bacon with a slotted spoon, reserving the drippings in the saucepan. Add the beef to the saucepan in batches and cook until brown on all sides, turning frequently. Remove with a slotted spoon.

Add the carrot and sliced onion to the drippings and cook until light brown. Skim the fat and return the bacon and beef to the saucepan. Sprinkle with 3 tablespoons flour, salt and pepper and toss to coat well.

Reserve 1/2 cup of the beef broth; add the remaining beef broth to the saucepan. Stir in the wine, tomato paste, garlic, thyme and bay leaf. Simmer, covered, for 3 hours or until the beef is very tender; do not boil.

Sauté the mushrooms in the oil and 3 tablespoons butter in a skillet for 5 minutes; remove with a slotted spoon. Add the whole onions to the skillet and sauté for 10 minutes, adding additional butter or oil if necessary. Add the reserved beef broth and simmer for 10 minutes or until the onions are tender but still hold their shape.

Skim the stew. Combine 1/4 cup flour and 2 tablespoons butter in a bowl and blend until smooth. Shape into very small balls. Add to the stew and cook over very low heat until the mixture thickens, stirring constantly. Add the mushrooms and onions. Bring just to a simmer; discard the bay leaf. Serve immediately with parslied potatoes and rice or buttered noodles.

Serves eight to ten

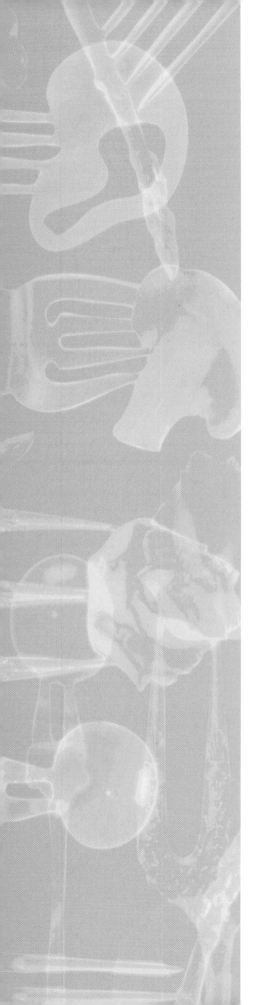

Teriyaki Flank Steak

1/4 CUP SOY SAUCE

1/4 CUP VINEGAR

3 TABLESPOONS HONEY

1/4 CUP VEGETABLE OIL

1 1/2 TEASPOONS GARLIC
   POWDER

1 1/2 TEASPOONS GROUND
   GINGER

1 OR 2 FINELY CHOPPED
   GREEN ONIONS

1 (1 1/2-POUND) FLANK
   STEAK

Combine the soy sauce, vinegar, honey, oil, garlic powder, ginger and green onions in a sealable plastic bag. Score the flank steak on both sides with a knife. Add to the marinade and seal the bag. Marinate in the refrigerator for 4 to 6 hours; drain.

Grill over hot coals for 5 minutes on each side for medium-rare. Cut diagonally into thin slices to serve.

You may reserve the marinade and bring to a boil to serve with the steak if desired.

Serves four

Curried Beef In Pastry

Beef

3 TABLESPOONS
   VEGETABLE OIL

1/2 CUP CHOPPED ONION

2 CUPS CHOPPED
   MUSHROOMS

1 POUND GROUND ROUND
   STEAK

1 TABLESPOON CURRY
   POWDER

2 TEASPOONS SALT

1/2 TEASPOON PEPPER

1 CUP THICK WHITE
   SAUCE

Wine Pastry

2 CUPS SIFTED FLOUR

2 TEASPOONS BAKING
   POWDER

1/2 TEASPOON SALT

1/4 CUP (1/2 STICK) BUTTER

1/2 CUP WHITE WINE

1 EGG YOLK, BEATEN

Chutney Sauce

1 CUP SOUR CREAM

1/4 CUP CHOPPED CHUTNEY

For the beef, heat the oil in a large skillet. Sauté the onion, mushrooms and ground round in the heated oil in the skillet for 10 minutes or until the beef is brown and crumbly; drain. Add the curry powder, salt, pepper and white sauce; mix well. Cool to room temperature.

For the pastry, sift the flour, baking powder and salt into a bowl. Cut in the butter. Add the wine gradually, stirring to form a dough. Roll into a rectangle 1/3 inch thick on a floured surface.

Spread the beef mixture down the center of the dough. Fold the edges over the beef and press to seal. Brush with the beaten egg yolk. Place on a baking sheet. Bake at 400 degrees for 35 minutes or until golden brown.

For the sauce, mix the sour cream with the chutney in a small bowl. Serve with the beef.

Serves eight

$\mathcal{L}$ASAGNA

1 ONION, CHOPPED
VEGETABLE OIL
1 1/2 POUNDS GROUND
   BEEF
1 (12-OUNCE) CAN
   TOMATO PASTE
1 (20-OUNCE) CAN
   TOMATOES
1 CUP WATER
1 GARLIC CLOVE,
   CHOPPED
3 TABLESPOONS CHOPPED
   PARSLEY
1 TEASPOON OREGANO
1 TEASPOON BASIL
2 TEASPOONS SALT
2 CUPS COTTAGE CHEESE
1 EGG, BEATEN
16 OUNCES UNCOOKED
   LASAGNA NOODLES
SALT TO TASTE
6 OUNCES MOZZARELLA
   CHEESE, SLICED
8 OUNCES CHEDDAR
   CHEESE, SLICED
GRATED PARMESAN
   CHEESE

Sauté the onion in a small amount of oil in a saucepan. Add the ground beef and cook until brown and crumbly, stirring constantly. Add the tomato paste, tomatoes, water, garlic, parsley, oregano, basil and 2 teaspoons salt and mix well. Simmer for 30 minutes or until thickened to the desired consistency.

Mix the cottage cheese and egg in a small bowl. Cook the noodles in salted water in a saucepan until tender; drain.

Layer the noodles, cottage cheese mixture, meat sauce, mozzarella cheese and Cheddar cheese $1/2$ or $1/3$ at a time in a greased rectangular 3-quart baking dish, ending with the sliced cheeses. Sprinkle with Parmesan cheese.

Bake at 350 degrees for 30 minutes or until bubbly. Let stand for 5 minutes before serving.

Serves eight

POLISHED PLATTERS

entrées

5 SLICES BACON

1 CUP CHOPPED CELERY

1/2 CUP CHOPPED ONION

1/2 CUP CHOPPED GREEN
   BELL PEPPER

3 POUNDS LEAN GROUND
   BEEF

1 (10-OUNCE) CAN
   CHOPPED TOMATOES
   WITH GREEN CHILES

1 (28-OUNCE) CAN WHOLE
   TOMATOES, CHOPPED

1 (8-OUNCE) CAN
   TOMATO SAUCE

2 TABLESPOONS SUGAR

1 TEASPOON CHOPPED
   PARSLEY

1 GARLIC CLOVE, MINCED,
   OR 1/4 TEASPOON
   GARLIC POWDER

3 TABLESPOONS CHILI
   POWDER

1 TEASPOON CELERY SEEDS

1 TEASPOON CRUSHED
   DRIED BASIL

1/2 TEASPOON CRUSHED
   DRIED ROSEMARY

2 OR 3 BAY LEAVES

1 TABLESPOON LEMON
   PEPPER

4 1/2 CUPS SLICED FRESH
   MUSHROOMS, ABOUT
   12 OUNCES

SALT TO TASTE

2 POUNDS UNCOOKED
   VERMICELLI

8 QUARTS WATER

3 TABLESPOONS BUTTER
   OR MARGARINE

Garnish

GRATED PARMESAN CHEESE

Cook the bacon in a heavy saucepan until crisp; drain, reserving 3 tablespoons drippings. Crumble the bacon.

Add the celery, onion and bell pepper to the drippings in the saucepan. Sauté until the vegetables are tender-crisp.

Add the ground beef and cook until brown and crumbly, stirring frequently; drain.

Add the undrained tomatoes with green chiles, undrained tomatoes, tomato sauce, sugar, parsley, garlic, chili powder, celery seeds, basil, rosemary, bay leaves and lemon pepper and mix well. Simmer, covered, for 1 hour.

Add the mushrooms and bacon. Cook for 15 minutes longer. Season with salt.

Cook the pasta in salted water in a 12-quart stockpot for 5 to 7 minutes or until al dente; drain.

Add the pasta to the meat sauce and mix gently. Add the butter and stir to melt; remove and discard the bay leaves.

Spoon into two 3-quart baking dishes. Bake at 350 degrees for 30 minutes or until bubbly. Garnish servings with Parmesan cheese.

Store in the refrigerator for 8 hours or longer before baking to enhance the flavor.

Serves sixteen

Shish Kabob

1 (5- TO 6-POUND) LEG OF
   LAMB
1/2 CUP SHERRY OR WINE
   VINEGAR
1/4 CUP OLIVE OIL OR
   PEANUT OIL
2 LARGE ONIONS, SLICED
1 TEASPOON OREGANO
1 TABLESPOON SALT
1/2 TEASPOON PEPPER

Trim the leg of lamb and cut into 1-inch pieces. Combine with the wine, olive oil, onions, oregano, salt and pepper in a shallow dish. Marinate, covered, in the refrigerator for 1 to 24 hours; drain.

Thread the lamb onto skewers. Grill or broil until brown and done to taste.

You may substitute chicken or beef for the lamb. You may also alternate the lamb with tomatoes, onions and bacon on the skewers.

Serves eight

Barbecued Leg Of Lamb

Barbecue Sauce

1 CUP KETCHUP
1 CUP VINEGAR
1 CUP WATER
1 TEASPOON
   WORCESTERSHIRE
   SAUCE
1 TABLESPOON OLIVE OIL
2 TABLESPOONS BUTTER,
   MELTED
1 GARLIC CLOVE, MINCED
1 TEASPOON SUGAR
1 TEASPOON DRY MUSTARD
1 TEASPOON SALT
1/8 TEASPOON CELERY SALT
1 TEASPOON CRUSHED RED
   PEPPER

Lamb

1 LEG OF LAMB
SALT AND PEPPER TO TASTE
BUTTER

For the sauce, combine the ketchup, vinegar, water, Worcestershire sauce, olive oil and melted butter in a medium saucepan and mix well. Add the garlic, sugar, dry mustard, salt, celery salt and crushed red pepper and mix well. Simmer for 20 minutes.

For the lamb, ask the butcher to bone and butterfly the leg of lamb. Season the lamb with salt and pepper and place in a roasting pan. Dot butter over the top. Roast at 300 degrees for 45 minutes.

Brush the lamb with the sauce. Grill over heated coals for 45 minutes or until done to taste, basting with the sauce.

Serves eight to ten

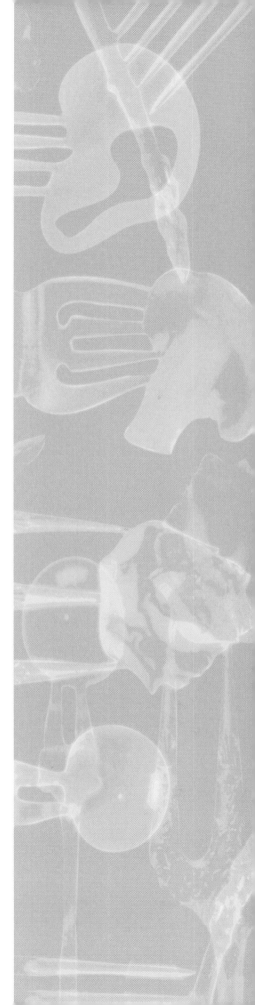

Sweet and Spicy Pork Tenderloin

Slice a pork tenderloin across the grain and pound the slices flat with a meat mallet. Coat with a mixture of flour, salt and pepper. Sauté in a small amount of oil in a large skillet until golden brown on both sides. Remove to a plate and drain the drippings. Add water or bouillon to the skillet, stirring to deglaze the bottom. Add 3 tablespoons each prepared mustard and black currant jelly and mix well. Return the pork and any accumulated juices to the skillet and simmer for 2 to 3 minutes. Serve with white rice.

PLASTERED PORKERS' SHOULDER

Basting Sauce

4 CUPS VINEGAR
1/4 CUP (1/2 STICK) BUTTER
    OR MARGARINE
1/4 CUP KETCHUP
1 TABLESPOON GROUND
    RED PEPPER
1 TABLESPOON BLACK
    PEPPER

Pork

1 (6- TO 8-POUND) PORK
    SHOULDER ROAST
GARLIC POWDER, SALT
    AND PEPPER TO TASTE

Barbecue Sauce

4 CUPS KETCHUP
1/2 CUP (1 STICK) BUTTER
    OR MARGARINE
1/2 CUP CHOPPED ONION
1/2 CUP PACKED BROWN
    SUGAR
2 TABLESPOONS LEMON
    JUICE
1 TABLESPOON PREPARED
    MUSTARD
3 GARLIC CLOVES, MINCED

For the basting sauce, combine the vinegar, butter, ketchup, red pepper and black pepper in a saucepan. Bring to a boil and remove from the heat.

For the pork, rub the shoulder roast with the garlic powder, salt and pepper. Place on a rack 10 to 12 inches from heated coals. Open the grill cover vents and close the cover. Grill for 3 hours, brushing with the basting sauce; add fresh coals every 45 to 60 minutes as needed to maintain the temperature.

Turn the pork and grill for 5 hours longer, brushing with the basting sauce once each hour and continuing to add coals.

For the barbecue sauce, combine the ketchup, butter, onion, brown sugar, lemon juice, mustard and garlic in a 3-quart saucepan. Bring to a boil and reduce the heat. Simmer over medium-low heat for 15 minutes. Serve with the pork.

If the grill is too shallow to allow 10 to 12 inches of space between the rack and coals, arrange the preheated coals in a circle or on the sides and place the pork in the center.

The Plastered Porkers are a fun-loving championship team in the Memphis in May Barbecue Contest.

Serves ten to fourteen

Prune- And Apricot-Stuffed Pork Roast

Fruit Stuffing

3/4 CUP DRIED APRICOTS

5 TO 8 PITTED PRUNES, CHOPPED

2 TEASPOONS FINELY SHREDDED ORANGE ZEST

1 1/2 CUPS HOT WATER

3 TABLESPOONS APRICOT BRANDY

Pork

1 (4- TO 5-POUND) BONELESS CENTER-CUT PORK LOIN ROAST

1/2 TEASPOON GROUND GINGER

1/4 TEASPOON DRY MUSTARD

1 TEASPOON SALT

1/2 TEASPOON COARSELY CRACKED BLACK PEPPER

1/4 TEASPOON GROUND RED PEPPER

Apricot Sauce

2 TABLESPOONS WATER

1 TABLESPOON FLOUR

DRIPPINGS

1 TABLESPOON SUGAR

RESERVED FRUIT LIQUID

1/2 CUP CHOPPED DRIED APRICOTS

1/2 TEASPOON COARSELY CRACKED PEPPER

Garnish

PURPLE BASIL SPRIGS

For the stuffing, combine the apricots, prunes and orange zest in a bowl. Combine the hot water and apricot brandy in a 2-cup measure; pour over the fruit. Let stand for 1 to 2 hours; drain, reserving the liquid.

For the pork, butterfly the loin by splitting it horizontally, cutting to within 1/2 inch of 1 long side; spread the sides open on a work surface. Spoon the fruit mixture down the center and bring the sides together to enclose the fruit; secure with string.

Combine the ginger, dry mustard, salt, black pepper and red pepper in a small bowl. Rub over the pork. Place on a rack in a shallow roasting pan and insert a meat thermometer into the thickest portion. Roast at 400 degrees for 10 minutes. Reduce the oven temperature to 325 degrees and roast for 1 1/2 to 2 hours or to 160 degrees on the meat thermometer. Cover and let stand.

For the sauce, blend the water, flour and any drippings from the roast in a 1-quart saucepan. Stir in the sugar and liquid reserved from the fruit. Bring to a boil and reduce the heat, stirring constantly. Cook for 1 to 2 minutes or until thickened, stirring constantly. Add the apricots and pepper.

Slice the roast and serve with the sauce. Garnish with the basil.

Serves twelve

The King's Grilled Tenders

1¹/₂ CUPS VEGETABLE OIL

³/₄ CUP SOY SAUCE

¹/₂ CUP RED WINE VINEGAR

¹/₃ CUP FRESH LEMON JUICE

¹/₄ CUP WORCESTERSHIRE
   SAUCE

2 TABLESPOONS CHOPPED
   PARSLEY

2 GARLIC CLOVES, MINCED

2 TABLESPOONS DRY
   MUSTARD

1 TABLESPOON PEPPER

3 (1-POUND) PORK
   TENDERLOINS

Combine the oil, soy sauce, vinegar, lemon juice, Worcestershire sauce, parsley, garlic, dry mustard and pepper in a bowl and mix well. Chill, covered, for 3 hours.

Place the tenderloins in a sealable plastic bag and place in a shallow dish. Add the marinade and seal the bag. Marinate in the refrigerator for 8 hours or longer, turning the bag occasionally.

Drain the pork and place on a grill rack over medium coals. Grill, covered, for 14 to 20 minutes or roast, uncovered, at 350 degrees for 1 to 1¹/₂ hours or until cooked through.

This was served at the kickoff party for *Heart & Soul,* held on the grounds of Graceland, the home of "The King."

Serves ten to twelve

Orange Pork Tenderloin

2 TABLESPOONS COARSE-
   GRAIN MUSTARD

2 TABLESPOONS SLICED
   GREEN ONIONS

1 GARLIC CLOVE, MINCED

1 TEASPOON CHOPPED
   FRESH ROSEMARY

1 TEASPOON CHOPPED
   FRESH TARRAGON

¹/₈ TEASPOON FRESHLY
   GROUND PEPPER

1 (1-POUND) PORK
   TENDERLOIN

¹/₃ CUP ORANGE
   MARMALADE

¹/₂ CUP WATER

¹/₄ CUP CHICKEN BROTH

Garnish

FRESH ROSEMARY SPRIGS

Combine the mustard, green onions, garlic, rosemary, tarragon and pepper in a small bowl and mix well. Make a horizontal cut lengthwise down the center of the tenderloin, cutting halfway through the tenderloin. Spread the mustard mixture on the cut surfaces. Close the sides and secure with string.

Place on a rack in a shallow roasting pan. Brush with 2 tablespoons of the marmalade and pour the water into the pan. Roast at 400 degrees for 40 to 45 minutes or until cooked through.

Combine the remaining orange marmalade with the chicken broth in a 1-quart saucepan. Bring to a boil and reduce the heat. Simmer for 2 to 3 minutes or until thickened and bubbly.

Slice the tenderloin and spoon the marmalade sauce over the slices. Garnish with rosemary.

Serves four

Cox's Championship Memphis In May Ribs

Cox's Barbecue Sauce

2 CUPS WHITE VINEGAR

2 CUPS WATER

2 CUPS KETCHUP

1/2 CUP CHOPPED ONION

3 TABLESPOONS SUGAR

3 TABLESPOONS CHILI
POWDER

3 TABLESPOONS SALT

3 TABLESPOONS PEPPER

Ribs

1/4 CUP PAPRIKA

2 TEASPOONS ONION
POWDER

2 TEASPOONS GARLIC
POWDER

2 TEASPOONS SALT

2 TEASPOONS WHITE
PEPPER

1 TEASPOON GROUND
RED PEPPER

2 TEASPOONS BLACK
PEPPER

4 TO 6 POUNDS PORK LOIN
BACK RIBS OR SPARERIBS

For the sauce, combine the vinegar, water, ketchup, onion, sugar, chili powder, salt and pepper in a 3-quart saucepan and mix well. Bring to a boil and reduce the heat. Simmer for 1 1/2 hours, stirring every 10 minutes.

Cool and store in the refrigerator for up to 4 weeks to blend the flavors.

For the ribs, mix the paprika, onion powder, garlic powder, salt, white pepper, red pepper and black pepper in a small bowl. Rub into the ribs.

Preheat the coals and arrange in a circle or on the sides of the grill. Place the ribs in the center of the grill rack.

Grill, covered, for 5 to 6 hours or until tender, turning the ribs every 30 minutes and adding coals every 45 to 60 minutes to maintain the grill temperature.

Brush the ribs with the barbecue sauce and grill for 20 minutes longer, turning and brushing again with the sauce after 10 minutes.

Serves four to six

Piggie Party

The Memphis in May International Festival, started in the '70s, provided an occasion to highlight Memphis as "hands down, no questions asked, THE pork barbecue capital of the world."

On May 5, 1978, 20 teams competed in a vacant lot downtown for a total prize of $1000. In May of 1999, 238 contestants brought incredible equipment and theatrical settings to an expanded Tom Lee Park, vying for $50,000 in prize money. Competitors have come from 42 states and from other countries, including Ireland, Estonia, Great Britain, Canada, and New Zealand. Today, the fun goes way beyond cooking. A crowd of more than 100,000 roars its delight as competitions in hog-calling, showmanship, and Ms. Piggie look-alikes entertain in outrageous style. Exceeding its planners' wildest dreams for success, the Memphis in May Barbecue Contest is a carnival of food and fun, and it will be working its riverside magic for years to come.

PORK CHOPS WITH BROWNED GARLIC BUTTER

Pork

1/2 TEASPOON ONION
    POWDER
1/4 TEASPOON GARLIC
    POWDER
1/4 TEASPOON DRY
    MUSTARD
1/4 TEASPOON GROUND
    SAGE
1/4 TEASPOON GROUND
    CUMIN
1/4 TEASPOON CRUSHED
    DRIED THYME
1 1/2 TEASPOONS SALT
1/4 TEASPOON WHITE
    PEPPER
6 (1/2-INCH) CENTER-CUT
    PORK CHOPS
2/3 CUP FLOUR
3 TABLESPOONS
    VEGETABLE OIL

Browned Garlic Butter

6 TABLESPOONS (3/4 STICK)
    BUTTER
2 GARLIC CLOVES, MINCED
1 TEASPOON CHOPPED
    PARSLEY
1 TEASPOON LEMON JUICE
1 TEASPOON HOT PEPPER
    SAUCE
1 TEASPOON PEPPER

For the pork, combine the onion powder, garlic powder, dry mustard, sage, cumin, thyme, salt and white pepper in a small bowl. Sprinkle 1/4 teaspoon of the mixture on each side of the pork chops and rub in with fingers.

Combine the remaining seasoning mixture with the flour in a small bowl. Coat the pork chops with the flour mixture.

Cook the pork chops in the heated oil in a large skillet for 4 to 5 minutes on each side or until golden brown on both sides. Drain the pork chops on paper towels.

For the butter, heat the butter in a saucepan until nearly melted. Add the garlic and cook over medium-high heat for 2 to 3 minutes or until the foam on the surface of the butter is light brown. Stir in the parsley, lemon juice, pepper sauce and pepper. Cook until light brown. Drizzle over the pork chops.

Serves six

Stuffed Pork Chops

6 THICK PORK CHOPS
1 CUP BREAD CRUMBS
1/4 CUP CHOPPED CELERY
1/4 CUP CHOPPED ONION
2 TABLESPOONS CHOPPED
   PARSLEY
1/2 TEASPOON SAGE OR
   POULTRY SEASONING
1/8 TEASPOON PAPRIKA
1/4 TEASPOON SALT
MILK OR CREAM

Cut a horizontal pocket in each pork chop, cutting from the outer edge to the bone and leaving the ends intact. Combine the bread crumbs, celery, onion, parsley, sage, paprika and salt in a bowl and mix well. Add enough milk to moisten the mixture. Stuff into the pockets in the pork chops.

Heat a nonstick ovenproof skillet and add the pork chops. Sear on both sides. Drizzle with additional milk or cream. Bake, covered, at 350 degrees for 45 to 60 minutes or until cooked through. Serve with cooking juices.

You may thicken the cooking juices with flour if preferred.

Serves six

Sweet-And-Sour Pork

1 EGG, BEATEN
2 TABLESPOONS FLOUR
1 TEASPOON SALT
1/4 TEASPOON PEPPER
2 POUNDS BONELESS PORK,
   CUT INTO 1-INCH CUBES
3/4 CUP VEGETABLE OIL
1 (20-OUNCE) CAN
   PINEAPPLE CHUNKS
1 MEDIUM CARROT, THINLY
   SLICED
1 MEDIUM ONION, CUT
   INTO HALVES, SLICED
1 GARLIC CLOVE, MINCED
1/2 CUP SUGAR
3 TABLESPOONS
   CORNSTARCH
1/2 CUP CHICKEN BROTH
1/2 CUP VINEGAR
2 TEASPOONS SOY SAUCE

Mix the egg, flour, salt and pepper in a medium bowl until smooth. Add the pork and toss to coat well. Cook the pork 1/2 at a time in the heated oil in a 12-inch skillet for 4 to 5 minutes or until golden brown. Remove the pork to paper towels and drain the skillet.

Add the undrained pineapple, carrot, onion and garlic to the skillet. Bring to a boil and reduce the heat. Simmer over low heat for 5 minutes.

Mix the sugar and cornstarch in a small bowl. Add the chicken broth, vinegar and soy sauce and mix until smooth. Add to the skillet and cook over medium heat until thickened and bubbly, stirring constantly. Cook for 2 minutes longer, stirring constantly. Stir in the pork and cook until heated through. Serve over hot cooked rice.

Serves six to eight

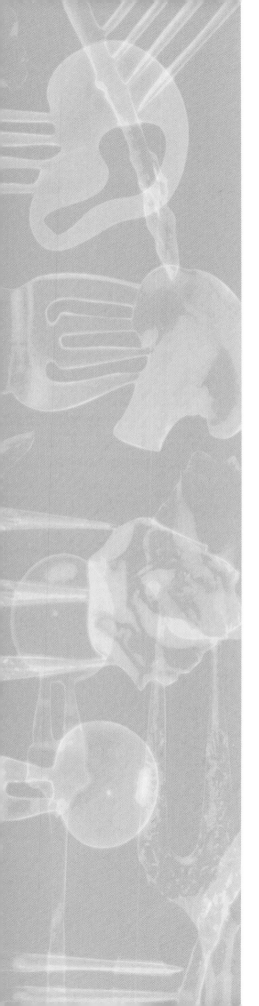

*L*OUISIANA *R*ED *B*EANS *A*ND *R*ICE

1 POUND DRIED KIDNEY
  BEANS, OR 1 (32-OUNCE)
  CAN RED BEANS
4 CUPS COLD WATER
3 SLICES BACON
8 CUPS COLD WATER
1 LARGE ONION, CHOPPED
1/2 CUP SLICED CELERY
2 GREEN BELL PEPPERS,
  SLICED
1 LARGE ONION, SLICED
6 GARLIC CLOVES,
  CRUSHED
2 TABLESPOONS MINCED
  PARSLEY
1/3 CUP CHOPPED CHIVES
  OR GREEN ONIONS
2/3 CUP OLIVE OIL
2 TABLESPOONS KETCHUP
1 1/2 TEASPOONS
  WORCESTERSHIRE
  SAUCE
2 BAY LEAVES
2 TEASPOONS CHILI
  POWDER
1 TEASPOON SALT
1 TEASPOON SEASONED
  SALT
CAYENNE PEPPER TO TASTE
1/8 TEASPOON BLACK PEPPER
1 1/2 POUNDS KIELBASA OR
  SMOKED SAUSAGE,
  SLICED
1 TABLESPOON VINEGAR
1 TABLESPOON SUGAR
HOT COOKED WHITE RICE

Rinse and sort the beans. Combine with 4 cups cold water in a bowl and let stand for 8 hours; rinse and drain.

Fry the bacon in a skillet until crisp; remove and crumble the bacon, reserving the drippings. Combine the bacon, beans, 8 cups cold water and 1 chopped onion in a large saucepan.

Sauté the celery, bell peppers, 1 sliced onion, garlic, parsley and chives in the reserved drippings in the skillet until tender but not brown. Add to the beans.

Add the olive oil, ketchup, Worcestershire sauce, bay leaves, chili powder, salt, seasoned salt, cayenne pepper and black pepper to the beans in the saucepan.

Simmer over low heat for several hours or until the beans are tender and the mixture begins to thicken, adding the sausage during the last hour of the cooking process.

Stir in the vinegar and sugar just before serving; remove and discard the bay leaves.

Serve immediately or store in the refrigerator for 24 hours to improve the flavor. Serve over hot cooked white rice.

Serves eight

Zucchini And Sausage Manicotti

Sausage Sauce

8 OUNCES BULK ITALIAN
   SAUSAGE
1/4 CUP CHOPPED ONION
1 GARLIC CLOVE, MINCED
3 CUPS SLICED FRESH
   MUSHROOMS
1 (16-OUNCE) CAN WHOLE
   TOMATOES, CHOPPED
1 (6-OUNCE) CAN TOMATO
   PASTE
1/2 CUP DRY WHITE WINE
1 TABLESPOON CHOPPED
   FRESH OREGANO
1 1/2 TEASPOONS CHOPPED
   FRESH BASIL

Manicotti

14 UNCOOKED MANICOTTI
   SHELLS, ABOUT
   8 OUNCES
SALT TO TASTE
4 QUARTS WATER
15 OUNCES RICOTTA
   CHEESE
1 CUP (4 OUNCES)
   SHREDDED MOZZARELLA
   CHEESE
1 CUP (4 OUNCES)
   SHREDDED MONTEREY
   JACK CHEESE
1/4 CUP (1 OUNCE) GRATED
   PARMESAN CHEESE
2 EGGS, BEATEN
3 TABLESPOONS CHOPPED
   PARSLEY
2 SMALL ZUCCHINI, FINELY
   CHOPPED
1/2 CUP CHOPPED ONION
2 TABLESPOONS OLIVE OIL

Garnish

GRATED PARMESAN CHEESE

For the sauce, cook the Italian sausage with the onion and garlic in a 3-quart saucepan, stirring until the sausage is brown and crumbly; drain.

Add the mushrooms, undrained tomatoes, tomato paste, wine, oregano and basil and mix well. Simmer for 45 minutes.

For the manicotti, cook the pasta shells in salted boiling water in a 6-quart saucepan for 18 minutes or until tender; drain.

Combine the ricotta cheese, mozzarella cheese, Monterey Jack cheese, Parmesan cheese, eggs and parsley in a large bowl.

Cook the zucchini and onion in the heated olive oil in a 10-inch skillet for a few minutes or just until tender, stirring constantly. Add to the cheese mixture and mix gently.

To assemble and bake, spoon the zucchini and cheese mixture into the manicotti shells. Arrange in a greased 9×13-inch baking dish. Pour the sauce over the top.

Bake at 375 degrees for 45 minutes. Garnish with additional Parmesan cheese.

Serves six or seven

Veal Grillades

2 POUNDS (1/4-INCH) VEAL
    OR BEEF ROUND STEAKS
SALT AND PEPPER
    TO TASTE
1/2 CUP FLOUR
2 TABLESPOONS
    SHORTENING
2 ONIONS, CHOPPED
6 RIBS CELERY, CHOPPED
2 TABLESPOONS CHOPPED
    GREEN BELL PEPPER
1 GARLIC CLOVE, CRUSHED
1 (28-OUNCE) CAN
    TOMATOES
3 OR 4 DROPS OF TABASCO
    SAUCE

Pound the veal thin with a meat mallet and cut into 4×4-inch pieces. Season generously with salt and pepper and coat with flour. Sauté in the heated shortening in a heavy saucepan until brown on both sides; remove to a plate.

Add the onions, celery, bell pepper and garlic to the drippings in the saucepan and sauté until golden brown. Add the tomatoes and veal with any accumulated juices. Add enough water to cover, Tabasco sauce, salt and pepper and mix gently. Simmer for 1 1/2 hours. Serve over cooked grits or rice.

Serves four to six

Veal Cutlets In Wine Sauce

1 1/2 POUNDS VEAL CUTLETS
3 TABLESPOONS BUTTER
    OR MARGARINE
2 TABLESPOONS OLIVE OIL
1/2 CUP SLICED FRESH
    MUSHROOMS
1/4 CUP SLICED GREEN
    ONIONS
2 GARLIC CLOVES, MINCED
1/4 CUP DRY SHERRY,
    MADEIRA OR MARSALA
3/4 CUP CREAM

Pound the veal cutlets 1/8 inch thick with a meat mallet. Melt the butter with the olive oil in a heavy 12-inch skillet. Add the veal cutlets and sauté for 1 1/2 minutes on each side or just until cooked through; do not overcook. Remove to a plate.

Add the mushrooms, green onions and garlic to the skillet and sauté over low heat for 5 to 6 minutes or until the vegetables are tender but not brown. Add the sherry, stirring to deglaze the skillet. Stir in the cream.

Bring to a boil and reduce the heat. Simmer until slightly thickened, stirring frequently. Add the veal and simmer for 2 minutes longer or just until heated through. Serve immediately.

Serves six

New-Mommy Roast Chicken

1 (3- TO 4-POUND)
   CHICKEN
SALT AND PEPPER
   TO TASTE
1/2 LEMON, CUT INTO
   4 WEDGES
1/2 MEDIUM ONION, CUT
   INTO 4 WEDGES
6 GARLIC CLOVES
1/4 CUP (1/2 STICK) BUTTER
   OR MARGARINE, SLICED

Garnish

CHOPPED PARSLEY
SHALLOTS
SWEET POTATO SLICES

Sprinkle the cavity of the chicken with salt and pepper. Place the lemon wedges, onion wedges, garlic and butter in the cavity. Skewer the neck skin to the back and tie the legs to the tail. Place breast side down in a foil-lined shallow roasting pan. Sprinkle with salt and pepper.

Roast, uncovered, at 475 degrees for 45 minutes or until the juices run clear when pierced with a fork and the leg moves easily. Garnish with parsley, shallots and sweet potato slices.

Serves six

Photograph for this recipe is on pages 78–79.

Eden Isle Breast Of Chicken

6 BONELESS SKINLESS
   CHICKEN BREASTS
PEPPER TO TASTE
6 SLICES BACON
1 PACKAGE DRIED BEEF,
   TORN
2 (10-OUNCE) CANS CREAM
   OF CHICKEN SOUP
1 1/2 CUPS SOUR CREAM
8 OUNCES CREAM CHEESE,
   SOFTENED

Sprinkle the chicken with pepper and wrap each with a slice of bacon. Sprinkle the dried beef in a baking dish. Arrange the chicken in the dish. Combine the soup, sour cream and cream cheese in a bowl and mix until smooth. Spoon evenly over the chicken.

Bake, covered loosely with foil, at 325 degrees for 2 hours or until tender. Remove the cover and bake just until light brown. Serve over rice.

Do not substitute corned beef for dried beef in this recipe.

Serves six

Rooted deep in the tradition of southern hospitality is the custom of taking food on special occasions. Friends and neighbors bearing cakes and casseroles are as customary at southern births as are flowers and cards. New mothers always appreciate the gift of food, for very few of them have the time or energy to cook, and that roasted chicken or chocolate pound cake may do more for their spirits than any other baby gift!

New-Mommy Roast Chicken is not too spicy for a nursing mother, yet it has enough personality for everyone in the family to enjoy. Served with a salad, bread, and dessert, it's light enough to be considered sinless and ample enough to include grandmothers, baby nurses, and all.

CHICKEN WITH BLACK BEANS

Black Beans

1/2 CUP CHOPPED ONION

2 GARLIC CLOVES, MINCED

1 TABLESPOON
VEGETABLE OIL

2 (16-OUNCE) CANS BLACK
BEANS, DRAINED, RINSED

1 (16-OUNCE) CAN
TOMATOES, DRAINED

1 (8-OUNCE) CAN TOMATO
SAUCE

1 (4-OUNCE) CAN CHOPPED
GREEN CHILES, DRAINED

2 TABLESPOONS WHITE
WINE VINEGAR

1 TABLESPOON GROUND
CUMIN

1 TEASPOON GROUND
CORIANDER

1 TABLESPOON CHILI
POWDER

Chicken

1 CUP FLOUR

1/2 TEASPOON SALT

1 TEASPOON CHILI POWDER

6 BONELESS SKINLESS
CHICKEN BREASTS

VEGETABLE OIL

3 CUPS HOT COOKED RICE

Garnish

PLAIN YOGURT OR SOUR
CREAM

SALSA

SLICED GREEN ONIONS

CHOPPED TOMATOES

SHREDDED CHEDDAR
CHEESE

For the beans, sauté the onion and garlic in the heated oil in a 3-quart saucepan until tender. Stir in the black beans, tomatoes, tomato sauce, green chiles, vinegar, cumin, coriander and chili powder.

Simmer for 25 minutes or until reduced to the desired consistency.

For the chicken, mix the flour, salt and chili powder in a sealable plastic bag. Add the chicken in batches and shake until evenly coated, shaking off the excess.

Heat 1/2 inch oil in a 10-inch skillet and add the chicken. Sauté for 4 to 5 minutes on each side or until brown; drain on paper towels.

Arrange the chicken in a 7×12-inch baking dish. Spoon the bean mixture over the top of the chicken. Bake at 400 degrees for 20 minutes or until heated through.

Spoon the rice onto serving plates and top with the chicken. Spoon the beans over the chicken. Garnish with yogurt, salsa, green onions, tomatoes and cheese.

Serves six

CHICKEN PIQUANT

3 CUPS DRY RED WINE
1 CUP SOY SAUCE
1 CUP VEGETABLE OIL
1/2 CUP WATER
4 GARLIC CLOVES, SLICED
1/4 CUP PACKED BROWN
    SUGAR
4 TEASPOONS GROUND
    GINGER
1 TEASPOON OREGANO
8 CHICKEN BREASTS OR
    PIECES OF CUT-UP
    CHICKEN

Combine the wine, soy sauce, oil, water, garlic, brown sugar, ginger and oregano in a bowl and mix well. Arrange the chicken in a rectangular 3-quart baking dish and pour the wine mixture over the top. Bake, covered, at 375 degrees for 1 hour. Serve over rice.

Serves eight

CHICKEN CORDON BLEU

6 WHOLE BONELESS
    SKINLESS CHICKEN
    BREASTS
6 THIN SLICES
    COOKED HAM
6 THIN SLICES SWISS
    CHEESE
1/2 CUP (1 STICK) BUTTER
1 CUP BREAD CRUMBS
1 TEASPOON PAPRIKA
1 TEASPOON SALT
1 TEASPOON PEPPER

Place the chicken flat on a work surface. Layer 1 slice of ham and 1 slice of cheese on each and roll the chicken to enclose the ham and cheese; secure with wooden picks.

Melt the butter in a shallow dish. Mix the bread crumbs, paprika, salt and pepper in a shallow dish. Dip the chicken rolls in the butter and coat with the crumb mixture.

Arrange in a buttered baking dish and chill, covered, for several hours. Uncover and bake at 400 degrees for 40 minutes.

Serves six

Gilding the Lily

Food tastes better and is more festive when it is beautifully garnished and presented.

For garnishing entrée platters, try:

- lemon cups filled with tartar sauce for fish
- cranberry sauce or chutney in peach halves for poultry
- mincemeat baked in orange cups for meat
- small pickled beets stuffed with seasoned cream cheese
- scored mushroom caps
- orange or pineapples slices topped with cranberry sauce cutouts
- fruit brochettes coated with lime juice and maple syrup for ham

To dress up chicken salad, serve it in:

- hollowed-out pineapple boats
- tomato shells
- cooked and chilled artichokes with the choke removed

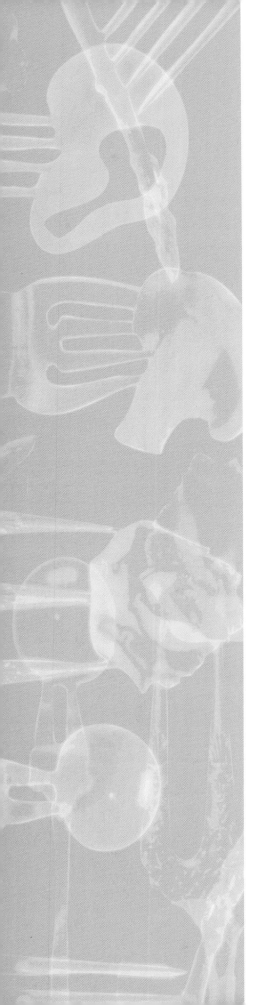

CHICKEN DIVAN

4 WHOLE CHICKEN
  BREASTS
2 CUPS WATER
1 ONION, CUT INTO
  QUARTERS
1 TABLESPOON SALT
2 (10-OUNCE) PACKAGES
  FROZEN ASPARAGUS
  OR BROCCOLI SPEARS
1/4 CUP (1/2 STICK) BUTTER
1/4 CUP FLOUR
1 CUP MILK
JUICE OF 1 LEMON
4 EGG YOLKS, BEATEN
2 TABLESPOONS SHERRY
GRATED PARMESAN
  CHEESE

Combine the chicken with the water, onion and salt in a saucepan and cook until tender. Drain, reserving 1 cup of the broth. Remove the chicken from the bones in large pieces; discard the skin and bones. Cook the asparagus using the package directions; drain. Arrange the asparagus in a buttered shallow baking dish.

Melt the butter in a saucepan and stir in the flour. Cook until bubbly. Add the milk and reserved chicken broth. Cook until thickened, stirring constantly. Stir in the lemon juice. Stir a small amount of the hot mixture into the egg yolks; stir the egg yolks into the hot mixture. Cook over low heat for several seconds, stirring constantly. Remove from the heat and stir in the sherry.

Spoon half the sauce over the asparagus and sprinkle with cheese. Arrange the chicken over the top and spoon the remaining sauce over the chicken. Sprinkle with additional cheese. Chill, covered, until time to bake. Bake at 400 degrees for 20 minutes or until heated through.

Serves eight

CHICKEN WITH SOUR CREAM

2 CUPS SOUR CREAM
2 TABLESPOONS LEMON
  JUICE
4 GARLIC CLOVES, SLICED
2 TABLESPOONS
  WORCESTERSHIRE
  SAUCE
2 TEASPOONS PAPRIKA
2 TEASPOONS CELERY SALT
1 TEASPOON SALT
6 CHICKEN BREASTS
CRACKER CRUMBS

Combine the sour cream, lemon juice, garlic, Worcestershire sauce, paprika, celery salt and salt in a bowl and mix well. Let stand for 1 hour or longer. Dip the chicken in the sour cream mixture, coating well. Arrange in a shallow foil-lined baking pan. Sprinkle with cracker crumbs. Bake at 350 degrees for 1 hour. Serve with rice.

Serves four to six

Chicken And Artichoke Casserole

1 (10-OUNCE) PACKAGE
    FROZEN CHOPPED
    SPINACH

1 (8-OUNCE) CAN SLICED
    WATER CHESTNUTS,
    DRAINED

6 LARGE SKINLESS
    CHICKEN BREASTS

1/2 CUP SHERRY

1 BAY LEAF

1 (14-OUNCE) CAN
    ARTICHOKE HEARTS,
    DRAINED, CHOPPED

2 TABLESPOONS BUTTER
    OR MARGARINE

8 OUNCES FRESH
    MUSHROOMS, SLICED

1/2 CUP SLICED GREEN
    ONIONS

1 GARLIC CLOVE, MINCED

3/4 CUP MAYONNAISE

1/2 CUP SOUR CREAM

1/2 CUP SHERRY

1 CUP (4 OUNCES) GRATED
    PARMESAN CHEESE

Cook the spinach using the package directions; drain and press to remove excess moisture. Add the water chestnuts and mix well. Spread evenly in a 9×13-inch baking dish.

Combine the chicken, 1/2 cup sherry and bay leaf in a 12-inch skillet. Bring to a boil and reduce the heat. Simmer, covered, for 18 to 20 minutes or until cooked through; drain. Arrange over the spinach mixture. Sprinkle the artichokes over the chicken.

Melt the butter in the skillet. Add the mushrooms, green onions and garlic and sauté over medium-high heat for 4 to 5 minutes or until the mushrooms and green onions are tender. Spread over the artichokes.

Combine the mayonnaise, sour cream, 1/2 cup sherry and half the cheese in a bowl and mix well. Spread over the layers in the baking dish. Top with the remaining Parmesan cheese. Bake at 350 degrees for 20 minutes or until heated through.

Serves six

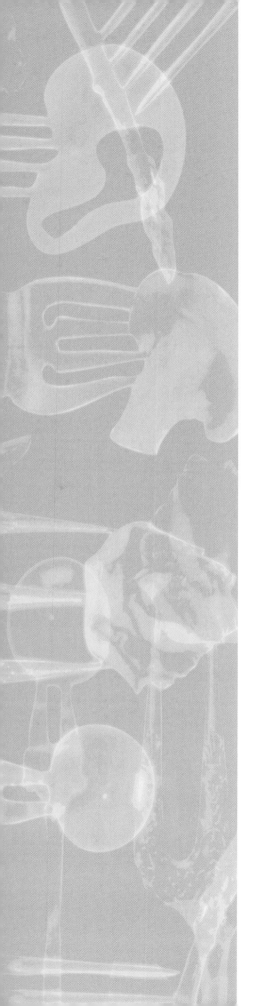

LIGHT-AND-EASY ITALIAN CHICKEN

6 BONELESS SKINLESS
    CHICKEN BREASTS
1/2 CUP REDUCED-CALORIE
    ITALIAN SALAD
    DRESSING
1 TEASPOON CHOPPED
    FRESH TARRAGON OR
    BASIL, OR 1/2 TEASPOON
    CRUSHED DRIED
    TARRAGON OR BASIL
1/4 TEASPOON CRACKED
    PEPPER
1/3 CUP (ABOUT
    1 1/2 OUNCES) GRATED
    PARMESAN CHEESE

Garnish

FRESH TARRAGON OR
    BASIL SPRIGS

Arrange the chicken in a 7×12-inch baking dish. Add 1/4 inch water. Pour the salad dressing over the chicken and sprinkle with the tarragon, pepper and cheese.

Bake at 350 degrees for 20 minutes or until tender. Garnish with tarragon or basil. Serve with hot or cold pasta, bread and wine for an easy meal on a busy day.

Serves six

CHICKEN AND WILD RICE

1 CUP UNCOOKED WILD
    RICE
2 CUPS CHICKEN BROTH
BUTTER
SALT AND PEPPER
    TO TASTE
1 (3-OUNCE) CAN
    MUSHROOMS, DRAINED
6 CHICKEN BREASTS
1/2 ENVELOPE ONION
    SOUP MIX
1 (10-OUNCE) CAN CREAM
    OF MUSHROOM SOUP
PAPRIKA TO TASTE

Soak the wild rice in enough water to cover in a bowl for 8 hours or longer; drain. Combine the rice with the chicken broth in a large shallow baking dish. Dot with butter and sprinkle with salt, pepper and mushrooms. Arrange the chicken over the rice.

Sprinkle the onion soup mix over the chicken. Mix the cream of mushroom soup with a small amount of water in a bowl. Spoon evenly over the chicken and sprinkle with paprika. Bake, uncovered, at 350 degrees for 1 hour. Bake, covered, for 30 minutes longer.

You may substitute a package of wild rice and long grain rice mix for the wild rice, discarding the seasoning packet; do not soak the wild rice mix.

Serves six

CHICKEN ENCHILADAS WITH CREMA FRESCA

Crema Fresca

1 CUP SOUR CREAM

1 CUP HEAVY CREAM

Enchiladas

16 TO 20 (10-INCH) FLOUR
TORTILLAS

4 CUPS COARSELY CHOPPED
COOKED CHICKEN

2 CUPS (8 OUNCES)
SHREDDED MONTEREY
JACK CHEESE

1 CUP CHOPPED ONION

Garnish

PICANTE SAUCE

For the crema fresca, mix the sour cream and cream in a small bowl. Let stand, covered, at room temperature for 8 hours. Chill for 24 hours.

For the enchiladas, dip 1 tortilla at a time into boiling water. Place on a work surface and spoon about 1/4 cup chicken onto each tortilla. Top with the cheese and onion. Roll the tortillas to enclose the filling and arrange seam side down in a greased 9×13-inch baking dish.

Bake, covered, at 350 degrees for 25 to 30 minutes or until heated through. Spoon the chilled crema fresca over the enchiladas and garnish with picante sauce.

Serves eight to ten

COUNTRY-STYLE CHICKEN PIE

2 CARROTS, SLICED
DIAGONALLY 1/4 INCH
THICK

1 MEDIUM POTATO, PEELED,
CHOPPED

1 MEDIUM ONION, CHOPPED

1/2 CUP PEAS

6 TABLESPOONS FLOUR

6 TABLESPOONS (3/4 STICK)
BUTTER, MELTED

2 1/2 CUPS CHICKEN BROTH

1 1/2 CUPS HEAVY CREAM

1/2 TEASPOON CRUSHED
DRIED THYME

1/8 TO 1/4 TEASPOON SAGE

1 TEASPOON SALT

1/2 TEASPOON PEPPER

4 CUPS CHOPPED COOKED
CHICKEN OR TURKEY

1 RECIPE (1-CRUST)
PIE PASTRY

Combine the carrots, potato, onion and peas with a small amount of water in a 2-quart saucepan and cook, covered, for 10 minutes or until tender-crisp; drain.

Stir the flour into the melted butter in a 2-quart saucepan. Cook until golden brown, stirring constantly. Stir in the chicken broth and cream gradually. Add the thyme, sage, salt and pepper. Cook for 5 minutes or until thickened, stirring constantly.

Layer the chicken, cooked vegetables and sauce in a 3-quart baking dish; mix gently. Place the pastry over the top; flute the edge and cut vents in the top. Bake at 425 degrees for 25 to 30 minutes or until golden brown.

Serves eight

MEXICAN CHICKEN CASSEROLE

1 LARGE ONION, CHOPPED
MARGARINE
1 (8-OUNCE) CAN CHOPPED
  GREEN CHILES
2 CUPS (8 OUNCES)
  SHREDDED CHEDDAR
  CHEESE
1 (10-COUNT) PACKAGE
  FLOUR TORTILLAS
4 CUPS CHOPPED COOKED
  CHICKEN
1 (10-OUNCE) CAN
  ENCHILADA SAUCE
1 (10-OUNCE) CAN CREAM
  OF CHICKEN SOUP
1 CUP MILK, OR 1 (5-OUNCE)
  CAN EVAPORATED MILK
2 CUPS CHICKEN BROTH

Sauté the onion in a small amount of margarine in a skillet. Stir in the green chiles.

Reserve 1/3 of the cheese. Line a 3-quart baking dish with 5 of the tortillas. Tear the remaining tortillas into bite-size pieces. Layer the chicken, remaining cheese, onion mixture and torn tortillas 1/2 at a time in the prepared dish and top with the reserved cheese.

Combine the enchilada sauce, soup, milk and chicken broth in a bowl and mix well. Spoon over the layers. Chill, covered, for 8 hours or longer. Uncover and bake at 350 degrees for 1 hour.

Serves eight to ten

CHICKEN TETRAZZINI

8 OUNCES MUSHROOMS,
  SLICED
1/4 CUP CHOPPED ONION
5 TABLESPOONS
  MARGARINE
1/4 CUP FLOUR
2 CUPS CHICKEN BROTH
11/4 CUPS HALF-AND-HALF
1 CUP (4 OUNCES)
  SHREDDED CHEDDAR
  CHEESE
1 TEASPOON LEMON JUICE
2 TEASPOONS SALT
1/8 TEASPOON PEPPER
8 OUNCES UNCOOKED
  VERMICELLI
3 CUPS CHOPPED COOKED
  CHICKEN
1/4 CUP (1 OUNCE) GRATED
  PARMESAN CHEESE

Sauté the mushrooms and onion in the margarine in a skillet until tender. Add the flour and cook until bubbly, stirring constantly. Add the chicken broth and half-and-half. Cook until thickened, stirring constantly. Stir in the Cheddar cheese, lemon juice, salt and pepper and cook until the cheese melts. Reduce the heat and simmer for 10 to 15 minutes, stirring frequently.

Cook the vermicelli using the package directions; drain. Add to the sauce with the chicken and mix gently. Spoon into a greased 2-quart baking dish and sprinkle with the Parmesan cheese. Bake at 400 degrees for 20 to 30 minutes or until bubbly.

You may substitute turkey or ham for the chicken.

Serves six

Chicken And Sun-Dried Tomato Fettuccini

4 BONELESS SKINLESS
   CHICKEN BREASTS

1 (7-OUNCE) JAR OIL-PACK
   SUN-DRIED TOMATOES

1/2 CUP CHOPPED ONION

2 GARLIC CLOVES, MINCED

2 TABLESPOONS CHOPPED
   FRESH BASIL, OR 2
   TEASPOONS CRUSHED
   DRIED BASIL

1/4 CUP SLICED BLACK
   OLIVES

2 TABLESPOONS CAPERS
   (OPTIONAL)

2 TABLESPOONS OLIVE OIL

1/2 TEASPOON SALT

1/4 TEASPOON BLACK
   PEPPER

1/4 TEASPOON CRUSHED
   RED PEPPER

8 OUNCES UNCOOKED
   FETTUCCINI

SALT TO TASTE

3 QUARTS WATER

Garnish

GRATED PARMESAN CHEESE

Cut the chicken into 1/2-inch strips. Drain the sun-dried tomatoes, reserving the oil; chop the tomatoes coarsely.

Heat 1 tablespoon of the reserved oil in a 12-inch skillet over medium heat and add the onion and garlic. Sauté until tender.

Add the chicken and cook for 8 minutes or until tender, stirring occasionally.

Add the basil and sun-dried tomatoes. Cook for 1 minute. Stir in the black olives, capers, olive oil, 2 tablespoons reserved oil, 1/2 teaspoon salt, black pepper and red pepper. Cook until the mixture is heated through.

Cook the fettuccini in the salted boiling water in a 6-quart saucepan for 8 to 10 minutes or until al dente; drain and return to the saucepan.

Add the chicken mixture and toss to mix well. Garnish with Parmesan cheese.

Serves four

Table Settings

A formal table setting doesn't have to be stiff and traditional. Use your imagination to add a touch of drama!

- Mix Grandmother's antique flatware with your own up-to-date table setting
- Mix and match plates and glasses, combining crystal, china, and pottery
- Add napkins of any material or design, such as bandanas or dish towels
- Place napkins in unexpected places, such as in the water goblets or on the dinner plates
- Practice folding napkins in interesting shapes and tying with ribbon, raffia, or ivy
- Make place cards from large green leaves and a paint pen, small individual potted plates, or vases holding a single flower with a card attached

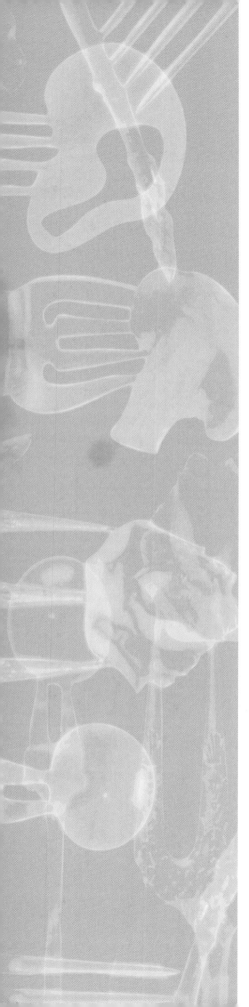

DIANE'S CURRY

5 CUPS CHOPPED COOKED
   TURKEY OR CHICKEN
1/2 CUP (1 STICK)
   MARGARINE
3 MEDIUM ONIONS,
   CHOPPED
1/2 GARLIC CLOVE, CRUSHED
1 1/4 TABLESPOONS CURRY
   POWDER
1 1/2 CUPS (OR MORE)
   POULTRY STOCK
1/2 CUP RAISINS
2 TABLESPOONS CHOPPED
   CHUTNEY
2 TEASPOONS SUGAR
1/2 TEASPOON GINGER
8 WHOLE PEPPERCORNS
1/4 CUP CHOPPED ALMONDS
MARGARINE
1/2 CUP CREAM
1 CUCUMBER, CUT INTO
   1/2-INCH PIECES
JUICE OF 1 LEMON
SALT TO TASTE

Sauté the turkey in 1/2 cup margarine in a skillet until golden brown; remove to a large saucepan with a slotted spoon, reserving the drippings. Add the onions and garlic to the drippings in the skillet and sauté until golden brown; remove to the saucepan with a slotted spoon, reserving the drippings.

Stir the curry powder into the drippings in the skillet. Add 1 1/2 cups poultry stock, raisins, chutney, sugar, ginger and peppercorns and sauté for several minutes. Add to the saucepan. Cover and bring to a simmer.

Toast the almonds in a small amount of margarine in a skillet until golden brown. Add the cream and cook for 5 minutes. Add to the turkey mixture in the saucepan. Simmer for 30 minutes; do not boil. Add the cucumber and additional turkey stock if necessary. Simmer, uncovered, for 4 hours or until the mixture is thickened to the desired consistency. Adjust the seasonings and stir in the lemon juice and salt. Serve over hot cooked saffron or white rice with assorted condiments.

Place the desired condiments in individual serving bowls and serve with the curry.

Serves six or seven

Condiments

Serve any or all of the following: crumbled crisp-fried bacon; chopped green bell pepper, cucumber, onion and tomato; chopped preserved gingerroot; chopped hard-cooked egg white; chopped peanuts or cashews; sieved hard-cooked egg yolks; grated coconut; raisins; chutney; and preserved kumquats.

DUCK WITH ORANGE SAUCE

Duck

1 (5- TO 6-POUND) DUCK
SALT TO TASTE
1 TABLESPOON BUTTER
1 TABLESPOON FLOUR
1 CUP POULTRY STOCK
1/2 CUP DRY WHITE WINE

Orange Sauce

PAN DRIPPINGS
2 ORANGES
2 TABLESPOONS SUGAR
2 TABLESPOONS WATER
JUICE OF 1/2 LEMON
2 TABLESPOONS BRANDY
SALT TO TASTE

Garnish

ORANGE SLICES
PARSLEY SPRIGS

For the duck, season the duck with salt and truss. Place on its side in a roasting pan. Roast at 475 degrees for 20 to 30 minutes or until golden brown, turning to brown evenly. Remove the duck to a platter and drain the pan, reserving 1 tablespoon of the drippings. Reduce the oven temperature to 375 degrees.

Melt the butter in the reserved drippings in the roasting pan and stir in the flour. Cook on the stove top until the mixture is dark brown, stirring constantly. Add the stock and wine and cook until thickened, stirring constantly.

Return the duck to the pan. Roast for 1 1/2 hours longer. Remove the duck to a plate.

For the sauce, pour the pan drippings from the duck into a small saucepan. Cook until reduced to 1 cup.

Cut the zest from the oranges and cut into very fine strips. Cut the remaining peel from the oranges and discard; squeeze and reserve the juice from the oranges. Combine the orange zest with enough water to cover in a saucepan and cook for 3 minutes; drain.

Combine the sugar and 2 tablespoons water in a small saucepan and cook until the mixture is light brown. Add to the reduced drippings from the duck. Add the orange zest, reserved orange juice, lemon juice and brandy. Season with salt to taste.

To serve, carve the duck and arrange on a serving platter. Spoon the orange sauce over the top. Garnish the platter with alternating slices of orange and sprigs of parsley.

Serves four to six

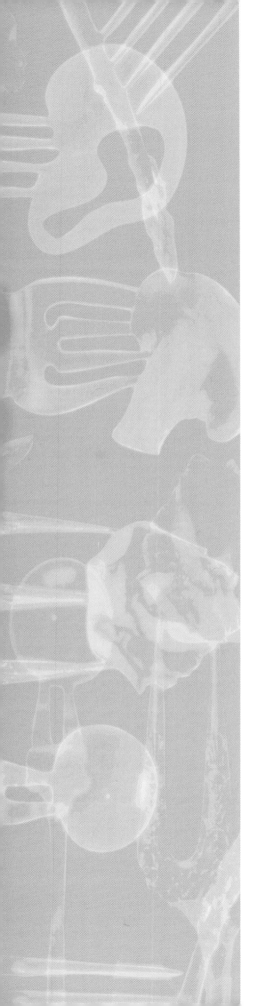

$\mathcal{S}$ALMI $\mathcal{O}$F $\mathcal{D}$UCK

3 OR 4 DUCKS

SALT TO TASTE

1 TABLESPOON (OR MORE)
FINELY CHOPPED ONION

1 RIB CELERY, FINELY
CHOPPED

1 CARROT, FINELY CHOPPED

1/4 CUP (1/2 STICK) BUTTER

1/4 CUP FLOUR

2 CUPS (OR MORE) BEEF
CONSOMMÉ

1 BAY LEAF

CHOPPED PARSLEY
TO TASTE

2 WHOLE CLOVES

PEPPER TO TASTE

1/2 CUP SHERRY

GREEN OLIVES (OPTIONAL)

CHOPPED MUSHROOMS
(OPTIONAL)

Cook the ducks in enough salted water to cover in a saucepan for 3 hours; drain. Cut the duck into bite-size pieces, discarding the skin and bones.

Sauté the onion, celery and carrot in the butter in a saucepan until the butter is light brown. Stir in the flour and cook until brown, stirring constantly. Stir in the consommé, olives, mushrooms, bay leaf, parsley, cloves, salt and pepper. Simmer for 30 minutes.

Add the duck and sherry and mix well. Remove from the heat and cool. Chill, covered, for 8 hours or longer.

Uncover and cook until heated through to serve, adding the olives and mushrooms. Add additional consommé if needed; discard the bay leaf and cloves.

Serves six

$\mathcal{G}$RILLED $\mathcal{D}$UCK

1 CUP DRY WHITE WINE

2/3 CUP VEGETABLE OIL

1/3 CUP WHITE VINEGAR

2 TABLESPOONS
WORCESTERSHIRE
SAUCE

1/2 TEASPOON DRY
MUSTARD

1/2 TEASPOON PAPRIKA

2 TABLESPOONS SEASONED
SALT

1 TEASPOON SALT

1/2 TEASPOON PEPPER

1 TEASPOON LEMON PEPPER

12 TO 16 MEDIUM DUCK
BREAST HALVES

12 TO 16 SLICES BACON

Combine the wine, oil, white vinegar, Worcestershire sauce, dry mustard, paprika, seasoned salt, salt, pepper and lemon pepper in a bowl and mix well. Combine with the duck in a sealable plastic bag and place in a large bowl, mixing well. Marinate in the refrigerator for 8 hours or longer, turning the bag occasionally; drain.

Arrange preheated coals in a circle or on the sides of the grill. Wrap a slice of bacon around each duck breast and secure with a wooden pick. Place in the center of the grill and grill, covered, for 1 hour or until tender, turning occasionally.

You may vary the amounts of herbs and seasonings to suit your taste.

Serves six to eight

Dove Au Vin

1 CUP FLOUR
1 TEASPOON SALT
1 TEASPOON PEPPER
12 DOVE, DRESSED
1/3 CUP BUTTER OR
   MARGARINE
1 CUP CHOPPED CELERY
1 CUP CHOPPED ONION
1 SMALL GREEN BELL
   PEPPER, CHOPPED
1 (10-OUNCE) CAN BEEF
   CONSOMMÉ
1/2 CUP DRY RED WINE

Mix the flour, salt and pepper in a sealable plastic bag. Add the dove a few at a time and shake to coat well. Sauté the dove in the melted butter in a large nonstick skillet over medium-high heat until brown, turning once; remove to a lightly greased 9×13-inch baking dish and sprinkle with the celery, onion and bell pepper. Pour the consommé over the dove.

Bake, covered with foil, at 350 degrees for 1½ hours. Pour the wine over the dove and bake, covered, for 30 minutes longer. Serve with hot cooked noodles or rice.

Serves six

Quail With Bacon

4 QUAIL
1 TABLESPOON VINEGAR
1/2 CUP (1 STICK) BUTTER,
   SLICED
SALT AND PEPPER
   TO TASTE
8 SLICES BACON

Combine the quail with the vinegar and enough water to cover in a bowl and soak for several minutes; rinse and drain. Place 2 tablespoons of the butter in the cavity of each quail and sprinkle with salt and pepper. Wrap the quail with bacon and secure with wooden picks. Place on a rack in a broiler pan and broil under a low heat for 30 to 40 minutes or until cooked through.

Serves four

Marinated Catfish

FILLETS OF 1¹/₂ TO
  2¹/₂ POUNDS CATFISH
1 SMALL BOTTLE
  WORCESTERSHIRE
  SAUCE
1 SMALL BOTTLE SOY
  SAUCE
JUICE OF 6 LEMONS
1 TEASPOON CINNAMON
2 TABLESPOONS
  GARLIC SALT
2 TABLESPOONS PEPPER
RED ONION SLICES

Cut the fillets into 1-inch strips. Combine the Worcestershire sauce, soy sauce, lemon juice, cinnamon, garlic salt and pepper in a blender container and process until smooth. Combine with the catfish in a bowl and mix well. Marinate, covered, in the refrigerator for 3 to 10 hours; drain.

Thread the catfish strips and onion slices alternately onto skewers. Grill for 15 minutes or until the catfish flakes easily.

Serves four to six

Fish In White Wine

5 MUSHROOMS, SLICED
2 GREEN SCALLIONS,
  CHOPPED
1 TABLESPOON BUTTER
6 WHITE FISH FILLETS
SALT AND PEPPER
  TO TASTE
¹/₂ CUP (OR MORE) DRY
  WHITE WINE OR DRY
  VERMOUTH
1 TABLESPOON FLOUR
2 TABLESPOONS BUTTER,
  MELTED

Garnish

CHOPPED FRESH CHERVIL
  OR DILL

Sauté the mushrooms and scallions in 1 tablespoon butter in a skillet until tender. Arrange the fish fillets over the mushroom mixture and sprinkle with salt and pepper. Add the wine to the skillet. Simmer, tightly covered, for 12 minutes. Remove the fish to a heated serving platter, reserving the cooking liquid.

Blend the flour into 2 tablespoons melted butter in a saucepan. Cook until smooth and bubbly, stirring constantly. Add the reserved cooking liquid. Cook until thickened, stirring constantly. Season with pepper and pour over the fish. Garnish with chervil or dill.

Serves four to six

RED SNAPPER WITH TOASTED PECAN BUTTER

Toasted Pecan Butter

2/3 CUP PECANS

1/8 TEASPOON WHITE PEPPER

1/8 TEASPOON GROUND RED PEPPER

1/4 CUP (1/2 STICK) BUTTER

2 TABLESPOONS FINELY CHOPPED PARSLEY

1 TABLESPOON FRESH LEMON JUICE

Red Snapper

1/2 CUP FLOUR

4 TEASPOONS PAPRIKA

2 TEASPOONS GARLIC POWDER

1/4 TEASPOON GROUND THYME

1 1/2 TEASPOONS SALT

1/4 TEASPOON GROUND RED PEPPER

4 (6-OUNCE) FRESH OR THAWED FROZEN RED SNAPPER FILLETS

1/2 CUP MILK

1/4 CUP PEANUT OIL

For the butter, toss the pecans with the white pepper and red pepper. Toast in the butter in an 8-inch skillet for 3 minutes or until light brown. Remove from the heat and stir in the parsley and lemon juice; keep warm.

For the snapper, combine the flour, paprika, garlic powder, thyme, salt and red pepper in a medium bowl and mix well.

Dip the fillets in the milk and coat with the flour mixture. Sauté in the heated peanut oil in a 12-inch skillet for 6 minutes or until golden brown on both sides, turning once.

Arrange the fillets on a serving plate; spoon the pecans and butter over the top. Serve immediately.

Serves four

Destin-ation

No Memphis cookbook could be complete without a mention of Destin, Florida— also known as Memphis South. Destin is so much the home-away-from-home for a vast number of Mid-Southerners that it is impossible to go to the grocery store there without running into an acquaintance from Memphis! On everyone's shopping list will be delicious fresh seafood from the Gulf, to be served with roasted corn, French bread, and ice-cold beer. Finish the meal with Custard Ice Cream (page 158) topped with Chocolate Sauce (page 157) for a perfect day at the beach.

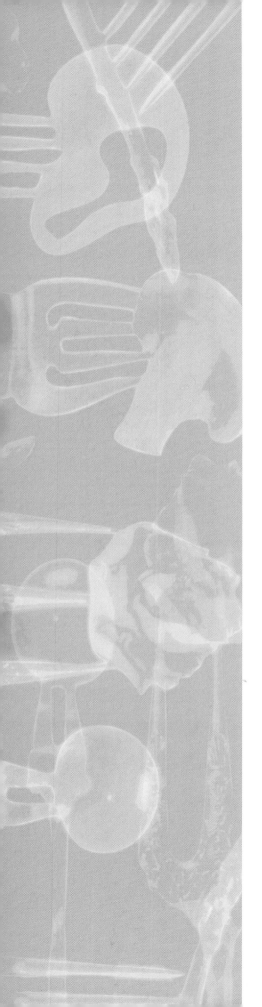

Mustard-Crusted Red Snapper

4 (6- TO 8-OUNCE) FRESH
    OR THAWED FROZEN RED
    SNAPPER FILLETS
SALT AND PEPPER
    TO TASTE
1/2 CUP OLIVE OIL
1/4 CUP MINCED ONION
3 LARGE GARLIC CLOVES,
    MINCED
1/3 CUP COARSE-GRAIN
    MUSTARD
1/2 CUP FLOUR
1/4 CUP (1/2 STICK)
    UNSALTED BUTTER

Score the skin side of the fillets and season both sides with salt and pepper; brush with a small amount of the olive oil. Mix the onion and garlic in a small bowl. Press the mixture into the scored sides of the fillets and spread with the mustard. Coat the fillets gently with the flour, shaking off the excess.

Heat the remaining olive oil with the butter in a 12-inch skillet until hot but not smoking. Add the fillets skin side down and cook for 3 to 4 minutes or until the bottom is golden brown. Turn the fillets and cook for 4 to 5 minutes longer or until they flake easily.

Serves four

Grilled Salmon With Caper And Lemon Butter

Caper and Lemon Butter

2 TABLESPOONS DRAINED
    CAPERS
1/2 CUP (1 STICK) BUTTER
1 TABLESPOON LEMON
    JUICE
WORCESTERSHIRE SAUCE
    TO TASTE
SEASONED SALT TO TASTE

Salmon

1/3 CUP MAYONNAISE
1 TABLESPOON CHOPPED
    FRESH DILLWEED, OR
    1 TEASPOON DRIED
    DILLWEED
2 POUNDS (1-INCH) SALMON
    FILLETS WITH SKIN, OR
    4 (1-INCH) SALMON
    STEAKS

For the butter, combine the capers, butter, lemon juice, Worcestershire sauce and seasoned salt in a blender container and process until smooth. Pour into a 1-quart saucepan. Cook until heated through; keep warm.

For the salmon, combine the mayonnaise and dillweed in a small bowl. Spread over both sides of the salmon. Place skin side down on a greased rack over medium coals. Grill, covered, for 10 minutes or until the salmon flakes easily; do not turn.

Remove the salmon to a serving platter. Spoon some of the butter over the salmon and pour the remaining butter into a serving bowl to serve at the table.

Serves eight

Fillets Of Sole Stuffed With Crab Meat

Sole

6 (4-OUNCE) FRESH OR
   THAWED FROZEN SOLE
   FILLETS
3 (4-OUNCE) SLICES SWISS
   CHEESE, CUT INTO
   HALVES LENGTHWISE
8 OUNCES LUMP
   CRAB MEAT
1 TABLESPOON CHOPPED
   FRESH BASIL, OR
   1 TEASPOON CRUSHED
   DRIED BASIL

Mushroom Wine Sauce

2 TABLESPOONS BUTTER
   OR MARGARINE
1/4 CUP CHOPPED
   MUSHROOMS
2 TEASPOONS CHOPPED
   SHALLOTS
3 TABLESPOONS DRY
   WHITE WINE
1 TEASPOON LEMON JUICE
2 TABLESPOONS BUTTER
   OR MARGARINE
3 TABLESPOONS FLOUR
1 CUP CLAM JUICE
1/2 CUP LIGHT CREAM
1 TEASPOON LEMON JUICE
SALT AND PAPRIKA TO
   TASTE

Garnish

1 TABLESPOON CHOPPED
   PARSLEY

For the sole, place the fillets skin side up on a work surface. Top each fillet with 1/2 slice of the Swiss cheese, 3 tablespoons of the crab meat and 1/2 teaspoon of the fresh basil. Roll the fillets to enclose the filling and arrange seam side down in a shallow baking dish.

For the sauce, melt 2 tablespoons butter in a heavy skillet over medium heat and add the mushrooms, shallots, wine and 1 teaspoon lemon juice. Cook until the liquid evaporates, stirring frequently.

Add 2 tablespoons butter and heat until the butter melts. Add the flour and mix well. Add the clam juice. Cook until thickened and bubbly, stirring constantly.

Add the cream, 1 teaspoon lemon juice and salt to the skillet and mix well. Pour over the fish and sprinkle with paprika.

Bake, covered, at 400 degrees for 16 to 20 minutes or until the fish flakes easily. Remove the fish rolls to serving plates and spoon the sauce over the top. Garnish with parsley.

Serves six

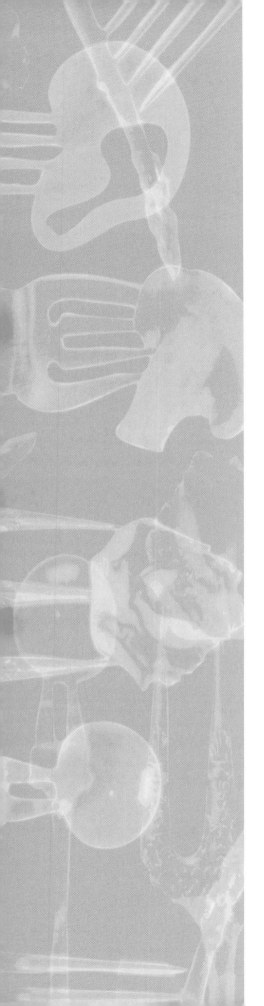

MEMPHIS HEART AND SOLE

4 MEDIUM TOMATOES,
    PEELED, THINLY SLICED
1/2 TEASPOON CRUSHED
    DRIED BASIL
1/2 CUP FINE DRY BREAD
    CRUMBS
6 (4-OUNCE) FRESH OR
    THAWED FROZEN
    SOLE FILLETS
1/2 TEASPOON SALT
1/2 TEASPOON FRESHLY
    GROUND PEPPER
1/2 CUP (1 STICK) BUTTER
    OR MARGARINE
3/4 CUP DRY WHITE WINE
1 TABLESPOON FRESH LIME
    JUICE
1/2 CUP (2 OUNCES) GRATED
    PARMESAN CHEESE

Arrange the tomato slices evenly over the bottom of a 9×13-inch baking dish and sprinkle with the basil and bread crumbs. Arrange the sole fillets over the bread crumbs and sprinkle with the salt and pepper.

Combine the butter, wine and lime juice in a 1-quart saucepan and cook over medium heat until the butter melts. Pour over the fillets and sprinkle with the cheese.

Bake at 400 degrees for 15 to 20 minutes or until the fish flakes easily.

You may substitute orange roughy for the sole.

Serves six

GRILLED TUNA STEAKS

Cilantro Marinade

1 CUP VEGETABLE OIL
1/4 CUP DRY VERMOUTH
2 TABLESPOONS LEMON
    JUICE
2 TABLESPOONS CHOPPED
    FRESH CILANTRO
1 TEASPOON SEASONED
    SALT
1/2 TEASPOON PEPPER

Tuna

6 TO 8 (6- TO 8-OUNCE)
    TUNA STEAKS, 1 INCH
    THICK
1 OR 2 RED BELL PEPPERS,
    SEEDED, SLICED INTO
    RINGS
LEAVES OF 1 LARGE HEAD
    ROMAINE LETTUCE

For the marinade, combine the oil, wine, lemon juice, cilantro, seasoned salt and pepper in a sealable plastic bag and mix well.

For the tuna, add the tuna steaks to the marinade and mix well; seal the bag and place in a shallow dish. Marinate in the refrigerator for 1 to 2 hours; drain.

Place several bell pepper rings on each steak and wrap each steak in 2 or 3 lettuce leaves and then in heavy-duty foil. Grill over medium coals for 10 minutes or until the fish flakes easily.

Serves six to eight

$\mathcal{T}$ROUT $\mathcal{A}$MANDINE

Trout

6 DROPS OF TABASCO
    SAUCE
1 TEASPOON SALT
MILK
8 TO 12 (8-OUNCE) FRESH
    RAINBOW TROUT,
    BROWN TROUT OR
    OTHER TROUT
2 CUPS FLOUR
1 TEASPOON SALT
1 TEASPOON WHITE
    PEPPER
2 CUPS (4 STICKS) BUTTER

Amandine Sauce

1 CUP (2 STICKS) BUTTER
3/4 CUP THINLY SLICED
    ALMONDS
2 TEASPOONS
    WORCESTERSHIRE SAUCE
1/4 CUP FRESH LEMON JUICE
1/4 CUP CHOPPED FRESH
    PARSLEY
1 TEASPOON SALT

Garnish

8 TO 12 LEMON SLICES

For the trout, combine the Tabasco sauce and 1 teaspoon salt with enough milk to cover the fish in a large bowl. Add the fish and let stand for 1 hour; drain.

Mix the flour with 1 teaspoon salt and the white pepper in a bowl. Coat the fish inside and out with the flour mixture. Melt 1 cup of the butter in each of 2 large skillets and heat until bubbly but not brown. Add half the fish to each skillet and sauté for 8 minutes or until golden brown, turning after 5 minutes; do not overcook. Remove to a warm platter.

For the sauce, wipe 1 of the skillets and melt the butter in it. Add the almonds and cook until golden brown. Add the Worcestershire sauce, lemon juice, parsley and salt.

Spoon some of the sauce over the fish and pour the remaining sauce into a serving bowl to serve at the table. Garnish with lemon slices. Serve with chilled dry white wine.

Serves four to six

New Orleans Barbecued Shrimp

2 CUPS (4 STICKS)
    MARGARINE
1 (16-OUNCE) BOTTLE
    ITALIAN SALAD
    DRESSING
JUICE OF 4 LEMONS
1 (2-OUNCE) CAN PEPPER
5 POUNDS UNCOOKED
    SHRIMP IN THE SHELL

Melt the margarine in a saucepan and stir in the salad dressing, lemon juice and pepper. Pour over the shrimp in a large baking pan. Bake at 350 degrees for 45 minutes. Remove to large platters with a slotted spoon and pour the margarine mixture from the pan over the shrimp. Serve with large napkins and bread for dipping into the sauce.

Serves eight to ten

Great Balls Of Fire Shrimp

GRATED ZEST AND JUICE
    OF 1 LARGE LEMON
1/2 CUP (1 STICK) BUTTER
    OR MARGARINE
2 TABLESPOONS PREPARED
    MUSTARD
3 GARLIC CLOVES, MINCED
2 BAY LEAVES, CRUSHED
1 1/2 TEASPOONS GROUND
    GINGER
1/2 TEASPOON SALT
2 TABLESPOONS BLACK
    PEPPER
1/2 TEASPOON GROUND
    RED PEPPER
1 1/2 POUNDS PEELED FRESH
    OR THAWED FROZEN
    JUMBO SHRIMP, DEVEINED

Combine the lemon zest, lemon juice, butter, mustard, garlic, bay leaves, ginger, salt, black pepper and red pepper in a 1-quart saucepan. Cook over medium-low heat until the butter melts, stirring to mix well. Cool to room temperature.

Combine the butter mixture with the shrimp in a sealable plastic bag and mix well. Place in a shallow dish. Marinate in the refrigerator for 2 to 24 hours, turning the bag several times.

Drain the shrimp and thread onto six 12-inch skewers, leaving space between shrimp. Place on a lightly greased rack over medium coals. Grill for 8 to 10 minutes or until the shrimp are pink, turning halfway through the grilling time.

Serves six

Shrimp Casserole With Mushrooms And Artichokes

8 OUNCES MUSHROOMS

2¹/₂ TABLESPOONS BUTTER

1 (20-OUNCE) CAN
   ARTICHOKE HEARTS,
   DRAINED

1¹/₂ POUNDS PEELED
   COOKED SHRIMP

4¹/₂ TABLESPOONS BUTTER

4¹/₂ TABLESPOONS FLOUR

³/₄ CUP MILK

³/₄ CUP HEAVY CREAM

1 TABLESPOON
   WORCESTERSHIRE
   SAUCE

¹/₂ CUP DRY SHERRY

SALT AND PEPPER TO TASTE

¹/₂ CUP (2 OUNCES) GRATED
   PARMESAN CHEESE

PAPRIKA TO TASTE

Sauté the mushrooms in 2¹/₂ tablespoons butter in a skillet. Layer the artichoke hearts, shrimp and mushrooms in a 2-quart baking dish.

Melt 4¹/₂ tablespoons butter in a saucepan. Whisk in the flour and cook until bubbly. Add the milk and cream and cook until thickened, whisking constantly. Stir in the Worcestershire sauce, sherry, salt and pepper. Pour over the layers in the baking dish.

Sprinkle with the cheese and paprika. Bake at 375 degrees for 20 to 30 minutes or until heated through. Serve over rice.

You may prepare the dish a day in advance to blend the flavors.

Serves six

Shrimp Creole

3 GREEN BELL PEPPERS

4 ONIONS

2 GARLIC CLOVES

4 CUPS CHOPPED CELERY

¹/₂ CUP MINCED PARSLEY

¹/₂ CUP (1 STICK) BUTTER

3 (16-OUNCE) CANS
   TOMATOES

1 TEASPOON CURRY
   POWDER

1 TEASPOON THYME

1 TEASPOON SALT

¹/₂ TEASPOON BLACK PEPPER

¹/₂ TEASPOON CAYENNE
   PEPPER

5 POUNDS UNCOOKED
   PEELED SHRIMP

Finely chop the bell peppers and onions. Chop the garlic. Sauté the bell peppers, onions, garlic, celery and parsley in the butter in a large saucepan.

Add the tomatoes, curry powder, thyme, salt, black pepper and cayenne pepper and mix well. Simmer for 30 minutes. Add the shrimp and simmer for 20 minutes longer. Serve with rice.

Serves eight to ten

Holiday Shrimp Creole

With festive red and green ingredients, Shrimp Creole makes a delicious make-ahead dish for Christmas Eve. It is a welcome change from the turkey, ham, and roast beef traditionally served for dinner on Christmas Day.

HEAVENLY SHRIMP PASTA

Herb Butter and Butter Sauce

1½ TEASPOONS DIJON
    MUSTARD
5 TEASPOONS MINCED
    GARLIC
5 TEASPOONS DRAINED
    CAPERS
5 TEASPOONS CHOPPED
    PIMENTOS
1 TABLESPOON CHOPPED
    PARSLEY
1½ TEASPOONS CHOPPED
    FRESH THYME
1½ TEASPOONS CHOPPED
    FRESH OREGANO
1½ TEASPOONS CHOPPED
    FRESH BASIL
¼ TEASPOON SALT
GROUND RED PEPPER
    TO TASTE
2 CUPS (4 STICKS)
    UNSALTED BUTTER,
    SOFTENED
1 CUP HEAVY CREAM
3 TABLESPOONS FRESH
    LEMON JUICE
SALT AND BLACK PEPPER
    TO TASTE

Pasta

¼ CUP (½ STICK) BUTTER
2 POUNDS FRESH OR
    THAWED FROZEN LARGE
    SHRIMP, PEELED,
    DEVEINED
SEAFOOD SEASONING
    TO TASTE
1 POUND ANGEL HAIR
    PASTA, COOKED,
    DRAINED

For the herb butter, combine the Dijon mustard, garlic, capers, pimentos, parsley, thyme, oregano, basil, ¼ teaspoon salt and red pepper with the butter in a mixing bowl and beat just until mixed; do not whip.

Spoon along 1 edge of a piece of waxed paper and roll up in the waxed paper. Wrap in plastic wrap and chill for up to 2 weeks or freeze for a longer period.

For the butter sauce, cut the herb butter into small pieces; keep cold. Bring the heavy cream to a simmer in a heavy 2-quart saucepan.

Whisk in the butter 1 or 2 pieces at a time, cooking until creamy; remove from the heat. Whisk in the lemon juice, salt and black pepper to taste.

For the pasta, melt the butter in a 12-inch skillet over medium heat. Add the shrimp and sprinkle with the seafood seasoning. Sauté for 2 to 4 minutes or until the shrimp are pink.

Spoon the pasta onto serving plates. Spoon the shrimp over the pasta and top with the sauce. Serve immediately.

Serves six

Pasta Ala Elfo

8 OUNCES UNCOOKED
   SPAGHETTI
SALT TO TASTE
3 QUARTS WATER
8 FRESH OR THAWED
   FROZEN JUMBO SHRIMP,
   PEELED, DEVEINED
1 CUP SLICED FRESH
   MUSHROOMS
10 GARLIC CLOVES,
   MINCED
1 CUP (2 STICKS) BUTTER
WHITE PEPPER TO TASTE
6 TABLESPOONS GRATED
   PARMESAN CHEESE

Cook the pasta in the salted boiling water in a 6-quart saucepan for 10 to 12 minutes or until al dente; drain well.

Cut each shrimp into thirds. Sauté the garlic in the butter in a 12-inch skillet until tender. Add the shrimp and mushrooms and sauté until the shrimp are pink. Add the pasta, salt and white pepper and mix well. Cook until heated through; do not allow the butter to brown. Spoon into a serving dish and top with the cheese.

Serves four

Seafood Casserole

¼ CUP (½ STICK) BUTTER
   OR MARGARINE
6 TABLESPOONS FLOUR
½ TEASPOON SALT
¼ TO ½ TEASPOON
   FRESHLY GROUND
   BLACK PEPPER
RED PEPPER TO TASTE
1¾ CUPS MILK
¼ CUP DRY WHITE WINE
¾ CUP (3 OUNCES)
   SHREDDED CHEDDAR
   CHEESE
1 CUP SLICED MUSHROOMS
2 TABLESPOONS BUTTER
   OR MARGARINE
12 OUNCES DEVEINED
   PEELED MEDIUM SHRIMP,
   COOKED
12 OUNCES LUMP
   CRAB MEAT
¼ CUP (1 OUNCE)
   SHREDDED CHEDDAR
   CHEESE

Melt ¼ cup butter in a 2-quart saucepan and stir in the flour, salt, black pepper and red pepper. Cook until bubbly, stirring constantly. Whisk in the milk and wine all at once. Cook over medium heat until thickened, whisking constantly. Stir in ¾ cup cheese until melted; remove from the heat.

Sauté the mushrooms in 2 tablespoons butter in an 8-inch skillet over medium heat for 4 or 5 minutes or until tender. Add the mushrooms, shrimp and crab meat to the cheese sauce and mix gently.

Spoon into a 2-quart baking dish and sprinkle with ¼ cup cheese. Bake at 350 degrees for 20 to 30 minutes or until heated through.

Serves four to six

Dynasty

"Life has its ups and downs and I cannot leave you much, but this recipe is mine to give. If you will cook it just like I tell you, you will always be able to make yourself a living." With these words, Elfo Grisanti set his son Rinaldo, or Ronnie, on a path of success as founder and owner of the popular Ronnie Grisanti & Sons Restaurant in the heart of Memphis. Ronnie follows in the footsteps of his father and grandfather in a dynasty begun in a small village in Tuscany, Italy. Ronnie is proud to be continuing the line of a centuries-old heritage of Italian cooking that is "Cucina Toscana"—in the style of the local kitchens of Tuscany.

ARTICHOKES AU GRATIN

2 (14-OUNCE) CANS
    ARTICHOKE HEARTS
3 TABLESPOONS BUTTER
    OR MARGARINE
3 TABLESPOONS FLOUR
1/2 TEASPOON SALT
1 3/4 CUPS MILK
1 CUP (4 OUNCES)
    SHREDDED CHEDDAR
    CHEESE
1/2 CUP MAYONNAISE
CRACKED PEPPER TO TASTE
2 TABLESPOONS BUTTER OR
    MARGARINE
3/4 CUP FINE DRY BREAD
    CRUMBS

Rinse and drain the artichokes. Coarsely chop the artichokes and set aside. Melt 3 tablespoons butter in a 2-quart saucepan and stir in the flour and salt until smooth. Cook for 1 minute, stirring constantly. Whisk in the milk gradually. Cook until thickened and bubbly, whisking constantly. Remove from the heat and add the artichoke hearts, cheese, mayonnaise and pepper; mix well. Spoon into a 1 1/2-quart baking dish.

Melt 2 tablespoons butter in a saucepan and add the bread crumbs; toss to coat well. Sprinkle over the artichoke mixture. Bake at 325 degrees for 45 minutes or until bubbly.

Serves six

CHEESY ASPARAGUS CASSEROLE

2 (16-OUNCE) CANS
    ASPARAGUS SPEARS
2 TABLESPOONS BUTTER
2 TABLESPOONS FLOUR
1 CUP (SCANT) CREAM
PAPRIKA, SALT, BLACK
    PEPPER AND RED PEPPER
    TO TASTE
12 OUNCES SHARP
    CHEDDAR CHEESE,
    CHOPPED
1 (4-OUNCE) CAN
    MUSHROOMS, DRAINED
2 HARD-COOKED EGGS,
    SLICED
GROUND BLANCHED
    ALMONDS

Drain the asparagus, reserving 2 tablespoons of the liquid. Melt the butter in a saucepan and stir in the flour. Cook until bubbly. Add the reserved asparagus liquid and blend to a paste. Whisk in the cream gradually. Cook until thickened and bubbly, whisking constantly. Season with paprika, salt, black pepper and red pepper. Add the cheese and cook until melted, stirring to blend well. Stir in the mushrooms.

Layer the asparagus, cheese sauce and eggs 1/2 at a time in a baking dish. Top with almonds. Bake at 350 degrees for 20 minutes or until heated through.

Serves eight to ten

MARINATED ASPARAGUS WITH PECANS

2 POUNDS FRESH
   ASPARAGUS SPEARS
2 TABLESPOONS WATER
1/4 CUP WHITE VINEGAR
1/4 CUP SOY SAUCE
2 TABLESPOONS
   VEGETABLE OIL
1/4 CUP SUGAR
1/4 CUP FINELY CHOPPED
   PECANS

Snap off and discard the tough ends of fresh asparagus; scrape off the scales if desired. Combine with the water in a microwave-safe 9×13-inch dish. Microwave on High for 5 to 7 minutes or until tender-crisp and bright green, rearranging once; rinse in cold water and drain. Arrange in the same dish.

Combine the vinegar, soy sauce, oil and sugar in a bowl and mix well. Add the pecans. Pour over the asparagus. Marinate, covered, in the refrigerator for 8 hours or longer.

Drain the asparagus, reserving the marinade. Arrange on a lettuce-lined serving platter and drizzle with some of the reserved marinade.

You may cook the fresh asparagus in boiling water for 6 to 8 minutes or until tender-crisp if preferred. You may also substitute three 10-ounce packages frozen asparagus for the fresh asparagus and cook according to the package directions.

Serves six to eight

ASPARAGUS DELIGHT

1 CUP CHENIN BLANC
1 CUP VEGETABLE OIL
1/4 CUP LEMON JUICE
1/2 TEASPOON DRY
   MUSTARD
1/2 TEASPOON PAPRIKA
1/2 TEASPOON THYME
1/2 TEASPOON OREGANO
1/2 TEASPOON ONION SALT
GARLIC SALT TO TASTE
1 TEASPOON SALT
40 FRESH OR FROZEN
   ASPARAGUS SPEARS,
   BLANCHED
40 THIN SLICES COOKED
   HAM

Combine the wine, oil, lemon juice, dry mustard, paprika, thyme, oregano, onion salt, garlic salt and salt in a large shallow dish and mix well. Add the asparagus.

Marinate, covered, in the refrigerator for 8 hours or longer; drain. Roll each asparagus spear in a slice of ham and secure with a wooden pick. Serve hot or cold.

Serves twenty

VENETIAN GREEN BEANS WITH TOMATOES

1 POUND FRESH GREEN
    BEANS, TRIMMED
SALT TO TASTE
1/4 CUP OLIVE OIL
3 LARGE TOMATOES,
    PEELED, SEEDED, CHOPPED
2 GARLIC CLOVES, MINCED
1 TABLESPOON CHOPPED
    FRESH BASIL
1 TABLESPOON CHOPPED
    FRESH OREGANO
1 TABLESPOON CHOPPED
    FRESH PARSLEY
FRESHLY GROUND PEPPER
    TO TASTE

Cook the beans, covered, in a small amount of salted boiling water in a 2-quart saucepan for 7 to 9 minutes or until tender-crisp; drain.

Heat the olive oil in a 10-inch skillet and add the beans, tossing to coat well. Add the tomatoes, garlic, basil, oregano and parsley. Cook for 1 minute or until the liquid evaporates. Reduce the heat and simmer for 5 to 10 minutes or until the beans are tender. Season with salt and pepper. Serve warm or chilled as a perfect accompaniment for cold ham and potato salad.

You may add 2 tablespoons grated Parmesan cheese if desired.

Serves four

Photograph for this recipe is on page 120.

GREEN BEANS Y'ALL WON'T BELIEVE

1 1/2 POUNDS FRESH GREEN
    BEANS, TRIMMED
SALT TO TASTE
10 SLICES BACON
6 TABLESPOONS SUGAR
6 TABLESPOONS VINEGAR
1/4 CUP SLIVERED ALMONDS

Leave the beans whole or cut into 1-inch pieces. Cook, covered, in a small amount of salted boiling water in a 2-quart saucepan for 20 to 25 minutes or until tender-crisp; drain.

Cook the bacon in a 10-inch skillet until crisp. Remove and crumble the bacon, reserving the drippings in the skillet. Stir the sugar and vinegar into the drippings.

Layer the beans, bacon and almonds 1/2 at a time in a 1 1/2-quart baking dish. Pour the vinegar mixture over the layers. Bake at 350 degrees for 45 minutes or until heated through.

You may substitute 2 drained and rinsed 16-ounce cans of green beans for the fresh beans.

Serves six to eight

Baked Green Beans

3 (16-OUNCE) CANS WHOLE
   GREEN BEANS
1 CUP CONSOMMÉ
2 CUPS FRESH MUSHROOMS,
   OR 1 (16-OUNCE) CAN
   MUSHROOMS, DRAINED
1/2 CUP (1 STICK) BUTTER
SALT AND MAGGI
   SEASONING TO TASTE

Drain the beans and combine with the consommé in a bowl. Let stand for 1 hour or longer. Sauté the mushrooms in the butter in a skillet until tender. Combine with the beans and add seasonings to taste. Spoon into a buttered baking dish. Bake at 325 degrees for 45 minutes.

This dish is better if prepared a day in advance.

Serves six to eight

Broccoli Soufflé

3 (10-OUNCE) PACKAGES
   FROZEN CHOPPED
   BROCCOLI
3/4 CUP BOUILLON
3/4 CUP HEAVY CREAM
1/2 CUP (1 STICK) BUTTER
1/2 CUP FLOUR
4 EGG YOLKS
2 TEASPOONS CHOPPED
   PARSLEY
1/4 CUP FINELY CHOPPED
   ONION
SALT AND FRESHLY
   CRACKED PEPPER TO
   TASTE
1/2 CUP (2 OUNCES)
   SHREDDED CHEDDAR
   CHEESE
4 EGG WHITES

Cook the broccoli using the package directions, drain. Combine the bouillon and cream in a saucepan and bring to a simmer.

Melt the butter in a saucepan and blend in the flour. Cook until bubbly. Add the cream mixture gradually. Cook until thickened, stirring constantly; remove from the heat.

Beat the egg yolks with the parsley, onion, salt and pepper in a bowl. Add the hot cream mixture gradually, whisking constantly. Add the broccoli and cheese and mix well.

Beat the egg whites in a mixing bowl until stiff peaks form. Fold into the broccoli mixture. Spoon into a buttered baking dish. Bake at 425 degrees for 25 to 30 minutes or until set.

The dish may be prepared in advance to the point that the beaten egg whites are added. Store, covered, in the refrigerator.

Serves ten

Broccoli "Oysters Rockefeller"

2 (10-OUNCE) PACKAGES
   FROZEN CHOPPED
   BROCCOLI
1 MEDIUM ONION, GRATED
1/2 CUP (1 STICK)
   MARGARINE
1 (10-OUNCE) CAN CREAM
   OF MUSHROOM SOUP
1 (4-OUNCE) CAN CHOPPED
   MUSHROOMS, DRAINED
1 (8-OUNCE) ROLL GARLIC
   CHEESE, CHOPPED
SLICED ALMONDS
   (OPTIONAL)

Cook the broccoli using the package directions; drain. Sauté the onion in the margarine in a saucepan until tender. Add the soup, mushrooms, broccoli and cheese and mix until the cheese melts. Stir in almonds.

Spoon into a baking dish and bake at 350 degrees for 30 minutes or until heated through.

You may serve this from a chafing dish as an appetizer. It can be prepared in advance and baked or reheated to serve.

Serves eight to ten

Summertime Carrots

3 MEDIUM CARROTS,
   SCRAPED
SALT TO TASTE
1/2 CUP (1 STICK) BUTTER
1/2 CUP SUGAR
1 TABLESPOON CHOPPED
   FRESH MINT LEAVES
BUTTER TO TASTE
PEPPER TO TASTE

Cut the carrots into 1/4-inch slices, strips or shapes as desired. Cook in salted boiling water in a saucepan for 15 minutes or until tender; drain. Add 1/2 cup butter, sugar and mint. Cook over low heat until glazed. Season with additional butter, salt and pepper.

Serves six

CARROTS WITH HORSERADISH

8 LARGE CARROTS,
    JULIENNED
1/2 CUP WATER
SALT TO TASTE
1/2 CUP MAYONNAISE OR
    MAYONNAISE-TYPE
    SALAD DRESSING
2 TABLESPOONS GRATED
    ONION
2 TABLESPOONS PREPARED
    HORSERADISH
1 TEASPOON LEMON JUICE
1/4 TEASPOON SALT
1/4 TEASPOON CRACKED
    PEPPER
1/2 CUP FINE DRY BREAD
    CRUMBS
1 TABLESPOON BUTTER OR
    MARGARINE, MELTED

Combine the carrots with the water and salt to taste in a 3-quart saucepan. Cook, covered, for 5 to 7 minutes or until tender-crisp; drain, reserving 1/4 cup of the cooking liquid. Spoon the carrots into a 7×12-inch baking dish.

Combine the mayonnaise, onion, horseradish, lemon juice, 1/4 teaspoon salt, pepper and reserved cooking liquid in a medium bowl and mix well. Spread over the carrots and sprinkle with the bread crumbs. Drizzle the butter over the top. Bake at 350 degrees for 15 to 20 minutes or until heated through.

Serves six

Photograph for this recipe is on page 120.

CARROT SOUFFLÉ

2 CUPS THINLY SLICED
    CARROTS
SALT TO TASTE
1 CUP SUGAR
3 EGGS
1/2 CUP (1 STICK) BUTTER
    OR MARGARINE, MELTED
3 TABLESPOONS FLOUR
1 TEASPOON BAKING
    POWDER
1/2 TEASPOON GROUND
    CINNAMON
1/4 TEASPOON GROUND
    NUTMEG

Garnish

SHREDDED ORANGE ZEST

Cook fresh carrots in a small amount of salted boiling water in a saucepan for 7 to 9 minutes or until tender, drain. Combine the carrots with the sugar, eggs, butter, flour, baking powder, cinnamon and nutmeg in a food processor container and process until smooth.

Spoon into a 1 1/2-quart baking dish. Bake at 350 degrees for 30 to 40 minutes or until a knife inserted near the center comes out clean. Garnish with orange zest.

You may substitute 1 drained 15-ounce can sliced carrots for the fresh carrots.

Serves six

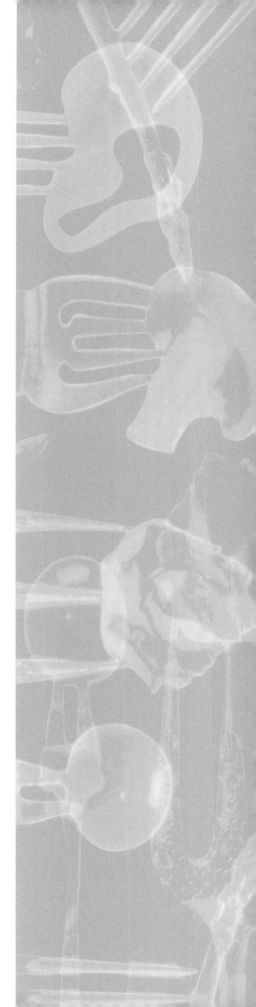

CRAZY CAULIFLOWER

1 CUP WATER
1 TABLESPOON LEMON
    JUICE
1 (2-POUND) HEAD
    CAULIFLOWER
3/4 CUP MAYONNAISE
1 TABLESPOON PREPARED
    MUSTARD
1 TEASPOON DRY
    MUSTARD
1/2 TO 1 TEASPOON CURRY
    POWDER
1 CUP (4 OUNCES)
    SHREDDED SHARP
    CHEDDAR CHEESE

Garnish

FRESH THYME SPRIGS

Bring the water and lemon juice to a boil in a 3-quart saucepan. Add the cauliflower stem side up. Bring to a boil and reduce the heat. Simmer, covered, for 15 minutes or until tender; drain. Place stem side down in a deep 3-quart baking dish.

Combine the mayonnaise, prepared mustard, dry mustard and curry powder in a small bowl and mix well. Spread over the cauliflower and sprinkle with the cheese. Bake at 350 degrees for 10 to 15 minutes or until the cheese melts. Garnish with thyme.

Serves six

CHICKASAW CORN PUDDING

4 EGGS
1/2 CUP LIGHT CREAM
1 1/2 TEASPOONS BAKING
    POWDER
1/4 CUP (1/2 STICK) BUTTER
    OR MARGARINE
2 TABLESPOONS SUGAR
2 TABLESPOONS FLOUR
3 CUPS FRESH OR FROZEN
    WHOLE KERNEL CORN,
    COOKED
2 TABLESPOONS BROWN
    SUGAR
1/4 TEASPOON CINNAMON
2 TABLESPOONS BUTTER
    OR MARGARINE, MELTED

Beat the eggs in a large mixing bowl. Add the cream and baking powder and mix well. Melt 1/4 cup butter in a 1 1/2-quart saucepan. Stir in the sugar and flour until smooth. Whisk into the egg mixture gradually. Stir in the corn.

Spoon into a greased shallow 1 1/2-quart baking dish. Bake at 350 degrees for 30 to 40 minutes or until set. Combine the brown sugar and cinnamon in a small bowl and mix well. Remove the pudding from the oven. Drizzle with 2 tablespoons melted butter. Sprinkle with the brown sugar mixture. Bake for 3 to 5 minutes longer or until the brown sugar melts.

Serves eight

$\mathcal{C}$ORN $\mathcal{F}$RITTERS

1 CUP FLOUR

1 TABLESPOON (SCANT)
SUGAR

1 TEASPOON SALT

1/2 TEASPOON PEPPER

2 EGGS

2 TABLESPOONS HEAVY
CREAM

2 TABLESPOONS CRUSHED
CORN FLAKES

1 (12-OUNCE) CAN CORN,
DRAINED

Sift the flour, sugar, salt and pepper together. Beat the eggs in a mixing bowl. Add the cream, corn flakes and sifted ingredients and mix well. Stir in the corn. Drop by small spoonfuls onto a lightly greased heated griddle and cook until light brown on both sides. Serve the fritters in stacks of 3, topped with butter.

You may substitute fresh corn kernels for the canned corn.

Serves four to six

$\mathcal{S}$AUTÉED $\mathcal{C}$UCUMBERS

4 LARGE CUCUMBERS

1 TABLESPOON SALT

1 CUP HEAVY CREAM

1 TO 2 TABLESPOONS
CHOPPED FRESH DILL,
OR 1/2 TO 1 TEASPOON
DRIED DILLWEED

FRESHLY GROUND PEPPER
TO TASTE

2 TABLESPOONS BUTTER
OR MARGARINE

Peel the cucumbers and cut into halves lengthwise. Remove the seeds with a spoon and cut into thin slices. Place in a colander and toss with the salt; drain for 20 minutes. Rinse under cold water and pat dry with paper towels.

Combine the cream, dill and pepper in a 1-quart saucepan and bring to a boil. Boil for 20 minutes or until reduce by 1/2.

Melt the butter in a 10-inch skillet over medium-high heat. Add the cucumbers and sauté for 3 to 5 minutes or until tender-crisp. Stir in the cream mixture and cook for 2 to 3 minutes longer or until heated through.

Serves four to six

Freezer Compost

Do you just hate to throw away those little bits of leftover vegetables? Great cooks seldom waste food of any kind and can create delectable dishes from rather ordinary ingredients—even leftovers. Try starting a freezer compost. Keep a plastic bag or container in the freezer and add leftover corn, green beans, onions, tomatoes, and even meats, until you have enough for vegetable soup.

Elvis Presley had the same cook, Mary, for more than 18 years. She knew his likes and dislikes and provided his favorite foods on demand, although his hours were erratic and his meal times unpredictable. She knew that Elvis' food tastes were simple and reflected his southern background. Perhaps it was the hectic urban pace of concerts, press appearances, and recording dates that drew him to the comfort of basic and familiar foods when he was at home at Graceland. Mary recalls watching television with Elvis on Sunday mornings as he enjoyed her sausage, scrambled eggs, homemade biscuits, and coffee, and she tells of two- or three-week food attachments to such southern goodies as corn bread and well-seasoned greens. Elvis once returned from a concert tour requesting a new food favorite—a peanut butter and banana sandwich grilled in butter. This stayed at the top of his chart along with his first dessert choice, banana pudding.

Extraordinary Eggplant Parmesan

Marinara Sauce

1 CUP CHOPPED ONION
2 GARLIC CLOVES, MINCED
1 TABLESPOON OLIVE OIL
2 (15-OUNCE) CANS
   TOMATO SAUCE
1/4 TEASPOON CRUSHED
   DRIED OREGANO
1/2 TEASPOON SALT
1/2 TEASPOON PEPPER

Eggplant

1 TABLESPOON OLIVE OIL
2 TABLESPOONS
   VEGETABLE OIL
2 GARLIC CLOVES, MINCED
2 CUPS FINE DRY BREAD
   CRUMBS
1 TABLESPOON DRIED
   PARSLEY FLAKES
1/4 TEASPOON CRUSHED
   DRIED OREGANO
1 TEASPOON SALT
1/2 TEASPOON PEPPER
1/2 CUP (2 OUNCES) GRATED
   PARMESAN CHEESE
VEGETABLE OIL FOR FRYING
1 LARGE EGGPLANT, PEELED,
   SLICED INTO 3/4×3-INCH
   STRIPS
2 EGGS, BEATEN
1 POUND MOZZARELLA
   CHEESE, SLICED
1 CUP (4 OUNCES)
   PARMESAN CHEESE

For the sauce, sauté the onion and garlic in the olive oil in a 3-quart saucepan until tender. Add the tomato sauce, oregano, salt and pepper. Bring to a boil and reduce the heat. Simmer for 30 minutes.

For the eggplant, heat the olive oil and 2 tablespoons vegetable oil in an 8-inch skillet over medium heat; remove from the heat.

Stir in the garlic, bread crumbs, parsley flakes, oregano, salt and pepper. Combine with 1/2 cup Parmesan cheese in a bowl and mix well.

Heat 2 inches vegetable oil in a wok or 12-inch skillet. Dip the eggplant into the eggs and coat with the bread crumb mixture.

Fry the coated eggplant in the heated oil for 30 seconds on each side or until golden brown; drain on paper towels.

Layer the eggplant, mozzarella cheese, 1 cup Parmesan cheese and marinara sauce 1/2 at a time in a 9×13-inch baking dish. Bake at 350 degrees for 30 minutes.

You may add 1 pound of cooked Italian sausage to the sauce or substitute one 32-ounce jar spaghetti sauce for the marinara sauce.

Serves eight to ten

EGGPLANT STICKS

3 EGGPLANT
1 CUP BREADING MIX
1 TEASPOON SALT
1 TEASPOON PEPPER
3 EGGS
1/4 CUP MILK
VEGETABLE OIL FOR
  DEEP-FRYING

Peel the eggplant and cut into 1/2×3-inch sticks. Combine with ice water to cover in a bowl and let stand for 30 minutes; drain and pat dry.

Combine the breading mix, salt and pepper in a bowl. Beat the eggs with the milk in a bowl. Dip the eggplant into the egg mixture and coat with the breading mixture. Arrange on a plastic wrap-lined tray and refrigerate for 30 minutes to set the breading. Deep-fry in the oil until golden brown.

This may also be served with salsa as an appetizer.

Serves eight to ten

CREAMED MUSHROOMS

2 POUNDS FRESH
  MUSHROOMS
1/4 CUP (1/2 STICK) BUTTER
1/4 CUP DRY SHERRY
2 CUPS SOUR CREAM
1 CUP (4 OUNCES) GRATED
  PARMESAN CHEESE
1 TEASPOON SALT
1/2 TEASPOON FRESHLY
  GROUND PEPPER
1 TEASPOON MSG
  (OPTIONAL)

Remove and chop the mushroom stems. Sauté the stems and caps in the butter in a skillet for 2 minutes. Add the sherry and cook for 1 minute. Stir in the sour cream, cheese, salt, pepper and MSG. Cook over low heat until thickened. Serve on buttered toast with rare roast beef.

You may also thicken this slightly with flour and serve from a chafing dish as an appetizer.

Serves eight

Stuffed Mushrooms

1½ POUNDS UNIFORM-SIZE
  MUSHROOMS
LEMON JUICE
½ CUP DRY BREAD
  CRUMBS
⅓ CUP (ABOUT
  1½ OUNCES) GRATED
  PARMESAN CHEESE
¼ CUP GRATED ONION
2 GARLIC CLOVES, MINCED
2 TABLESPOONS MINCED
  FRESH PARSLEY
½ TEASPOON DRIED
  OREGANO
2 TEASPOONS SALT
¼ TEASPOON FRESHLY
  GROUND PEPPER
⅔ CUP OLIVE OIL

Rinse the mushrooms in a mixture of water and lemon juice; pat dry. Remove and chop the stems, reserving the caps. Combine the chopped stems with the bread crumbs, cheese, onion, garlic, parsley, oregano, salt and pepper in a bowl; mix well. Spoon into the mushroom caps.

Spread a small amount of the olive oil in a shallow baking dish. Arrange the stuffed mushrooms in the dish and drizzle evenly with the remaining olive oil. Bake at 350 degrees for 25 minutes.

These may also be served as an appetizer.

Serves eight to ten

Vidalia Onion Casserole

6 LARGE VIDALIA OR
  OTHER MILD SWEET
  ONIONS
⅓ CUP BUTTER OR
  MARGARINE
½ TEASPOON SUGAR
½ TEASPOON SALT
½ TEASPOON PEPPER
½ CUP VERMOUTH
1 TEASPOON
  WORCESTERSHIRE SAUCE
½ CUP (2 OUNCES)
  SHREDDED GRUYÈRE,
  JARLSBERG OR SWISS
  CHEESE
¼ CUP FINE DRY BREAD
  CRUMBS
2 TABLESPOONS BUTTER
  OR MARGARINE, MELTED
1 TEASPOON PAPRIKA

Cut the onions into ⅜-inch-thick slices. Cook the onion slices in ⅓ cup butter in a 12-inch skillet until tender. Sprinkle with the sugar, salt and pepper. Stir in the vermouth and Worcestershire sauce and cook for 3 minutes longer. Spoon into a 9×13-inch baking dish and sprinkle with the cheese.

Combine the bread crumbs, 2 tablespoons melted butter and paprika in a small bowl and mix well. Sprinkle over the cheese. Bake at 350 degrees for 20 minutes.

Serves six

Boursin Potato Gratin

2/3 CUP HOMEMADE
    BOURSIN CHEESE
    (BELOW), OR 1 (5-OUNCE)
    PACKAGE PREPARED
    BOURSIN CHEESE WITH
    CRACKED BLACK PEPPER
2 CUPS HEAVY CREAM
2 TABLESPOONS MINCED
    SHALLOTS
1 GARLIC CLOVE, MINCED
2 1/2 POUNDS NEW
    POTATOES
SALT AND FRESHLY
    GROUND PEPPER
    TO TASTE
2 TABLESPOONS CHOPPED
    CHIVES

Garnish

2 TABLESPOONS CHOPPED
    PARSLEY

Combine the Homemade Boursin Cheese, cream, shallots and garlic in a heavy 1 1/2-quart saucepan. Cook over medium heat until the cheese melts, stirring to mix well.

Scrub the unpeeled potatoes. Cut the potatoes into 1/4-inch-thick slices. Arrange half the potato slices in a buttered 9×13-inch baking dish, slightly overlapping the slices. Sprinkle with salt and pepper. Spread half the cheese sauce over the potatoes and sprinkle with the chives. Add the remaining potato slices, sprinkle with salt and pepper and top with the remaining cheese sauce.

Bake at 400 degrees for 1 hour or until the potatoes are tender and the top is golden brown. Garnish with parsley.

Serves eight to ten

Homemade Boursin Cheese

3 GARLIC CLOVES, MINCED
1/2 TEASPOON SALT
8 OUNCES CREAM CHEESE,
    SOFTENED
1/4 CUP (1/2 STICK) BUTTER,
    SOFTENED
2 TABLESPOONS MINCED
    PARSLEY
1 TO 2 TABLESPOONS
    COARSELY GROUND
    PEPPER

Combine the garlic and salt in a small bowl and crush to form a paste. Combine the garlic mixture with the cream cheese, butter, parsley and pepper in a food processor container and process until smooth. Store, covered, in the refrigerator for up to 2 weeks.

To serve as an appetizer, spoon into a 2-cup baking dish or ramekin and bake at 350 degrees for 10 minutes or until warm. Serve with crackers or as a filling for bite-size hors d'oeuvre puffs.

Makes one and one-third cups

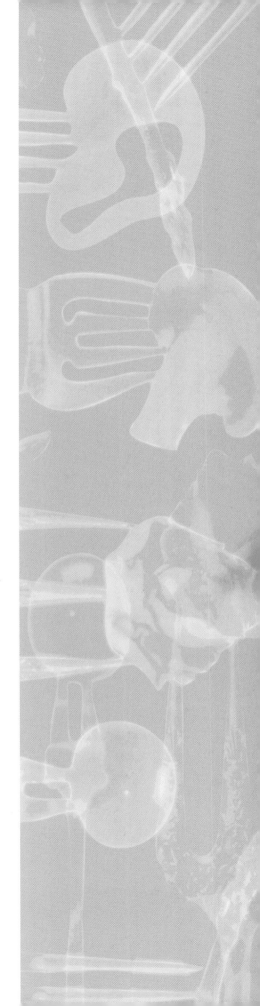

Cream of Any Vegetable Soup

Don't despair if you need soup in a hurry and there is no familiar red and white can in the pantry. Soup is always at your fingertips with this easy formula. It uses no special ingredients and can even provide a second life for last night's leftover vegetables!

Cook 2 to 3 cups of any chopped vegetable and 1 cup chopped onion in 3 tablespoons butter or margarine in a saucepan until tender-crisp. Add 4 cups chicken broth and 3 tablespoons quick-cooking rice and cook until the vegetables are tender. Purée the mixture in a blender or food processor and combine with 1 cup light cream, salt, white pepper and other seasonings of choice. Suggested seasonings or toppings include: thyme or shredded cheese for broccoli; nutmeg, Pernod or dry vermouth for spinach; hot pepper sauce, curry powder or dillweed for carrot; dillweed, leeks, chives, crumbled bacon or cheese for potato; and savory, basil or marjoram for green beans.

PATRICIAN POTATOES

6 MEDIUM POTATOES
MILK
3 CUPS CREAM-STYLE
   COTTAGE CHEESE
3/4 CUP SOUR CREAM
1 1/2 TABLESPOONS MINCED
   ONION
2 1/2 TEASPOONS SALT
1/3 TEASPOON WHITE
   PEPPER
BUTTER
CHOPPED TOASTED
   ALMONDS

Cook the potatoes in water to cover in a saucepan until tender; drain. Peel and coarsely chop the potatoes. Mash in a mixing bowl, adding a small amount of milk. Add the cottage cheese, sour cream, onion, salt and white pepper and mix until smooth.

Spoon into a greased 2-quart baking dish. Dot with butter and sprinkle with almonds. Bake at 350 degrees for 30 minutes.

Serves eight

POMMES HASSELBACK

8 MEDIUM RUSSET
   POTATOES
   (ABOUT 3 POUNDS)
6 TABLESPOONS (3/4 STICK)
   BUTTER OR MARGARINE,
   MELTED
1 TEASPOON CRUSHED
   DRIED BASIL
1/4 TEASPOON SALT
1/4 TEASPOON PEPPER
GRATED PARMESAN CHEESE

Garnish

CHOPPED PARSLEY

Peel the potatoes and cut a thin slice from the long side of each potato. Place flat side down on a work surface and slice crosswise at 1/4-inch intervals, cutting to within 1/4 inch of the bottom. Arrange the potatoes flat side down in a greased 9×13-inch baking dish.

Combine the butter, basil, salt and pepper in a bowl and mix well. Brush generously over the potatoes. Bake at 350 degrees for 45 minutes or until barely tender, brushing occasionally with the butter mixture.

Increase the oven temperature to 450 degrees. Sprinkle the potatoes generously with the cheese, filling the spaces between slices. Bake for 15 minutes longer or until golden brown. Remove to a serving platter with a slotted spoon and garnish with parsley.

Serves eight

Roquefort Tomatoes

3 TABLESPOONS
   CRUMBLED ROQUEFORT
   CHEESE
3 TABLESPOONS CREAM
   CHEESE, SOFTENED
1 TEASPOON
   WORCESTERSHIRE
   SAUCE
1/2 TEASPOON ONION
   POWDER
3 TOMATOES, CUT
   CROSSWISE INTO HALVES
1/3 CUP DRY BREAD CRUMBS
BUTTER
PAPRIKA TO TASTE

Garnish

6 PARSLEY SPRIGS

Combine the Roquefort cheese, cream cheese, Worcestershire sauce and onion powder in a small bowl and mix well.

Spread the cheese mixture on the cut sides of the tomatoes; sprinkle with the bread crumbs. Arrange in a broiler pan; dot with butter and sprinkle with paprika.

Broil the tomatoes for 10 minutes. Garnish with parsley.

Serves six

Spinach With Cheese

1 (10-OUNCE) PACKAGE
   FROZEN CHOPPED
   SPINACH
2 TABLESPOONS BUTTER
1 TABLESPOON FLOUR
1 TABLESPOON (OR MORE)
   GRATED ONION
1/2 CUP (2 OUNCES)
   SHREDDED SHARP
   CHEDDAR CHEESE
SALT AND PEPPER TO TASTE
3 EGGS, BEATEN

Cook the spinach using the package directions; drain well. Melt the butter in a skillet and stir in the flour until smooth. Add the onion and cook until light brown. Add the spinach, cheese, salt and pepper and mix well. Stir in the eggs. Cook for 5 minutes, stirring constantly.

You may pack the spinach into a ring mold and invert onto a serving platter; fill with creamed beets or mushrooms.

Serves four

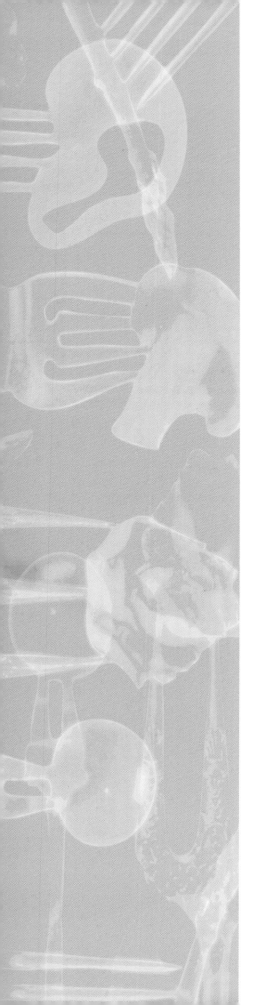

Spinach Symphony

2 (10-OUNCE) PACKAGES
   FROZEN CHOPPED
   SPINACH
3 CUPS SLICED FRESH
   MUSHROOMS
2 TABLESPOONS BUTTER
   OR MARGARINE
1 (14-OUNCE) CAN
   ARTICHOKE HEARTS,
   DRAINED, CHOPPED
1/2 CUP MAYONNAISE
1/2 CUP SOUR CREAM
5 TEASPOONS FRESH
   LEMON JUICE
1/3 CUP (ABOUT
   1 1/2 OUNCES) GRATED
   PARMESAN CHEESE

Cook the spinach using the package directions; drain and press to remove excess moisture. Sauté the mushrooms in the butter in a 10-inch skillet until tender. Layer the artichoke hearts, mushrooms and spinach in a 1 1/2-quart baking dish.

Combine the mayonnaise, sour cream and lemon juice in a bowl and mix well. Spread over the layers and sprinkle with the cheese. Bake at 350 degrees for 20 minutes or until bubbly and light brown.

Serves six

Squash Casserole

2 POUNDS SQUASH,
   CHOPPED
2 EGGS, BEATEN
6 TABLESPOONS (3/4 STICK)
   MARGARINE, MELTED
1/2 CUP (SCANT) MILK
1/2 MEDIUM ONION,
   MINCED OR GRATED
2 TABLESPOONS BROWN
   SUGAR
1 TEASPOON SALT
2 1/2 CUPS SOFT BREAD
   CRUMBS OR ZWIEBACK
   CRUMBS
1 CUP (4 OUNCES)
   SHREDDED CHEDDAR
   CHEESE
BUTTER

Cook the squash in water in a saucepan until tender; drain. Mash in a bowl. Add the eggs, margarine, milk, onion, brown sugar and salt and mix well.

Reserve 1/3 of the bread crumbs. Layer the remaining bread crumbs, squash mixture and cheese 1/2 at a time in a buttered baking dish. Top with the reserved bread crumbs and dot with butter. Bake at 350 degrees for 45 minutes.

Serves eight

Stuffed Squash

8 SMALL YELLOW SQUASH
1 (10-OUNCE) PACKAGE
   FROZEN GREEN PEAS
1/4 CUP (1/2 STICK) BUTTER,
   MELTED
1/4 CUP LIGHT CREAM,
   HEATED
SALT AND PEPPER
   TO TASTE
BREAD CRUMBS
BUTTER
GRATED PARMESAN
   CHEESE

Cut the squash into halves lengthwise. Cook in enough water to cover in a saucepan for 7 to 10 minutes or until tender-crisp; drain. Scoop out the seeds with a spoon, reserving the shells.

Cook the peas using the package directions; drain. Combine with 1/4 cup butter, light cream, salt and pepper in a bowl and mix gently. Spoon into the reserved squash shells. Sprinkle with bread crumbs, dot with additional butter and top with Parmesan cheese.

Arrange in a baking dish. Bake at 350 degrees for 15 minutes or until heated through. Broil just until golden brown.

The squash can be prepared in advance and baked at serving time. Broccoli, spinach, chopped tomatoes or green beans can be substituted for the peas; the squash can also be filled with creamed mushrooms, spinach or peas and carrots.

Serves eight

Summer Squash With Sour Cream

4 POUNDS SUMMER
   SQUASH, PEELED,
   JULIENNED
2 TABLESPOONS SALT
1/4 CUP (1/2 STICK) BUTTER
2 TABLESPOONS FLOUR
1 TEASPOON PAPRIKA
2 CUPS SOUR CREAM
2 MEDIUM ONIONS,
   CHOPPED

Sprinkle the squash with the salt in a colander and let stand for 1 hour; drain. Sauté in the butter in a skillet for 15 minutes or until tender-crisp.

Blend the flour and paprika with enough of the sour cream to make a paste in a small bowl. Add the remaining sour cream. Add to the squash with the onions. Simmer for 5 minutes, stirring gently. Serve immediately.

Serves six

Sweet Potato Casserole

6 MEDIUM SWEET POTATOES
1/4 CUP (1/2 STICK) BUTTER,
   MELTED
3 EGG YOLKS
1/2 CUP SUGAR
1/2 CUP MOLASSES
GRATED ZEST OF 1 ORANGE
1 TEASPOON GINGER
1 TEASPOON NUTMEG
1/4 TEASPOON SALT
3 EGG WHITES

Peel and grate the sweet potatoes. Combine the sweet potatoes, butter, egg yolks, sugar, molasses, orange zest, ginger, nutmeg and salt in a bowl and mix well. Beat the egg whites in a mixing bowl until stiff peaks form. Fold into the sweet potato mixture.

Spoon into a greased baking dish. Bake at 350 degrees for 20 to 30 minutes or until set.

Serves eight

Sweet Potatoes In Orange Cups

8 MEDIUM ORANGES
4 LARGE SWEET POTATOES,
   PEELED, CHOPPED
SALT TO TASTE
1 1/2 CUPS SUGAR
1/2 CUP (1 STICK) BUTTER
   OR MARGARINE
1 TEASPOON GROUND
   CINNAMON
GROUND NUTMEG
8 LARGE MARSHMALLOWS

Cut a slice from the tops of the oranges. Grate 1/4 teaspoon zest from the tops and reserve; discard the tops. Remove the orange sections with a grapefruit spoon or knife and reserve for another use. Cut the tops of the orange shells into a zigzag pattern with a sharp knife.

Cook the sweet potatoes in a small amount of salted boiling water in a 3-quart saucepan for 10 to 12 minutes or until tender; drain and cool. Combine with the sugar, butter, reserved orange zest, cinnamon, nutmeg and salt in a large mixing bowl; beat until smooth.

Spoon the sweet potato mixture into the orange cups. Arrange in a greased 7×12-inch baking dish. Bake at 350 degrees for 20 to 30 minutes or until heated through. Top each with a marshmallow and bake for 2 to 3 minutes longer or until the marshmallows are golden brown. Serve with wild duck, quail, chicken or turkey.

Serves eight

Tomatoes Stuffed With Spinach

12 TO 15 TOMATOES
SALT AND PEPPER
    TO TASTE
2 (10-OUNCE) PACKAGES
    FROZEN CHOPPED
    SPINACH
1 ENVELOPE ONION
    SOUP MIX
2 CUPS SOUR CREAM

Garnish

12 TO 15 CRISP-FRIED
    BACON CURLS

Place the tomatoes in boiling water in a saucepan for 5 seconds; remove to a bowl of cold water with a slotted spoon. Remove the peels. Cut a slice off the top of each tomato; scoop out some of the pulp and reserve for another use. Sprinkle the shells with salt and pepper and invert to drain.

Place the spinach in a large heavy saucepan; do not add water. Cook, covered, over very low heat for 10 to 15 minutes or until thawed, stirring occasionally to separate. Remove from the heat and add the soup mix, sour cream, salt and pepper; mix well. Spoon into the tomato shells.

Arrange in a baking dish and bake at 325 degrees for 25 minutes. Garnish with bacon curls.

You may spoon the spinach mixture into a 1 1/2-quart baking dish and bake at 300 degrees for 30 minutes if preferred.

Serves twelve to fifteen

Tomato Pie With Basil

1 FROZEN UNBAKED
    (9-INCH) DEEP-DISH
    PIE SHELL
3 OR 4 MEDIUM TOMATOES
SALT AND PEPPER
    TO TASTE
8 SLICES BACON, CRISP-
    FRIED, CRUMBLED
3 TABLESPOONS CHOPPED
    FRESH BASIL
3/4 CUP (3 OUNCES) GRATED
    PARMESAN CHEESE
3/4 CUP MAYONNAISE
1/3 CUP CRUSHED BUTTER
    CRACKERS

Thaw the frozen pie shell at room temperature for 10 minutes. Slice the tomatoes, drain and pat dry. Arrange a single layer of the tomato slices in the pie shell and season lightly with salt and pepper. Sprinkle with some of the bacon and basil. Repeat the layers until all layering ingredients are used.

Mix the cheese and mayonnaise in a small bowl. Spread over the layers and sprinkle with the cracker crumbs. Bake at 350 degrees for 30 minutes or until light brown.

You may omit the pie shell and bake in a greased pie pan. May substitute 1 tablespoon crushed dried basil for the fresh basil.

Serves eight

Beale Street

Beale Street is called the "Birthplace of the Blues." The night air swings with the sounds of great live music—blues, jazz, rock, and soul are all represented in the clubs that dot the famous street. On any given night you can spot a wanna-be playing for a crowd on the corner, or you can drop in to a club and catch a glimpse of a musical legend. Either way, Beale Street is a magical, musical kind of place.

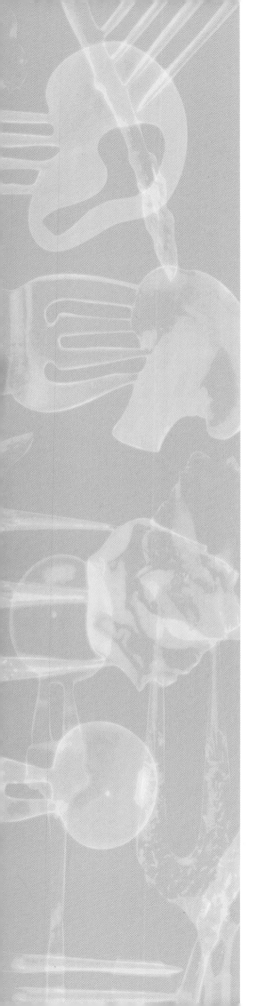

Zucchini Pie

4 GREEN ONIONS WITH
   TOPS, SLICED
BUTTER
2 MEDIUM ZUCCHINI
1 CUP (4 OUNCES)
   SHREDDED SWISS
   CHEESE
1 FROZEN UNBAKED
   (9-INCH) DEEP-DISH PIE
   SHELL, THAWED
1 CUP HEAVY CREAM
2 EGGS
SALT AND PEPPER TO TASTE
3 OR 4 SLICES BACON,
   CRISP-FRIED, CRUMBLED

Sauté the green onions in butter in a skillet until tender. Slice the unpeeled zucchini thinly. Layer the cheese and zucchini in the pie shell and sprinkle with the green onions.

Combine the cream, eggs, salt and pepper in a blender container and process for 4 or 5 seconds or until smooth. Pour over the layers and sprinkle with the bacon. Bake at 350 degrees for 45 minutes. Let stand for 10 to 15 minutes before serving.

Serves six to eight

Marinated Vegetables

Vegetable Marinade

9 TABLESPOONS
   VEGETABLE OIL
6 TABLESPOONS OLIVE OIL
3 GARLIC CLOVES
9 TABLESPOONS MIXED
   VINEGARS
3/4 TEASPOON DRY
   MUSTARD
SALT AND PEPPER TO TASTE

Vegetables

2 (16-OUNCE) CANS TINY
   WHOLE BEETS
2 (16-OUNCE) CANS GREEN
   BEANS
SLICED CARROTS
SLICED YELLOW SQUASH
SLICED ZUCCHINI
FLORETS OF 1 HEAD
   CAULIFLOWER
SALT TO TASTE
MINCED FRESH PARSLEY
PEPPER TO TASTE

For the marinade, combine the vegetable oil, olive oil and garlic in a bowl and let stand for several hours; remove and discard the garlic. Add the vinegars, dry mustard, salt and pepper and mix well.

For the vegetables, drain the beets and beans and place in separate containers. Cook the carrots, squash, zucchini and cauliflower separately in salted boiling water in saucepans for 4 to 5 minutes or until tender-crisp; drain and place in separate containers.

Add some of the marinade to the vegetables in each container. Marinate, covered, in the refrigerator for 8 hours or longer. Drain the vegetables and arrange on a serving platter. Sprinkle with parsley and pepper.

Serves a variable number

PUFFED ANGEL HAIR PASTA

4 OUNCES UNCOOKED
   ANGEL HAIR PASTA
SALT TO TASTE
3 QUARTS WATER
6 EGG YOLKS
1 CUP (4 OUNCES)
   SHREDDED GRUYÈRE,
   HAVARTI OR CHEDDAR
   CHEESE
1 CUP FINELY CHOPPED
   PROSCIUTTO OR
   CANADIAN BACON
3 TABLESPOONS CHOPPED
   CHIVES
3/4 TEASPOON WHITE PEPPER
1/8 TO 1/2 TEASPOON RED
   PEPPER
8 EGG WHITES

Cook the pasta in the salted water in a 6-quart saucepan for 2 to 4 minutes or until al dente; drain. Beat the egg yolks in a mixing bowl for 5 minutes or until thick and pale yellow. Add the pasta, cheese, prosciutto, chives, white pepper and red pepper and mix well.

Beat the egg whites in a mixing bowl until soft peaks form. Fold into the pasta mixture gradually. Spoon into a buttered 2-quart soufflé dish.

Smooth the top of the mixture and cut a circle about 2 inches deep and 2 inches from the edge of the dish with a sharp knife. Bake at 375 degrees for 15 to 20 minutes or until puffed and golden brown.

Serves six

FETTUCCINI CHARLES

1 CUP (2 STICKS) BUTTER
2 EGGS, BEATEN
1 CUP HEAVY CREAM
1 CUP SOUR CREAM
16 OUNCES UNCOOKED
   SPINACH FETTUCCINI OR
   EGG FETTUCCINI
SALT TO TASTE
4 QUARTS WATER
2 TABLESPOONS CHOPPED
   PARSLEY
2 GARLIC CLOVES, MINCED
1 TEASPOON CHOPPED
   FRESH OREGANO, OR 1/2
   TEASPOON CRUSHED
   DRIED OREGANO
PEPPER TO TASTE
1 CUP (4 OUNCES) FRESHLY
   GRATED PARMESAN
   CHEESE

Let the butter, eggs, cream and sour cream stand at room temperature for 1 hour. Cook the pasta in the salted water in a 6-quart saucepan for 8 to 10 minutes or until al dente; drain.

Melt half the butter in a 3-quart saucepan. Add the parsley, garlic, oregano and salt and pepper to taste. Add the pasta and mix to coat well.

Add the remaining butter. Cook over low heat until the butter melts, stirring constantly. Add the eggs, cream, sour cream and cheese. Cook until heated through, tossing to mix well.

Use only butter and freshly grated Parmesan cheese for the best results when preparing this dish.

Serves eight to ten

Bread Stuffings

For *Basic Bread Stuffing*, combine 4 cups soft bread crumbs or cubes with 1/4 to 1/2 cup melted butter or margarine, 1 teaspoon salt and 1 teaspoon pepper. Stuff lightly into the meat or poultry, allowing room for expansion.

For *Apple Stuffing*, use 1/2 cup butter and add 1 cup chopped tart apple.

For *Celery Stuffing*, add 1 cup minced celery and 2 tablespoons minced onion.

For *Chili Stuffing*, use 1/4 cup butter and add 1/2 cup chili sauce or tomato ketchup and 1 tablespoon minced onion.

For *Mushroom Stuffing*, add 3/4 cup chopped mushrooms to Onion Stuffing or Celery Stuffing.

For *Onion Stuffing*, add 2 tablespoons minced onion.

For *Sage Stuffing*, add 2 teaspoons sage, 2 tablespoons chopped onion and 1 tablespoon chopped parsley.

For *Sausage Stuffing*, omit the butter and add 1 1/2 cups browned sausage.

PASTA PRIMAVERA

1 POUND UNCOOKED
　FETTUCCINI OR LINGUINI
1 MEDIUM ONION,
　CHOPPED
1 LARGE GARLIC CLOVE,
　MINCED
1/2 CUP (1 STICK)
　UNSALTED BUTTER
1 POUND FRESH THIN
　ASPARAGUS, TRIMMED,
　SLICED DIAGONALLY
　INTO 1/2-INCH PIECES
8 OUNCES MUSHROOMS,
　THINLY SLICED
1 MEDIUM ZUCCHINI,
　SLICED INTO 1/4-INCH
　ROUNDS
1 SMALL CARROT,
　CUT INTO HALVES
　LENGTHWISE, CUT
　DIAGONALLY INTO
　1/8-INCH SLICES
6 OUNCES CAULIFLOWER
　FLORETS
1 CUP HEAVY CREAM
1/2 CUP CHICKEN STOCK
2 TABLESPOONS CHOPPED
　FRESH BASIL, OR
　2 TEASPOONS CRUSHED
　DRIED BASIL
1 CUP THAWED FROZEN OR
　FRESH TINY GREEN PEAS
2 OUNCES PROSCIUTTO OR
　COOKED HAM, CHOPPED
5 GREEN ONIONS, CHOPPED
SALT AND FRESHLY
　GROUND PEPPER
　TO TASTE
1 CUP (4 OUNCES) GRATED
　PARMESAN CHEESE

Cook the pasta al dente using the package directions; drain and keep warm. Sauté the onion and garlic in the heated butter in a large deep skillet over medium-high heat for 2 minutes or until tender.

Add the asparagus, mushrooms, zucchini, carrot and cauliflower to the skillet. Sauté for 2 minutes or until tender-crisp. Remove several asparagus tips, mushrooms and zucchini slices and reserve for garnish.

Increase the heat to high and add the cream, chicken stock and basil. Bring to a boil and cook for 3 minutes or until slightly reduced.

Stir the peas, prosciutto and green onions into the skillet. Cook for 1 minute longer. Season with salt and pepper.

Add the pasta to the vegetable mixture with the cheese and cook until heated through, tossing lightly to mix well. Spoon onto a serving platter and garnish with the reserved vegetables.

Add 1 pound of cooked peeled shrimp with the peas for a main dish.

Serves six to eight

Linguini With Tomatoes And Basil

8 VERY RIPE LARGE
    TOMATOES, PEELED,
    SEEDED, CHOPPED
1 CUP EXTRA-VIRGIN
    OLIVE OIL
1 CUP JULIENNED FRESH
    BASIL LEAVES
1 CUP (4 OUNCES) GRATED
    PARMESAN CHEESE
3/4 CUP SLICED BLACK
    OLIVES
1/2 CUP SLICED GREEN
    OLIVES
3 TO 6 GARLIC CLOVES,
    MINCED
1 TABLESPOON SALT
1 TEASPOON PEPPER
1½ POUNDS UNCOOKED
    LINGUINI
SALT TO TASTE
6 QUARTS WATER

Combine the tomatoes, olive oil, basil, cheese, black olives, green olives, garlic, salt and pepper in a large bowl and mix well. Let stand, covered, at room temperature for 2 hours.

Cook the linguini in the salted water in an 8-quart saucepan for 8 to 10 minutes or until al dente; drain and return to the saucepan. Add the tomato mixture and toss to mix well. Serve with additional Parmesan cheese.

You may substitute spaghetti for the linguini and cook for 10 to 12 minutes. Add cooked chicken or shrimp for a main dish.

Serves twelve to fifteen

Green Garlic Spaghetti

6 TABLESPOONS (3/4 STICK)
    BUTTER, MELTED
3 TABLESPOONS OLIVE OIL
6 TABLESPOONS MINCED
    FRESH PARSLEY
6 TABLESPOONS MINCED
    GREEN GARLIC
3 TABLESPOONS MINCED
    FRESH BASIL
1/4 TEASPOON SALT
1/2 TEASPOON BLACK PEPPER
CAYENNE PEPPER TO TASTE
12 OUNCES UNCOOKED
    SPAGHETTI
1½ CUPS (6 OUNCES)
    GRATED PARMESAN
    CHEESE

Combine the butter, olive oil, parsley, green garlic, basil, salt, black pepper and cayenne pepper in a bowl and mix well.

Cook the spaghetti al dente in water in a saucepan; drain. Add to the butter mixture with the cheese and toss to mix well.

You may substitute 5 garlic cloves, minced, for the green garlic.

Serves six

CREAMY VEGETABLE TORTELLINI

9 OUNCES UNCOOKED
    FRESH TORTELLINI
SALT TO TASTE
1 MEDIUM CARROT
1/2 CUP FRESH OR FROZEN
    SNOW PEAS
1/2 CUP WATER
3 TABLESPOONS BUTTER
    OR MARGARINE
1 GARLIC CLOVE, MINCED
2 CUPS SLICED FRESH
    MUSHROOMS
1 MEDIUM ZUCCHINI,
    SLICED 1/4 INCH THICK
1 CUP (4 OUNCES) GRATED
    PARMESAN CHEESE
3 TABLESPOONS BUTTER
    OR MARGARINE
1 CUP HEAVY CREAM
1 (14-OUNCE) CAN
    ARTICHOKE HEARTS,
    DRAINED, QUARTERED
2 TABLESPOONS CHOPPED
    PIMENTOS

Cook the pasta in salted water in a saucepan using the package directions; drain. Cut the carrot diagonally into 1/4-inch-thick slices. Trim the snow peas and cut into halves diagonally. Cook the carrot, covered, in 1/2 cup water in a 1-quart saucepan for 4 minutes. Add the snow peas and cook for 2 to 3 minutes longer; drain.

Melt 3 tablespoons butter in a 10-inch skillet over medium-high heat. Add the garlic and sauté for 30 seconds. Add the mushrooms and sauté for 3 minutes or until tender; remove with a slotted spoon. Add the zucchini to the skillet and sauté for 1 to 2 minutes or until tender-crisp. Remove with a slotted spoon.

Combine the pasta with the cheese and 3 tablespoons butter in a heavy 4-quart saucepan. Cook over low heat until the cheese melts, tossing to mix well. Add the cream, artichoke hearts, pimentos, carrot and snow peas mixture, mushrooms and zucchini and mix gently. Cook until heated through.

Serves four

HERBED RICE

1 CUP UNCOOKED RICE
2 BEEF BOUILLON CUBES
2 CUPS COLD WATER
1 TABLESPOON BUTTER
1 TEASPOON CHOPPED
    CHIVES
1/2 TEASPOON ROSEMARY
1/2 TEASPOON MARJORAM
1/2 TEASPOON THYME
1/2 TEASPOON SALT

Combine the rice, bouillon cubes, water, butter, chives, rosemary, marjoram, thyme and salt in a heavy saucepan.

Bring to a boil and reduce the heat; stir with a fork. Simmer, covered, for 14 minutes or until the rice is tender and the liquid is absorbed.

Serves six

Spanish Rice

1 CUP UNCOOKED RICE
2 TO 3 TABLESPOONS
    OLIVE OIL
1 SMALL ONION, CHOPPED
2 RIBS CELERY, CHOPPED
2 TABLESPOONS CHOPPED
    GREEN BELL PEPPER
1 SMALL GARLIC CLOVE,
    CHOPPED
1 (6-OUNCE) CAN TOMATO
    SAUCE
1 TEASPOON CHILI POWDER
1 TEASPOON SALT
GROUND RED PEPPER TO
    TASTE
2 CUPS BOILING WATER

Sauté the rice in the heated olive oil in a heavy skillet until golden brown. Add the onion, celery, bell pepper and garlic. Sauté until tender. Stir in the tomato sauce, chili powder, salt and red pepper. Cook until bubbly, stirring constantly. Add the boiling water; mix well.

Spoon into a preheated greased baking dish. Bake, covered, at 350 degrees for 1 hour or until the rice is tender and fluffy; do not stir.

You may add 1 to 2 cups cooked ground beef, leftover roast beef, cooked shrimp, cooked bacon or sausage, or cooked chicken or turkey just before the addition of the boiling water to make this a one-dish meal.

Serves four to six

Green Rice

1 (10-OUNCE) PACKAGE
    FROZEN CHOPPED
    SPINACH
4 CUPS COOKED RICE
1¹/₃ CUPS CHICKEN BROTH
4 EGGS, BEATEN
²/₃ CUP (ABOUT 3 OUNCES)
    SHREDDED SHARP
    CHEDDAR CHEESE
¹/₂ CUP MINCED FRESH
    PARSLEY
2 TEASPOONS GRATED
    ONION
¹/₂ CUP (1 STICK) BUTTER,
    MELTED
1¹/₂ TEASPOONS
    WORCESTERSHIRE SAUCE
2 TEASPOONS SALT

Thaw the spinach. Combine with the rice, chicken broth, eggs, cheese, parsley, onion, butter, Worcestershire sauce and salt in a bowl and mix well. Spoon into a buttered baking dish.

Bake at 325 degrees for 1 hour.

You may substitute 2¹/₂ chicken bouillon cubes dissolved in 1¹/₄ cups hot water for the chicken broth.

Serves ten

Decorate Olé

A great centerpiece can be made by using a sombrero as a planter. Place newspaper under the sombrero on the table and line the brim with plastic wrap. Fill with soil and fill with as many colorful bedding plants as possible. Then slide the newspaper out.

Make lanterns from aluminum or tin cans. Fill the cans with water and freeze until firm. Punch holes in a design with an ice pick. Place in the sink until the ice melts and dry. For a rustic look, place outside to rust if time permits, or spray-paint with bright colors. Place a candle in each lantern.

SHINING FINISH desserts

Bread Pudding

1/4 CUP (1/2 STICK) BUTTER
  OR MARGARINE
6 CUPS TORN FRENCH
  BREAD, ABOUT
  8 OUNCES
4 CUPS MILK
4 EGGS, BEATEN
2 CUPS SUGAR
2 TABLESPOONS VANILLA
  EXTRACT

Garnish

WHIPPED CREAM

Melt the butter in a 7×12-inch baking dish in a 350-degree oven. Sprinkle the bread in the dish and pour the milk over the bread. Combine the eggs, sugar and vanilla in a medium mixing bowl and mix until smooth. Pour over the bread mixture.

Bake at 350 degrees for 40 to 45 minutes or until a knife inserted near the center comes out clean. Serve warm with Winter Sauce or Summer Sauce. Garnish with whipped cream.

Serves eight

Winter Sauce

3/4 CUP SUGAR
1/2 CUP (1 STICK) BUTTER
  OR MARGARINE
1/2 CUP BOURBON

Combine the sugar, butter and bourbon in a 1-quart saucepan. Cook over medium heat until the butter melts and the sugar dissolves, stirring constantly. Serve warm.

Makes one and one-half cups

Summer Sauce

3 CUPS SLICED PEELED
  PEACHES
2 TABLESPOONS SUGAR
1 TEASPOON LEMON JUICE

Combine the peaches, sugar and lemon juice in a medium bowl and mix gently. Let stand for 2 hours before serving.

Makes two and one-half cups

SHINING FINISH

desserts

BANANA PUDDING

2 EGG YOLKS
1/2 CUP SUGAR
1 TABLESPOON FLOUR
2 CUPS MILK
SALT TO TASTE
1 TO 2 TEASPOONS
    VANILLA EXTRACT
VANILLA WAFERS
    (OPTIONAL)
3 OR 4 BANANAS, SLICED
2 EGG WHITES
3 TABLESPOONS SUGAR

Beat the egg yolks with 1/2 cup sugar in a saucepan until thick and pale yellow. Add the flour, milk and salt and mix well. Cook over low to medium heat until thickened, stirring constantly. Stir in the vanilla. Alternate layers of vanilla wafers, pudding mixture and bananas in a baking dish until all the ingredients are used.

Beat the egg whites with 3 tablespoons sugar in a mixing bowl until stiff peaks form. Spread over the pudding. Bake at 350 degrees just until the meringue is golden brown.

Serves six to eight

CHOCOLATE ALMOND TERRINE WITH RASPBERRY PURÉE

Terrine

3 EGG YOLKS, BEATEN
1/2 CUP HEAVY CREAM
16 (1-OUNCE) SQUARES
    SEMISWEET CHOCOLATE
1/2 CUP CORN SYRUP
1/2 CUP (1 STICK) BUTTER
1 1/2 CUPS HEAVY CREAM
1/4 CUP CONFECTIONERS'
    SUGAR
1 TEASPOON VANILLA
    EXTRACT
1/4 TEASPOON ALMOND
    EXTRACT

Raspberry Purée

1 (10-OUNCE) PACKAGE
    FROZEN RED
    RASPBERRIES, THAWED
1/4 CUP CORN SYRUP
1 TO 2 TABLESPOONS
    RASPBERRY LIQUEUR

Garnish

FRESH RED RASPBERRIES
MINT LEAVES

For the terrine, combine the egg yolks with 1/2 cup cream in a small bowl and mix well. Combine the chocolate, corn syrup and butter in a 3-quart saucepan. Cook over medium heat until the chocolate and butter melt, stirring to blend well. Whisk in the egg yolk mixture. Cook for 3 minutes, stirring constantly. Cool to room temperature.

Combine 1 1/2 cups cream, confectioners' sugar and flavorings in a small mixing bowl and beat until soft peaks form. Fold into the chocolate mixture. Pour into a 4×8-inch loaf pan lined with plastic wrap. Chill, covered, for 8 hours or longer.

For the purée, process the raspberries in a blender or food processor until smooth. Press through a sieve to remove the seeds. Combine the purée with the corn syrup and liqueur in a bowl and mix well. Spoon onto serving plates.

To serve, invert the terrine onto a plate and remove the plastic wrap. Cut into 5/8-inch slices. Place 1 slice on each plate. Garnish with raspberries and mint.

Serves twelve

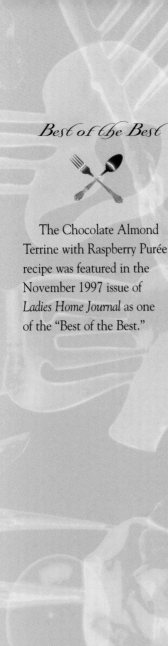

COFFEE MOUSSE IN CHOCOLATE CUPS

Chocolate Cups

3 (1-OUNCE) SQUARES
   SEMISWEET CHOCOLATE

1¹/₂ TEASPOONS
   SHORTENING

Mousse

1 TABLESPOON
   UNFLAVORED GELATIN

¹/₂ CUP MILK

1¹/₂ CUPS STRONG COFFEE

²/₃ CUP SUGAR

3 EGG YOLKS

¹/₄ TEASPOON SALT

3 EGG WHITES, STIFFLY
   BEATEN

¹/₂ TEASPOON VANILLA
   EXTRACT

Garnish

WHIPPED CREAM

SHAVED CHOCOLATE

CHOPPED NUTS

For the chocolate cups, melt the chocolate and shortening in a double boiler over hot water, stirring to blend well. Cool until thick enough to spread. Spread over the bottom and up the side of fluted or plain cup liners placed in muffin cups. Chill or freeze until firm.

For the mousse, soften the gelatin in the milk in a double boiler. Add the coffee and half the sugar and heat until the gelatin dissolves. Combine the remaining sugar with the egg yolks and salt in a mixing bowl and beat until smooth. Stir a small amount of the hot coffee mixture into the beaten egg yolks; stir the egg yolks into the hot coffee mixture. Cook until thickened, stirring constantly. Fold in the egg whites and vanilla. Cool to room temperature.

To assemble, remove the paper liners carefully from the chocolate cups. Spoon the mousse into the cups. Chill, covered, until serving time. Garnish with whipped cream, shaved chocolate and chopped nuts.

Serves six

QUICK CHOCOLATE POTS DE CRÈME

²/₃ CUP LIGHT CREAM

1 CUP (6 OUNCES)
   SEMISWEET CHOCOLATE
   CHIPS

3 TABLESPOONS VERY
   STRONG BREWED COFFEE

2 TABLESPOONS COFFEE
   LIQUEUR OR BRANDY

2 EGGS

SWEETENED WHIPPED
   CREAM

Garnish

CHOCOLATE CURLS,
   CHOPPED NUTS, CANDIED
   VIOLETS OR CANDIED
   ORANGE PEEL

Heat the cream just to a simmer in a small saucepan. Combine with the chocolate chips, coffee, liqueur and eggs in a blender container and process at high speed for 3 minutes. Pour into six 4-ounce demitasse cups or 6-ounce custard cups. Chill, covered, for 4 hours or longer. Top with sweetened whipped cream and garnish with chocolate curls, chopped nuts, candied violets or candied orange peel.

Serves six

CRÈME A RHUM

1 ENVELOPE UNFLAVORED
   GELATIN
1/4 CUP COLD WATER
1 1/4 CUPS SUGAR
1 CUP ORANGE JUICE
1/4 CUP LEMON JUICE
6 EGG YOLKS
1/2 CUP WHITE WINE
3 TO 4 TABLESPOONS RUM
PINCH OF SALT
2/3 CUP WHIPPING CREAM

Garnish

WHIPPED CREAM

Soften the gelatin in the cold water. Combine the sugar, orange juice, lemon juice, egg yolks, wine, rum and salt in a double boiler. Cook over hot water until foamy and thickened, beating constantly. Remove from the heat and add the gelatin mixture, stirring to dissolve completely. Cool until syrupy.

Beat the whipping cream in a mixing bowl until soft peaks form. Fold into the gelatin mixture. Spoon into an oiled 1-quart mold and chill, covered, for 3 hours or longer. Unmold onto a serving plate and garnish servings with additional whipped cream.

Serves six

CRÈME BRÛLÉE

2 CUPS HEAVY CREAM
3 TABLESPOONS BROWN
   SUGAR
1 TO 3 TABLESPOONS
   COGNAC
4 EGG YOLKS, BEATEN
BROWN SUGAR FOR
   TOPPING
COGNAC FOR TOPPING

Bring the cream just to a simmer in a double boiler; do not boil. Add 3 tablespoons brown sugar and 1 to 3 tablespoons Cognac and stir until the brown sugar dissolves. Stir a small amount of the hot mixture into the egg yolks; stir the egg yolks into the hot mixture.

Spoon into a round 8-inch baking dish and place in a larger pan of hot water. Bake at 250 degrees on the center oven rack for 1 1/2 hours or until set. Cool to room temperature and chill, covered, in the refrigerator.

Sprinkle 1/2 inch brown sugar over the top, covering evenly. Broil until the brown sugar melts and forms a crust, turning to brown evenly if necessary and watching carefully to prevent burning. Chill until serving time. Spoon a thin coating of Cognac over the top just before serving.

You may also bake this in individual ramekins; adjust the baking time accordingly.

Serves four to six

Toasted Spiced Pecans

Spread 2 cups pecan halves in a shallow baking pan. Toast at 325 degrees for 10 minutes. Add 1/4 cup butter and bake until the butter melts; stir to coat the pecans well. Beat 1 egg white until foamy. Add 1/2 cup sugar, 1 teaspoon cinnamon and 1/8 teaspoon nutmeg and beat until smooth. Spoon over the pecans and mix well. Bake for 30 minutes longer, stirring every 10 minutes. Cool to room temperature and store in an airtight container.

Frozen Soufflé With Hot Strawberry Sauce

Soufflé

1 QUART VANILLA ICE
    CREAM, SOFTENED
24 MACAROONS, CRUSHED
1/4 CUP ORANGE JUICE OR
    GRAND MARNIER
1 CUP WHIPPING CREAM,
    WHIPPED

Strawberry Sauce

1 QUART FRESH
    STRAWBERRIES, OR
    2 (10-OUNCE) PACKAGES
    FROZEN SLICED
    STRAWBERRIES, THAWED
SUGAR TO TASTE
1/4 CUP ORANGE JUICE OR
    GRAND MARNIER

Garnish

4 TEASPOONS
    CONFECTIONERS' SUGAR
1/4 CUP CHOPPED TOASTED
    ALMONDS

For the souflé, combine the ice cream, macaroons and orange juice in a large bowl and mix well. Fold in the whipped cream. Spoon into a 6-cup mold or metal dish. Freeze, covered with plastic wrap, for 4 hours or until firm.

For the sauce, cut fresh strawberries into halves. Combine the strawberries with sugar in a saucepan and simmer until tender but not mushy. Remove from the heat and add the orange juice.

To serve, loosen the side of the mold with a knife and wrap the mold with warm towels. Invert onto a serving plate and garnish with the confectioners' sugar and almonds. Serve with the warm sauce.

Serves eight

Cold Lemon Soufflé With Wine Sauce

Soufflé

1 ENVELOPE UNFLAVORED GELATIN

1/4 CUP COLD WATER

5 EGG YOLKS

3/4 CUP FRESH LEMON JUICE

2 TEASPOONS GRATED LEMON ZEST

3/4 CUP SUGAR

5 EGG WHITES

3/4 CUP SUGAR

1 CUP WHIPPING CREAM

Wine Sauce

1/2 CUP SUGAR

1 TABLESPOON CORNSTARCH

1/2 CUP WATER

3 TABLESPOONS FRESH LEMON JUICE

1 TEASPOON GRATED LEMON ZEST

2 TABLESPOONS BUTTER

1/2 CUP DRY WHITE WINE

For the soufflé, sprinkle the gelatin over the cold water and let stand until softened. Combine the egg yolks, lemon juice, lemon zest and 3/4 cup sugar in a double boiler and mix well. Cook over boiling water for 8 minutes or until slightly thickened, stirring constantly. Remove from the heat and add the gelatin mixture; stir until the gelatin dissolves completely. Chill for 30 to 40 minutes or until the mixture mounds slightly when dropped from a spoon.

Beat the egg whites until soft peaks form. Add 3/4 cup sugar gradually, beating constantly until stiff peaks form. Beat the whipping cream until soft peaks form. Fold the egg whites and whipped cream into the gelatin mixture. Spoon into a 2-quart soufflé dish or wine glasses and chill, covered, for 4 hours or longer.

For the sauce, mix the sugar and cornstarch in a small saucepan. Stir in the water, lemon juice and lemon zest. Add the butter. Bring to a boil and reduce the heat, stirring constantly. Simmer for 3 minutes or until thickened, stirring constantly. Remove from the heat and stir in the wine. Chill, covered, until serving time, stirring occasionally. Serve with the soufflé.

To avoid uncooked eggs that may carry salmonella, use an equivalent amount of pasteurized egg substitute, or meringue powder, sometimes sold as powdered egg whites.

Serves eight

SHINING FINISH *desserts*

Walnut Crust

2 CUPS CINNAMON
   GRAHAM CRACKER
   CRUMBS
6 TABLESPOONS (3/4 STICK)
   BUTTER OR MARGARINE,
   MELTED
2 TABLESPOONS SUGAR
1/2 CUP CHOPPED WALNUTS

Cheesecake

24 OUNCES CREAM
   CHEESE, SOFTENED
3/4 CUP SUGAR
3 EGGS
1/4 CUP LEMON JUICE
2 TEASPOONS GRATED
   LEMON ZEST
1 TEASPOON VANILLA
   EXTRACT

Sour Cream Topping

2 CUPS SOUR CREAM
2 TABLESPOONS SUGAR
2 TEASPOONS VANILLA
   EXTRACT

Lemon Glaze

1/2 CUP SUGAR
4 TEASPOONS CORNSTARCH
1/4 TEASPOON SALT
3/4 CUP WATER
1/3 CUP LEMON JUICE
1 EGG YOLK, LIGHTLY
   BEATEN
1 TABLESPOON BUTTER OR
   MARGARINE
1 TEASPOON GRATED
   LEMON ZEST

Garnish

WHITE ROSE PETALS,
   VIOLETS, ORANGE PEEL
   CURLS, MINT LEAVES
   AND/OR LEMON LEAVES

For the crust, combine the graham cracker crumbs, butter, sugar and walnuts in a bowl and mix well. Press evenly over the bottom and up the side of a lightly buttered 9-inch springform pan. Bake at 350 degrees for 5 minutes. Cool to room temperature.

For the cheesecake, beat the cream cheese with the sugar in a medium mixing bowl until light. Add the eggs 1 at a time, beating well after each addition. Add the lemon juice, lemon zest and vanilla and mix well. Pour into the cooled crust. Bake at 350 degrees for 35 minutes.

For the topping, mix the sour cream, sugar and vanilla in a small bowl. Spread over the cheesecake. Bake for 12 minutes longer. Cool on a wire rack for 30 minutes.

For the glaze, mix the sugar, cornstarch and salt in a heavy 1-quart saucepan. Combine the water, lemon juice and egg yolk in a small bowl and mix well. Add to the saucepan and mix well.

Cook the glaze over low heat until thickened and bubbly, stirring constantly. Stir in the butter and lemon zest. Cool slightly. Spread the glaze over the cheesecake.

Chill the cheesecake, covered, for several hours. Place on a serving platter and remove the side of the pan. Garnish with rose petals, violets, orange peel, mint leaves and/or lemon leaves.

Serves twelve to sixteen

Photograph for this recipe is on page 147.

Lemon Charlotte Russe

1 TABLESPOON
  UNFLAVORED GELATIN
$^1/_2$ CUP COLD WATER
4 LARGE EGG YOLKS
1 CUP SUGAR
$^1/_2$ CUP FRESH LEMON
  JUICE
GRATED LEMON ZEST
  TO TASTE
4 LARGE EGG WHITES
2 CUPS (1 PINT) WHIPPING
  CREAM
24 LADYFINGERS
$^1/_2$ CUP TOASTED
  ALMONDS, SLIVERED

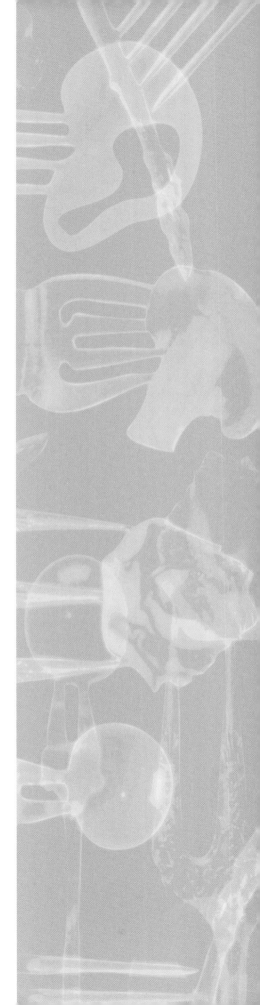

Sprinkle the gelatin over the cold water in a double boiler and let stand until softened. Heat over hot water, stirring until the gelatin dissolves completely.

Beat the egg yolks in a mixing bowl until pale yellow. Add the sugar gradually, beating constantly until thickened. Beat in the lemon juice and lemon zest. Add the gelatin mixture and beat until smooth.

Beat the egg whites in a mixing bowl until stiff peaks form. Beat the whipping cream in a mixing bowl until soft peaks form. Fold the egg whites and whipped cream into the lemon mixture.

Line the bottom and side of a crystal bowl with ladyfingers. Spoon half the custard mixture into the bowl and add a layer of ladyfingers. Add the remaining custard mixture and sprinkle with almonds. Chill, covered, for 24 hours.

To avoid uncooked eggs that may carry salmonella, use an equivalent amount of pasteurized egg substitute, or meringue powder, sometimes sold as powdered egg whites.

Serves ten

Lemon Icebox Cake

$^3/_4$ CUP SUGAR
1 TABLESPOON FLOUR
$^1/_4$ TEASPOON SALT
3 EGG YOLKS
$^1/_4$ CUP LEMON JUICE
GRATED ZEST OF 1 LEMON
1 CUP MILK
1 TABLESPOON BUTTER,
  MELTED
3 EGG WHITES
1 CUP WHIPPING CREAM
1 ANGEL FOOD OR POUND
  CAKE, TORN, OR 18
  LADYFINGERS

Mix the sugar, flour and salt in a bowl. Add the egg yolks and beat until smooth. Add the lemon juice, lemon zest, milk and butter and mix well. Spoon into a double boiler. Cook over low heat until thickened, stirring constantly.

Beat the egg whites until stiff peaks form. Fold into the custard. Cool to room temperature. Beat the whipping cream until soft peaks form. Fold into the custard. Pour over the cake in a serving bowl. Chill, covered, until serving time.

Serves six

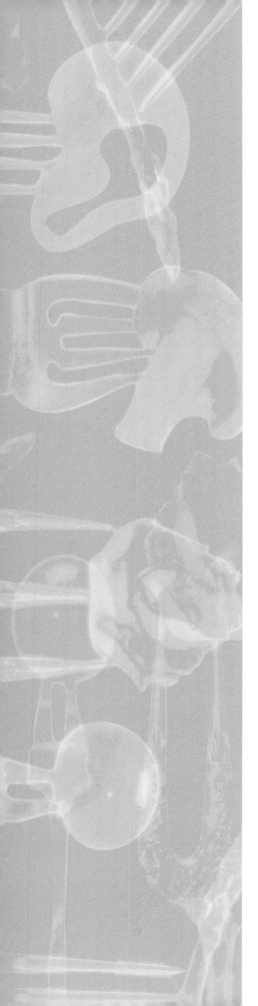

Schaum Torte

6 EGG WHITES
PINCH OF CREAM OF
    TARTAR
2 CUPS CONFECTIONERS'
    SUGAR, SIFTED
1 TABLESPOON VANILLA
    EXTRACT (OPTIONAL)
1 TABLESPOON VINEGAR
SWEETENED FRUIT
WHIPPED CREAM

Beat the egg whites until foamy. Add the cream of tartar and beat until stiff peaks form. Add the confectioners' sugar gradually, beating constantly until the confectioners' sugar dissolves and adding the vanilla and vinegar just before the last addition.

Spoon into a springform pan, shaping the outer edge to form a rim. Place in a cold oven and set the oven temperature to 250 degrees. Bake for 1 to $1^{1}/_{2}$ hours or until light brown. Cool to room temperature. Place on a serving plate and remove the side of the pan. Fill with fruit and top with whipped cream.

You may shape the meringue mixture into individual tortes on greased brown paper or baking parchment and bake for a shorter time.

Serves six to eight

Strawberries Romanoff

$^{1}/_{2}$ GRAPEFRUIT
1 ORANGE
4 TO 6 CUPS WATER
$1^{1}/_{2}$ QUARTS STRAWBERRIES,
    CUT INTO HALVES
6 OUNCES RUM
3 EGGS
6 TABLESPOONS SUGAR
2 CUPS (1 PINT) WHIPPING
    CREAM
12 MACAROONS, CRUSHED

Cut the peels from the grapefruit and orange, reserving the pulp for another use. Cut the peels into thin strips. Combine the peels with half the water in a saucepan and cook for 5 minutes. Drain and add the remaining water. Cook until tender. Cool to room temperature. Add the strawberries and rum. Let stand for 3 hours or longer.

Beat the eggs with the sugar in a mixing bowl until pale yellow. Bring half the cream just to a simmer in a double boiler. Stir a small amount of the hot cream into the egg mixture; stir the egg mixture into the hot cream. Cook until thickened, stirring constantly. Cool to room temperature.

Whip the remaining cream in a mixing bowl until soft peaks form. Fold into the cooled custard. Spoon the strawberry mixture into a serving bowl. Spoon the custard over the strawberry mixture. Top with the macaroon crumbs.

Serves six to eight

Chocolate Sauce

4 (1-OUNCE) SQUARES
   UNSWEETENED
   CHOCOLATE
1/2 CUP (1 STICK) BUTTER
   OR MARGARINE
1/3 CUP BAKING COCOA
1 1/2 CUPS SUGAR
1 CUP HEAVY CREAM
2 TEASPOONS VANILLA
   EXTRACT

Melt the chocolate with the butter in a double boiler. Add the baking cocoa and sugar and mix well. Cook for 45 minutes, stirring frequently. Stir in the cream and cook for 10 minutes longer, stirring constantly. Stir in the vanilla gradually. Cool to room temperature and store in the refrigerator for several weeks. Reheat to serve if desired. Serve on ice cream.

Mixture may appear curdled when the cream is added, but will become smooth.

Makes three cups

Lemon Sauce

3/4 CUP SUGAR
2 TABLESPOONS
   CORNSTARCH
1/8 TEASPOON SALT
2 CUPS BOILING WATER
2 TABLESPOONS LEMON
   JUICE
1/2 TEASPOON GRATED
   LEMON ZEST
2 TABLESPOONS BUTTER
1/2 TEASPOON NUTMEG

Mix the sugar, cornstarch and salt in a saucepan. Stir in the boiling water gradually. Cook for 5 minutes; do not stir. Remove from the heat and add the lemon juice, lemon zest, butter and nutmeg; mix well. Serve warm on gingerbread, pound cake or pudding.

Makes three cups

desserts

SHINING FINISH

Custard Ice Cream

6 EGGS
2 CUPS SUGAR
4 CUPS (1 QUART) MILK
1 TABLESPOON VANILLA
    EXTRACT
6 CUPS (1½ QUARTS) HALF-
    AND-HALF
2 CUPS (1 PINT) HEAVY
    CREAM

Beat the eggs in a mixing bowl until thick. Add the sugar and beat until pale yellow. Bring the milk just to a simmer in a double boiler. Stir a small amount of the hot milk into the egg mixture; stir the egg mixture into the hot milk. Cook until the mixture thickens enough to coat a spoon, stirring constantly. Remove from the heat and stir in the vanilla. Cool to room temperature.

Pour into an ice cream freezer container and add the half-and-half and cream. Freeze using the manufacturer's instructions.

Makes one gallon

Variations

For *Caramel Ice Cream*, sprinkle 2 cups sugar in a skillet and cook until golden brown, stirring constantly. Add to the mixture.

For *Peppermint Ice Cream*, add crushed peppermint candy to the cooled mixture.

For *Coffee Ice Cream*, add 1 or more cups very strong brewed coffee to the cooled mixture.

For *Fruit Ice Cream*, add the desired amount of fruit to the ice cream halfway through the freezing time.

As Close As I Can Come To Dorothy's Specials

BEST-QUALITY VANILLA
    ICE CREAM
½ CUP BRANDY
½ CUP CRÈME DE CACAO

Fill a blender container with ice cream and add the brandy and crème de cacao. Process until smooth. Spoon into serving bowls.

Serves four

SHINING FINISH *desserts*

MINETRY'S ICE CREAM MAGIC

24 ALMOND MACAROONS

1/4 CUP BOURBON

1/2 GALLON VANILLA ICE
   CREAM, SOFTENED

6 TO 8 CHOCOLATE-
   COVERED TOFFEE BARS,
   COARSELY CHOPPED

Dip the macaroons into the bourbon just until moistened. Layer the macaroons, ice cream and toffee candy 1/2 at a time in a 3-quart serving bowl. Freeze, covered, until firm.

Serves twelve

QUADRUPLE-CHOCOLATE CUPCAKES

1 CUP FLOUR

3 TABLESPOONS BAKING
   COCOA

SALT TO TASTE

1 CUP (2 STICKS) BUTTER
   OR MARGARINE

2 (1-OUNCE) SQUARES
   UNSWEETENED
   CHOCOLATE

2 (1-OUNCE) SQUARES
   SEMISWEET CHOCOLATE

1 1/2 CUPS SUGAR

4 EGGS, BEATEN

1 TEASPOON VANILLA
   EXTRACT

1/4 TEASPOON ALMOND
   EXTRACT

2 CUPS (12 OUNCES)
   SEMISWEET CHOCOLATE
   CHIPS

Mix the flour, baking cocoa and salt in a large bowl. Melt the butter, unsweetened chocolate and semisweet chocolate in a 2-quart saucepan, stirring to blend well. Add the sugar, eggs and flavorings and mix well. Add to the flour mixture and mix well. Stir in the chocolate chips.

Spoon into muffin cups lined with foil baking cups, filling half full. Bake at 350 degrees for 12 to 14 minutes or until cupcakes test done. Remove to a wire rack to cool.

Makes twenty

Party Rules for Small Fry

- Restrict the number of guests for preschoolers' parties. Six will seem like a large and fun group, and even four will be a party.
- Provide two adults for every six children. Too many adults interfere by chatting with one another or correcting the children too often.
- Do not use a child's party to discharge your social obligations.
- Do not plan a party to last overlong, for children tire easily: an hour and a half is sufficient.
- Never try to surprise a child with a party. Anticipation is half the fun.
- Have plenty of bright decorations, particularly balloons.
- Make the food festive and easy to eat. Always include a pitcher of water.
- Provide "goodie bags," but they do not have to be elaborate. Sidewalk chalk, bath sponges, bubbles, and candy are a few ideas, and most can be found at your local dollar store.

Siren's Chocolate Cake

2½ CUPS FLOUR

2 CUPS SUGAR

2 TEASPOONS BAKING SODA

½ TEASPOON SALT

2 EGGS

2 CUPS BUTTERMILK

2 TEASPOONS VANILLA EXTRACT

1 CUP (2 STICKS) BUTTER

8 (1-OUNCE) SQUARES UNSWEETENED CHOCOLATE

1 (5-OUNCE) CAN EVAPORATED MILK

2 TEASPOONS VANILLA EXTRACT

1 (1-POUND) PACKAGE CONFECTIONERS' SUGAR

Sift the flour, sugar, baking soda and salt together. Beat the eggs with the buttermilk in a mixing bowl and add 2 teaspoons vanilla. Add the dry ingredients and mix well.

Melt half the butter and chocolate in a double boiler, stirring to blend well. Add to the batter and mix well. Spoon into 2 greased 9-inch cake pans. Bake at 350 degrees for 30 minutes. Cool in the pans for 5 minutes; remove to wire racks to cool completely.

Combine the evaporated milk, 2 teaspoons vanilla and confectioners' sugar in a mixing bowl and mix until smooth. Melt the remaining chocolate and butter in a saucepan over low heat, stirring to blend well. Add to the confectioners' sugar mixture and mix until smooth. Add additional confectioners' sugar if necessary for a spreading consistency. Spread between the layers and over the top and side of the cake.

Serves sixteen

Chocolate Bar Cake

¼ TEASPOON BAKING SODA

1 CUP BUTTERMILK

8 SMALL CHOCOLATE CANDY BARS

1 CUP (2 STICKS) BUTTER, SOFTENED

2 CUPS SUGAR

4 EGGS

2½ CUPS SIFTED CAKE FLOUR

SALT TO TASTE

2 TEASPOONS VANILLA EXTRACT

1 CUP CHOPPED PECANS

Garnish

CONFECTIONERS' SUGAR

Dissolve the baking soda in the buttermilk. Melt the chocolate bars in a double boiler. Cream the butter and sugar in a mixing bowl until light and fluffy. Beat in the eggs 1 at a time. Add the flour, salt, vanilla, buttermilk mixture and melted chocolate and mix well. Stir in the pecans.

Spoon into a greased bundt pan. Bake at 300 degrees for 1 hour and 40 minutes. Cool in the pan for 10 minutes. Remove to a wire rack to cool completely. Garnish with sifted confectioners' sugar. Fill the center with sweetened whipped cream to serve, or serve with a scoop of ice cream.

Serves ten to twelve

EASY RUM CAKE

Cake

1 (2-LAYER) PACKAGE
    YELLOW CAKE MIX
1 (4-OUNCE) PACKAGE
    VANILLA INSTANT
    PUDDING MIX
1/2 CUP LIGHT RUM
1/2 CUP WATER
1/2 CUP VEGETABLE OIL
4 EGGS

Rum Sauce

1/2 CUP (1 STICK) BUTTER
1 CUP SUGAR
1/4 CUP WATER
1/4 CUP RUM

Garnish

SIFTED CONFECTIONERS'
    SUGAR

For the cake, combine the cake mix and pudding mix in a mixing bowl. Add the rum, water and oil and mix well. Beat in the eggs 1 at a time. Spoon into a greased bundt pan. Bake at 350 degrees for 1 hour. Cool on a wire rack.

For the sauce, combine the butter, sugar and water in a saucepan. Bring to a boil and cook for 1 minute, stirring constantly. Remove from the heat and cool slightly. Stir in the rum.

Invert the cake onto a plate lined with foil; turn up and crimp the edges of the foil. Pierce the cake with a wooden pick. Pour the sauce slowly over the cake.

Let the cake stand, covered, for 8 hours or longer. Scoop up sauce from the foil and spread over the cake with a knife. Garnish with confectioners' sugar.

You may substitute Kahlúa or amaretto for the rum if preferred.

Serves sixteen

EGGNOG FROSTED CAKE

1 PREPARED ROUND ANGEL
    FOOD CAKE
1/2 CUP (1 STICK) BUTTER,
    SOFTENED
2 CUPS CONFECTIONERS'
    SUGAR, SIFTED
2 EGG YOLKS
5 TABLESPOONS
    HALF-AND-HALF
2 TABLESPOONS SHERRY
2 TABLESPOONS WHISKEY
1 TEASPOON VANILLA
    EXTRACT
1/4 TEASPOON NUTMEG
1 1/2 CUPS WHIPPING
    CREAM, WHIPPED
NUTMEG

Cut the cake horizontally into 4 even layers with a serrated knife. Cream the butter and confectioners' sugar in a mixing bowl until light and fluffy. Beat in the egg yolks 1 at a time. Add the half-and-half, wine, whiskey, vanilla and 1/4 teaspoon nutmeg and mix well. Spread between the cake layers.

Spread the whipped cream over the top and side of the cake. Sprinkle with additional nutmeg. Chill, covered, for 6 hours or longer.

You may substitute 1/4 cup Scotch for the sherry and whiskey if preferred.

To avoid uncooked eggs that may carry salmonella, use an equivalent amount of pasteurized egg substitute, or meringue powder, sometimes sold as powdered egg whites.

Serves twelve

FRESH ORANGE CHIFFON CAKE

Cake

2¼ CUPS SIFTED CAKE
    FLOUR
1½ CUPS SUGAR
1 TABLESPOON BAKING
    POWDER
¼ TEASPOON SALT
½ CUP VEGETABLE OIL
5 EGG YOLKS
JUICE OF 2 ORANGES
2 TABLESPOONS GRATED
    ORANGE ZEST
1 CUP (7 OR 8) EGG WHITES
½ TEASPOON CREAM OF
    TARTAR

Orange Cream Frosting

½ CUP (1 STICK) BUTTER,
    SOFTENED
4 TEASPOONS FLOUR
SALT TO TASTE
½ CUP ORANGE JUICE
¼ CUP GRATED
    ORANGE ZEST
3½ CUPS CONFECTIONERS'
    SUGAR

For the cake, sift the cake flour, sugar, baking powder and salt into a bowl; make a well in the center. Add the oil gradually, mixing well. Stir in the egg yolks 1 at a time.

Mix the orange juice with enough water to measure ¾ cup. Add to the batter with the orange zest; beat with a spoon until smooth.

Beat the egg whites with the cream of tartar in a mixing bowl until stiff peaks form. Fold into the batter.

Spoon into an ungreased 9-inch tube pan. Bake at 325 degrees for 50 to 60 minutes or until the cake tests done.

Invert on a bottle to cool. Loosen from the pan with a knife and remove to a serving plate.

For the frosting, combine the butter, flour and salt in a mixing bowl and mix until smooth. Add the orange juice and orange zest.

Add the confectioners' sugar gradually, beating constantly until smooth. Spread over the top and side of the cake.

Serves sixteen

Georgia Peach Pound Cake

3 CUPS FLOUR
1/4 TEASPOON BAKING SODA
1/2 TEASPOON SALT
1 1/4 CUPS (2 1/2 STICKS) BUTTER, SOFTENED
2 1/2 CUPS SUGAR
6 EGGS, AT ROOM TEMPERATURE
1 TEASPOON VANILLA EXTRACT
1/2 TEASPOON ALMOND EXTRACT
1/2 CUP PLAIN YOGURT
2 CUPS CHOPPED PEELED FRESH PEACHES

Garnish

SWEETENED WHIPPED CREAM
FRESHLY GRATED NUTMEG

Mix the flour, baking soda and salt together. Cream the butter and sugar in a large mixing bowl until light and fluffy. Add the eggs 1 at a time, beating for 1 minute after each addition. Stir in the flavorings. Add the dry ingredients alternately with the yogurt, mixing well after each addition. Fold in the peaches.

Spoon into a greased and floured 10-inch tube pan. Bake at 350 degrees for 1 to 1 1/4 hours. Cool in the pan for 20 minutes. Remove to a wire rack to cool completely. Garnish servings with sweetened whipped cream and nutmeg.

Serves sixteen

Strawberry Shortcakes

2 CUPS FLOUR
4 TEASPOONS BAKING POWDER
1/2 TEASPOON SALT
2 TABLESPOONS SUGAR
1/2 CUP (1 STICK) BUTTER
3/4 CUP MILK
1 QUART FRESH STRAWBERRIES
SUGAR TO TASTE
1 CUP WHIPPING CREAM, WHIPPED

Mix the flour, baking powder, salt and sugar in a bowl. Cut in the butter until crumbly. Stir in the milk. Roll into a circle on a floured surface. Cut out with a biscuit cutter or roll large enough for 2 round pans.

Bake at 425 degrees for 12 to 15 minutes or until golden brown.

To serve, split the shortcakes and top with sweetened strawberries and whipped cream.

Serves six to eight

Spice Cake With Caramel Frosting

Cake

2 1/4 CUPS SIFTED CAKE
   FLOUR
1 2/3 CUPS SUGAR
1 TEASPOON BAKING
   POWDER
3/4 TEASPOON BAKING
   SODA
2 TEASPOONS GROUND
   CINNAMON
1 TEASPOON GROUND
   NUTMEG
3/4 TEASPOON GROUND
   CLOVES
1/4 TEASPOON SALT
PEPPER TO TASTE
1 CUP (2 STICKS) BUTTER
   OR MARGARINE,
   MELTED
1 CUP BUTTERMILK
3 EGGS
1 TEASPOON VANILLA
   EXTRACT
1 CUP CHOPPED WALNUTS

Caramel Frosting

1 1/3 CUPS PACKED BROWN
   SUGAR
1/2 CUP MILK
1/4 TEASPOON SALT
3 TABLESPOONS BUTTER
   OR MARGARINE
1 TEASPOON VANILLA
   EXTRACT
3 CUPS SIFTED
   CONFECTIONERS' SUGAR

For the cake, mix the flour, sugar, baking powder, baking soda, cinnamon, nutmeg, cloves, salt and pepper in a large mixing bowl. Add the butter, buttermilk, eggs and vanilla and stir with a wooden spoon to mix well. Stir in the chopped walnuts.

Spoon into 2 greased and floured 9-inch cake pans. Bake at 350 degrees for 25 to 30 minutes or until a wooden pick inserted near the center comes out clean.

Cool in the pans on wire racks for 10 minutes. Remove to the wire racks to cool completely.

For the frosting, combine the brown sugar, milk and salt in a 2-quart saucepan and mix well. Bring to a boil and reduce the heat. Simmer for 5 minutes or until slightly thickened.

Remove from the heat and stir in the butter and vanilla. Cool slightly. Add the confectioners' sugar and beat until smooth and of spreading consistency. Spread between the layers and over the top and side of the cake.

Serves twelve

CHOCOLATE BUTTER TOFFEE

1 CUP (2 STICKS) BUTTER
1¹/₃ CUPS SUGAR
1 (16-OUNCE) BOTTLE
    CORN SYRUP
3 TABLESPOONS WATER
1 CUP TOASTED BLANCHED
    ALMONDS, FINELY
    CHOPPED
4 (4¹/₂-OUNCE) CHOCOLATE
    CANDY BARS
1 CUP FINELY CHOPPED
    PECANS

Melt the butter in a large saucepan. Add the sugar, corn syrup and water and mix well. Cook to 300 degrees on a candy thermometer, hard crack stage, stirring occasionally. Stir in the almonds. Spread in a greased 9×13-inch pan. Let stand until cool.

Melt the chocolate bars in a double boiler, stirring until smooth. Invert the toffee onto waxed paper. Spread half the chocolate over the top and sprinkle with half the pecans. Invert onto a second sheet of waxed paper and spread the remaining side with the remaining chocolate; sprinkle with the remaining pecans. Let stand until firm and break into pieces. Store in an airtight container.

Serves sixteen

PEPPERMINT MERINGUES

2 EGG WHITES
SALT TO TASTE
¹/₄ TEASPOON CREAM OF
    TARTAR
³/₄ CUP SUGAR
1 CUP (6 OUNCES)
    CHOCOLATE CHIPS
PEPPERMINT EXTRACT
    TO TASTE
SEVERAL DROPS OF GREEN
    FOOD COLORING

Preheat the oven to 350 degrees. Beat the egg whites with salt and cream of tartar in a mixing bowl until frothy. Add the sugar gradually, beating constantly for 15 minutes. Fold in the chocolate chips, peppermint extract and food coloring.

Drop by spoonfuls onto an ungreased baking sheet. Turn off the oven and place the meringues in the oven. Let stand in the oven for 1¹/₂ hours without opening the oven door.

You may substitute 1 teaspoon vanilla and ¹/₄ cup chopped nuts for the peppermint extract and food coloring if preferred.

Makes three dozen

Perfect Meringues

- Choose a dry day to make meringues; humidity can sabotage the texture of meringue and keep it from drying properly, even in our modern climate-controlled homes.
- Treat the beaten egg whites with a light hand to maintain their volume. Keep the beater from touching the side of the bowl, as this will cause some loss of volume.
- Add 1 teaspoon of cold water or ¹/₄ teaspoon vinegar for every 3 egg whites to increase the volume.
- Watch the oven carefully to see that meringues are not baking too fast. A slow oven, or even a turned-off oven, cooks meringues without browning.

Sour Cream Fudge

1 CUP SUGAR
2 CUPS PACKED BROWN
  SUGAR
1 CUP SOUR CREAM
3 (1-OUNCE) SQUARES
  UNSWEETENED
  CHOCOLATE
1/4 CUP LIGHT CORN SYRUP
1/4 CUP (1/2 STICK) BUTTER
SALT TO TASTE
1 TEASPOON VANILLA
  EXTRACT
1 CUP CHOPPED NUTS

Combine the sugar, brown sugar, sour cream, chocolate and corn syrup in a large saucepan. Cook over very low heat to 234 degrees on a candy thermometer, soft ball stage. Remove from the heat and stir in the butter. Let stand until cool.

Beat the mixture until it is thickened and begins to lose its gloss. Stir in the salt, vanilla and nuts. Spread in a buttered 8×8-inch pan. Let stand until firm. Cut into squares.

Makes twenty-five squares

Apricot Almond Squares

1 1/2 CUPS FLOUR
1 TEASPOON BAKING
  POWDER
1/2 CUP GROUND ALMONDS
1/2 CUP (1 STICK) BUTTER,
  SOFTENED
1/2 CUP SUGAR
1 EGG
1 TEASPOON ALMOND
  EXTRACT
APRICOT JAM

Mix the flour, baking powder and almonds together. Cream the butter and sugar in a mixer bowl until light and fluffy. Add the egg and almond extract and mix well. Add the flour mixture and mix to form a stiff dough.

Press half the mixture into a greased 8×8-inch baking pan. Spread with a thin layer of apricot jam and spread the remaining almond mixture over the top. Bake at 350 degrees for 30 minutes. Cool on a wire rack and cut into 2-inch squares.

Makes sixteen squares

SHINING FINISH *desserts*

Death-To-The-Diet Brownies

1 CUP FLOUR

2 CUPS SUGAR

4 (1-OUNCE) SQUARES
    UNSWEETENED
    CHOCOLATE

1 CUP (2 STICKS) BUTTER
    OR MARGARINE

4 EGGS, BEATEN

2 TEASPOONS COFFEE
    LIQUEUR, BRANDY OR
    VANILLA EXTRACT

1 CUP (6 OUNCES)
    CHOCOLATE CHIPS

1 CUP CHOPPED NUTS

Mix the flour and sugar in a large bowl. Melt the chocolate and butter in a heavy 1-quart saucepan, stirring to blend well. Add to the flour mixture with the eggs and liqueur; mix well. Stir in the chocolate chips and nuts.

Spread in a greased 9×13-inch baking pan. Bake at 325 degrees for 35 minutes or until the edges are firm; the center will be soft. Cool on a wire rack for 30 to 60 minutes before cutting. Cut into small squares and chill for 2 hours or longer before serving.

For an even deadlier-to-the-diet treat, microwave the squares for 30 seconds and top with a scoop of vanilla ice cream.

Makes four dozen squares

Grandmother's Brownies

½ CUP BAKING COCOA

2 CUPS SUGAR

1 CUP (2 STICKS) BUTTER
    OR MARGARINE,
    SOFTENED

4 EGGS

1 CUP SIFTED FLOUR

2 CUPS CHOPPED PECANS
    (OPTIONAL)

2 TEASPOONS VANILLA
    EXTRACT

½ TEASPOON BAKING
    POWDER

Garnish

CONFECTIONERS' SUGAR

Mix the baking cocoa and sugar in a mixing bowl. Add the butter and beat until light and fluffy. Beat in the eggs 1 at a time. Add the flour and mix well. Stir in the pecans and vanilla and then the baking powder.

Spread in a greased 10×15-inch baking pan. Bake at 350 degrees for 40 minutes. Cool on a wire rack. Garnish with confectioners' sugar and cut into squares.

Makes thirty-five squares

Family Mystery

The recipe for Grandmother's Brownies was submitted by a daughter of the grandmother in question to *Party Potpourri* when it was published in 1971. It had always been referred to as an old family recipe and has been prepared hundreds of times. When questioned later about the recipe, however, the grandmother replied that she had never heard of that brownie recipe before! It is still a family mystery.

Brown Sugar Pecan Brownies

1/2 CUP (1 STICK) BUTTER
1 (1-POUND) PACKAGE
    DARK BROWN SUGAR
2 EGGS, BEATEN
1 1/2 CUPS FLOUR
2 TEASPOONS BAKING
    POWDER
SALT TO TASTE
1 TEASPOON VANILLA
    EXTRACT
1 CUP CHOPPED PECANS

Melt the butter with the brown sugar in a saucepan, stirring to mix well. Cool to room temperature. Add the eggs, flour and baking powder and mix well. Stir in the salt, vanilla and pecans.

Spread in a greased shallow baking pan. Bake at 350 degrees for 45 to 60 minutes or until a wooden pick inserted in the center comes out clean. Cool on a wire rack. Cut into squares.

Makes two dozen squares

White Chocolate Brownies

1 CUP (2 STICKS) BUTTER
    OR MARGARINE,
    MELTED
1 CUP SUGAR
2 EGGS, BEATEN
2 TEASPOONS VANILLA
    EXTRACT
1/4 TEASPOON SALT
1 CUP FLOUR
2 (3 1/2-OUNCE) WHITE
    CHOCOLATE CANDY
    BARS, CHOPPED
1 CUP ROASTED SALTED
    MACADAMIAS, CHOPPED

Combine the butter, sugar, eggs, vanilla and salt in a medium bowl and mix well. Stir in the flour. Add the chopped candy and macadamias; mix well.

Spread in an 8×8-inch baking pan. Bake at 350 degrees for 20 to 25 minutes or until the edges are firm. Cool on a wire rack. Cut into squares.

Makes two dozen squares

Cocoons

1 CUP (2 STICKS) BUTTER,
SOFTENED
1/4 CUP SUGAR
1 TABLESPOON SHERRY
SALT TO TASTE
2 1/2 CUPS SIFTED FLOUR
1 CUP CHOPPED PECANS
OR ALMONDS
CONFECTIONERS' SUGAR
(OPTIONAL)

Cream the butter and sugar in a mixing bowl until light and fluffy. Beat in the sherry and salt. Add the flour gradually, beating constantly until smooth. Mix in the pecans.

Shape into small balls, logs or crescents and place on an ungreased cookie sheet. Bake at 275 degrees for 45 minutes. Roll in confectioners' sugar. Remove to a wire rack to cool.

Makes seven dozen

Gingerbread Men

Cookies

5 CUPS SIFTED FLOUR
1 1/2 TEASPOONS BAKING
SODA
1 TABLESPOON GINGER
1 TEASPOON CINNAMON
1 TEASPOON GROUND
CLOVES
1 CUP SHORTENING
1 CUP SUGAR
1/2 TEASPOON SALT
1 EGG
1 CUP MOLASSES
2 TABLESPOONS VINEGAR

Confectioners' Sugar Icing

2 CUPS CONFECTIONERS'
SUGAR
HALF-AND-HALF

Garnish

RED HOT CINNAMON
CANDIES

For the cookies, sift the flour, baking soda, ginger, cinnamon and cloves together. Cream the shortening, sugar and salt in a mixing bowl until light and fluffy. Beat in the egg, molasses and vinegar. Add the dry ingredients and mix well. Chill, covered, for 3 hours.

Roll 1/8 inch thick on a lightly floured surface. Cut with a gingerbread man cutter. Arrange 1 inch apart on a greased cookie sheet. Bake at 375 degrees for 6 minutes. Cool on the cookie sheet for several minutes. Remove to a wire rack to cool completely.

For the icing, combine the confectioners' sugar with enough half-and-half to make an icing that can be piped through a pastry tube. Spoon into the pastry tube and decorate the gingerbread men as desired. Garnish with red hot cinnamon candies.

Makes four dozen

HELLO DOLLIES

¹/₂ CUP (1 STICK) BUTTER
1 CUP GRAHAM CRACKER
 CRUMBS
1 CUP SHREDDED
 COCONUT
2 CUPS (12 OUNCES)
 SEMISWEET CHOCOLATE
 CHIPS
1 (14-OUNCE) CAN
 SWEETENED CONDENSED
 MILK
1 CUP CHOPPED NUTS

Melt the butter in a 9×13-inch baking pan and sprinkle the graham cracker crumbs evenly in the butter. Layer the coconut and chocolate chips over the crumbs. Drizzle with the condensed milk and sprinkle with the nuts; do not mix.

Bake at 350 degrees for 30 minutes. Cool on a wire rack and cut into squares.

You may substitute butterscotch for half or all of the chocolate chips.

Makes two and one-half dozen squares

FROSTED HIGH TEA LEMON COOKIES

Cookies

2 CUPS (4 STICKS) BUTTER,
 SOFTENED
²/₃ CUP CONFECTIONERS'
 SUGAR
1 TEASPOON GRATED
 LEMON ZEST
¹/₂ TEASPOON VANILLA
 EXTRACT
2 CUPS FLOUR
1¹/₃ CUPS CORNSTARCH

Lemon Frosting

¹/₃ CUP BUTTER, SOFTENED
1 TEASPOON GRATED
 LEMON ZEST
4 CUPS CONFECTIONERS'
 SUGAR
¹/₃ CUP FRESH LEMON JUICE

For the cookies, beat the butter in a large bowl until light. Add the confectioners' sugar and beat until fluffy. Add the lemon zest and vanilla and mix well. Add a mixture of the flour and cornstarch and mix until smooth.

Shape into 1-inch balls and place on ungreased cookie sheets. Bake at 350 degrees for 15 minutes or just until the bottoms are light brown. Cool on the cookie sheets for several minutes. Remove to a wire rack to cool completely.

For the frosting, beat the butter and lemon zest in a medium mixing bowl until light. Add the confectioners' sugar and beat until smooth. Mix in the lemon juice. Spread over the cookies.

Makes six dozen

LEMON ICEBOX COOKIES

2 CUPS SIFTED FLOUR

1/4 TEASPOON BAKING
   SODA

1/4 TEASPOON SALT

1/2 CUP (1 STICK)
   MARGARINE, SOFTENED

1/2 CUP SHORTENING

1/2 CUP SUGAR

1/2 CUP PACKED BROWN
   SUGAR

1 EGG

2 TABLESPOONS LEMON
   JUICE

1 TABLESPOON GRATED
   LEMON ZEST

1/2 CUP CHOPPED NUTS

Mix the flour, baking soda and salt together. Cream the margarine, shortening, sugar and brown sugar in a mixing bowl until light and fluffy. Beat in the egg, lemon juice and lemon zest. Add the dry ingredients and mix well. Mix in the nuts. Chill, covered, in the refrigerator.

Shape into a log and wrap in floured waxed paper. Store in the refrigerator for up to 1 week. Cut into thin slices and place on a cookie sheet. Bake at 400 degrees for 10 minutes. Cool on the cookie sheet for several minutes. Remove to a wire rack to cool completely.

Makes four dozen

Variations

For *Coconut Icebox Cookies*, substitute 1 cup shredded coconut for the lemon juice and lemon zest.

For *Chocolate Icebox Cookies*, substitute 2 melted squares of chocolate and 1/2 teaspoon vanilla for the lemon juice and lemon zest.

For *Vanilla Icebox Cookies*, substitute 1/2 teaspoon vanilla for the lemon juice and lemon zest.

For *Orange Icebox Cookies*, reduce the sugar to 2/3 cup and add 2 tablespoons orange marmalade.

For *Date Icebox Cookies*, substitute 1/2 cup finely chopped dates and 1/2 teaspoon vanilla for the lemon juice and lemon zest.

LEMON SQUARES

1 CUP (2 STICKS) BUTTER, SOFTENED
1/2 CUP CONFECTIONERS' SUGAR
2 CUPS FLOUR
2 CUPS SUGAR
4 EGGS, LIGHTLY BEATEN
1/4 CUP FLOUR
2 TEASPOONS BAKING POWDER
1/4 TEASPOON SALT
1/4 CUP FRESH LEMON JUICE
2 TABLESPOONS GRATED LEMON ZEST
CONFECTIONERS' SUGAR

Combine the butter, 1/2 cup confectioners' sugar and 2 cups flour in a mixing bowl and mix well. Press into a 9×13-inch baking pan. Bake at 325 degrees for 20 minutes or until brown around the edges.

Combine the sugar, eggs, 1/4 cup flour, baking powder, salt, lemon juice and lemon zest in a mixing bowl and mix until smooth. Spoon over the baked layer.

Bake at 325 degrees for 25 to 30 minutes or until set. Cool on a wire rack and sift additional confectioners' sugar over the top. Cut into small squares. Do not use substitutions for the butter in this recipe. May use Key lime juice and grated lime zest instead of the lemon juice and lemon zest if desired.

Makes three dozen squares

MOLASSES LACE COOKIES

1 1/2 CUPS SIFTED FLOUR
1 1/2 TEASPOONS BAKING POWDER
1 1/4 TEASPOONS CINNAMON
3/4 CUP SUGAR
1/2 CUP DARK MOLASSES
1/2 CUP WATER
3/4 CUP (1 1/2 STICKS) BUTTER OR MARGARINE
1 CUP CHOPPED PECANS

Sift the flour, baking powder and cinnamon together. Combine the sugar, molasses, water and butter in a saucepan. Bring to a boil. Remove from the heat and stir until the butter melts completely. Add the dry ingredients gradually, mixing well. Mix in the pecans.

Drop by teaspoonfuls 3 inches apart onto a greased cookie sheet. Bake at 325 degrees for 12 to 15 minutes or until golden brown. Cool on the cookie sheet for 1 minute. Remove to waxed paper with a spatula to cool completely.

Makes four dozen

PEANUT BUTTER COOKIES

2 CUPS FLOUR
1 1/2 TEASPOONS BAKING
   SODA
1/2 TEASPOON SALT
2/3 CUP BUTTER OR
   MARGARINE, SOFTENED
1 CUP SUGAR
1 CUP PACKED BROWN
   SUGAR
2 EGGS
1 CUP PEANUT BUTTER

Sift the flour, baking soda and salt together. Cream the butter, sugar and brown sugar in a mixing bowl until light and fluffy. Beat in the eggs and peanut butter. Add the dry ingredients and mix well.

Shape into small balls and place on a cookie sheet. Press with a fork to flatten. Bake at 350 degrees for 10 to 20 minutes or until golden brown. Cool on the cookie sheet for 5 minutes. Remove to a wire rack to cool completely.

Makes six dozen

RAISIN HONEY CHEWS

3/4 CUP SHORTENING
3/4 CUP SUGAR
1/2 CUP HONEY
1 EGG
1/2 TEASPOON GRATED
   ORANGE ZEST
1 1/4 CUPS FLOUR
1 TEASPOON BAKING
   SODA
1/2 TEASPOON SALT
2 CUPS QUICK-COOKING
   OATS
1 CUP RAISINS

Combine the shortening, sugar, honey, egg and orange zest in a mixing bowl and beat until smooth. Add the flour, baking soda and salt and mix well. Stir in the oats and raisins.

Drop by tablespoonfuls onto greased cookie sheets. Bake at 375 degrees for 8 to 10 minutes or until evenly brown. Cool on the cookie sheets for 2 or 3 minutes. Remove to wire racks to cool completely.

Makes three dozen

Whiskey Balls

2 POUNDS VANILLA
   WAFERS, FINELY
   CRUSHED
$^{1}/_{2}$ CUP LIGHT CORN
   SYRUP
1 CUP SUGAR
$^{3}/_{4}$ CUP BOURBON
$1^{1}/_{2}$ CUPS CRUSHED PECANS
CONFECTIONERS' SUGAR

Combine the vanilla wafer crumbs, corn syrup and sugar in a bowl and mix well. Mix in the whiskey and pecans. Shape into balls and roll in confectioners' sugar.

Makes four dozen

Mixed-Up Popcorn

6 CUPS POPPED POPCORN
3 CUPS BITE-SIZE RICE
   CEREAL SQUARES
2 CUPS TOASTED ROUND
   OAT CEREAL
$1^{1}/_{2}$ CUPS SALTED PEANUTS
1 CUP PECANS
1 CUP PACKED BROWN
   SUGAR
$^{1}/_{2}$ CUP (1 STICK) BUTTER
   OR MARGARINE
$^{1}/_{4}$ CUP LIGHT CORN SYRUP
$^{1}/_{4}$ TEASPOON BAKING SODA
1 TEASPOON VANILLA
   EXTRACT

Mix the popcorn, rice cereal, oat cereal, peanuts and pecans in a large baking pan. Combine the brown sugar, butter and corn syrup in a heavy 2- or 3-quart saucepan. Bring to a boil over medium heat, stirring constantly. Boil for 5 minutes without stirring. Remove from the heat and beat in the baking soda and vanilla.

Pour the hot syrup over the popcorn mixture and toss to coat well. Bake at 250 degrees for 1 hour. Cool to room temperature and store in an airtight container.

Makes fourteen cups

SHINING FINISH *desserts*

Garden Of Eden Apple Pie

Cheese Pastry

2 CUPS FLOUR
3/4 TEASPOON SALT
1/2 CUP SHORTENING
1 CUP (4 OUNCES)
    SHREDDED CHEDDAR
    CHEESE
6 TO 8 TABLESPOONS
    COLD WATER
MELTED BUTTER

Filling

5 OR 6 LARGE TART
    APPLES, PEELED, SLICED
3/4 CUP SUGAR
2 TABLESPOONS FLOUR
1 TEASPOON CINNAMON
1 TEASPOON NUTMEG
    (OPTIONAL)
1/8 TEASPOON SALT
2 TABLESPOONS (OR MORE)
    BUTTER

For the pastry, sift the flour and salt into a bowl. Cut in the shortening until crumbly. Add the cheese and mix lightly with a fork. Add just enough cold water to bind the mixture and mix to form a dough. Divide into 2 equal portions and roll each portion into a circle on a floured surface. Fit 1 circle into a 9-inch pie plate and brush with butter.

For the filling, arrange the apples in the prepared pie plate. Mix the sugar, flour, cinnamon, nutmeg and salt in a bowl. Sprinkle over the apples and dot with the butter.

Place the remaining pastry circle over the apple mixture; trim and crimp the edges and cut vents in the top. Bake at 450 degrees for 10 minutes or until the edge begins to brown. Reduce the oven temperature to 350 degrees and bake for 30 minutes longer.

You may substitute American cheese for half of the Cheddar cheese if preferred.

Serves six to eight

Chocolate Chip Pecan Pie

1 CUP SUGAR
4 EGGS
1 CUP LIGHT CORN SYRUP
1 TEASPOON VANILLA
    EXTRACT
1/2 CUP (1 STICK) BUTTER,
    MELTED
1 CUP CHOPPED PECANS
    OR ENGLISH WALNUTS
1 CUP (6 OUNCES)
    CHOCOLATE CHIPS
1 UNBAKED (10-INCH)
    PIE SHELL

Combine the sugar, eggs, corn syrup and vanilla in a mixing bowl and mix until smooth. Stir in the butter, pecans and chocolate chips. Spoon into the pie shell. Bake at 350 degrees for 50 minutes or until set. Do not substitute for the butter in this recipe.

Serves eight

LEROY'S CHESS PIES

3 CUPS SUGAR
1 CUP (2 STICKS) BUTTER
2 TABLESPOONS VINEGAR
6 EGGS
2 TEASPOONS VANILLA
    EXTRACT
SALT TO TASTE
2 UNBAKED (9-INCH)
    PIE SHELLS

Combine the sugar, butter and vinegar in a saucepan and bring to a boil. Beat the eggs with the vanilla and salt in a bowl. Stir a small amount of the hot mixture into the eggs; stir the eggs into the hot mixture. Cook for several minutes, stirring constantly. Spoon into the pie shells. Bake at 350 degrees for 40 minutes.

Serves twelve to sixteen

COCONUT CREAM PIE

Pie

3 EGG YOLKS
1/3 CUP SUGAR
2 1/2 TABLESPOONS
    CORNSTARCH
1 TABLESPOON BUTTER,
    MELTED
1/4 TEASPOON SALT
2 CUPS MILK
1 CUP SHREDDED
    COCONUT
1 TEASPOON VANILLA
    EXTRACT OR RUM
1/4 TEASPOON NUTMEG
1 BAKED (9-INCH)
    PIE SHELL

Meringue

3 EGG WHITES
1/4 TEASPOON CREAM OF
    TARTAR
6 TABLESPOONS SUGAR

Beat the egg yolks in a mixing bowl. Add the sugar, cornstarch, butter and salt gradually, beating constantly until smooth. Bring the milk just to a simmer in a double boiler. Stir a small amount of the hot milk into the egg yolk mixture; stir the egg yolk mixture into the hot milk. Cook over boiling water until thickened, stirring constantly. Stir in the coconut. Let stand until cool.

Stir in the vanilla and nutmeg. Spoon into the pie shell.

For the meringue, beat the egg whites in a mixing bowl until frothy. Add the cream of tartar and sugar gradually, beating until stiff peaks form. Spread over the pie, sealing to the edge of the pie plate. Bake at 300 degrees for 15 to 20 minutes or just until golden brown.

For Banana Cream Pie, substitute 2 or 3 sliced bananas for the coconut.

Serves six to eight

LUSCIOUS CRACKER PIE

18 SALTINE CRACKERS,
   FINELY CRUSHED
1 CUP CHOPPED PECANS
1 TEASPOON VANILLA
   EXTRACT
3 EGG WHITES
1/4 TEASPOON CREAM OF
   TARTAR
1 CUP SUGAR

Mix the cracker crumbs, pecans and vanilla in a bowl. Beat the egg whites in a mixing bowl until frothy. Add the cream of tartar and sugar gradually, beating constantly until stiff peaks form. Fold in the cracker mixture. Spoon into a greased 9-inch pie plate. Bake at 325 degrees for 30 minutes.

Serves six to eight

PUMPKIN CHIFFON PIE

1 ENVELOPE UNFLAVORED
   GELATIN
1/4 CUP COLD WATER
1 1/2 CUPS CANNED
   PUMPKIN
3/4 CUP PACKED BROWN
   SUGAR
1 TABLESPOON CINNAMON
1/2 TEASPOON GINGER
1/2 TEASPOON ALLSPICE
1/2 TEASPOON SALT
3 LARGE EGG YOLKS
1/2 CUP MILK
3 LARGE EGG WHITES
1/4 TEASPOON CREAM OF
   TARTAR
6 TABLESPOONS SUGAR
1 BAKED (10-INCH) PIE
   SHELL, OR 2 BAKED (8-
   INCH) PIE SHELLS

Garnish

WHIPPED CREAM

Sprinkle the gelatin over the cold water and let stand until softened. Mix the pumpkin, brown sugar, cinnamon, ginger, allspice and salt in a saucepan. Beat the egg yolks with the milk in a small bowl. Add to the pumpkin mixture. Bring to a boil over low heat and boil for 1 minute, stirring constantly.

Remove from the heat and add the gelatin mixture; stir until the gelatin dissolves completely. Spoon into a bowl and chill until partially set.

Beat the egg whites with the cream of tartar until frothy. Add the sugar gradually and beat until stiff peaks form. Fold into the pumpkin mixture. Spoon into the pie shell. Chill for 3 hours or longer. Garnish servings with whipped cream.

To avoid uncooked eggs that may carry salmonella, use an equivalent amount of pasteurized egg substitute, or meringue powder, sometimes sold as powdered egg whites.

Serves eight to twelve

SHARKIE PIE

1 CUP BLACKBERRY JAM

1/2 CUP SUGAR

3 EGGS, BEATEN

2²/3 TABLESPOONS
    (¹/3 STICK) BUTTER

1/4 CUP BOURBON

1 TEASPOON VANILLA
    EXTRACT

1 UNBAKED (9-INCH) PIE
    SHELL

1 CUP WHIPPING CREAM,
    WHIPPED

Combine the blackberry jam, sugar, eggs, butter, whiskey and vanilla in a mixing bowl and mix well. Spoon into the pie shell. Bake at 375 degrees for 25 minutes. Cool on a wire rack and top with the whipped cream to serve.

Serves six to eight

CREAM CHEESE TARTS

Tart Crust

1¹/2 CUPS GRAHAM
    CRACKER CRUMBS

1/4 CUP SUGAR

1/4 TEASPOON CINNAMON

1/4 CUP (¹/2 STICK) BUTTER,
    MELTED

Filling

16 OUNCES CREAM
    CHEESE, SOFTENED

1/4 CUP SOUR CREAM

1/2 CUP SUGAR

2 EGGS

1 TEASPOON VANILLA
    EXTRACT

Garnish

SOUR CREAM

FRESH BERRIES OR BERRY
    PRESERVES

For the crust, mix the graham cracker crumbs, sugar and cinnamon in a bowl. Add the butter and mix well. Press the mixture into 12 paper-lined muffin cups.

For the filling, combine the cream cheese, sour cream and sugar in a mixing bowl and beat until smooth. Beat in the eggs and vanilla. Spoon into the prepared muffin cups. Bake at 350 degrees for 16 minutes. Cool to room temperature. Chill, covered, in the refrigerator.

Remove the paper liners carefully and place the tarts on dessert plates. Garnish with sour cream and berries.

You may freeze these tarts. Let stand for 1¹/2 hours at room temperature before serving.

Serves twelve

KEY LIME TART

Ginger Pecan Crust

1/2 CUP FINELY CRUSHED
    GINGERSNAPS
1/2 CUP FINELY CRUSHED
    GRAHAM CRACKERS
1/2 CUP FLAKED COCONUT
1/4 CUP FINELY CHOPPED
    PECANS
5 TABLESPOONS BUTTER
    OR MARGARINE, MELTED

Filling

4 EGG YOLKS
1 (14-OUNCE) CAN
    SWEETENED CONDENSED
    MILK
1/3 CUP KEY LIME JUICE OR
    LIME JUICE
1 1/2 TEASPOONS FINELY
    SHREDDED LIME ZEST

Whipped Cream Topping

1 CUP WHIPPING CREAM
2 TABLESPOONS SUGAR
1/2 TEASPOON VANILLA
    EXTRACT

Garnish

TWISTED LIME SLICES

For the crust, mix the gingersnap crumbs, graham cracker crumbs, coconut and pecans in a bowl. Add the butter and mix well. Press over the bottom and 3/4 inch up the side of a 9-inch springform pan. Bake at 350 degrees for 5 minutes. Cool to room temperature and chill, covered, in the refrigerator.

For the filling, whisk the egg yolks in a large bowl until pale yellow. Add the condensed milk, lime juice and lime zest and mix well. Spoon into the chilled crust. Chill, covered, for 4 hours or until firm.

For the topping, combine the whipping cream, sugar and vanilla in a chilled small mixing bowl. Beat at medium speed until soft peaks form. Spread over the tart. Store, covered, in the refrigerator. Garnish with lime twists.

To avoid uncooked eggs that may carry salmonella, use an equivalent amount of pasteurized egg substitute, or meringue powder, sometimes sold as powdered egg whites.

Serves eight

A Sterling Idea

Add an extra-festive touch to your dessert course by giving your guests *Chocolate-Dipped Spoons* with their coffee. It's a wonderful way to display a variety of silver patterns, and surprised guests will leave your party remembering this sweet idea.

To prepare Chocolate-Dipped Spoons, melt four 1-ounce squares of semisweet or dark sweet chocolate with 1 1/2 tablespoons heavy cream in a double boiler or a microwave set at Medium power. Add 1/8 teaspoon almond, peppermint or orange extract and stir to blend well. Dip each spoon into the mixture, coating the bowl and 1/2 inch up the handle; allow the excess to drip off. Place on waxed paper until set and freeze for 15 minutes. Place 2 ounces vanilla candy coating in a plastic bag and Microwave on Medium until melted. Cut off 1 corner of the bag and drizzle the coating over the spoons. Freeze until serving time.

A *Sterling Collection* is grateful to all the following individuals and businesses who generously gave their cherished recipes, ideas, expertise, and invaluable time. There are more than four generations of cooks represented here and countless number of calories consumed. Our deepest gratitude goes to all those listed here and to anyone we may have inadvertently failed to mention. Our deepest thanks.

The Memphis Cookbook Original Committee

EDITOR	CO-EDITORS	COMMITTEE CHAIRMEN	
Mrs. Archibald McClure	Mrs. Charles B. Dudley, Jr. Mrs. Nancy B. Cook	Mrs. Paul Gillespie—*Publicity* Mrs. George S. Miles—*Selection & Testing* Mrs. Marcus J. Stewart—*Distribution*	Mrs. Howard Willey, Jr.—*Promotion* Mrs. John McDonough—*Composition* Mrs. John Coulter Wycoff II—*Typist*

The Memphis Cookbook Contributors

Mrs. Dunbar Abston
Mrs. Ben C. Adams, Jr.
Mrs. Richard Alcott
Mrs. F. Pearson Allen
Mrs. F. Pearson Allen, Jr.
Mrs. J. Seddon Allen, Jr.
Mrs. D. Harbert Anthony
Mrs. Robert Z. T. Anthony
Mrs. Walter P. Armstrong
Mrs. Walter P. Armstrong, Jr.
Mrs. Albert M. Austin III
Mrs. William W. Aycock
Mrs. Eric Babendreer
Mrs. John F. Barbee
Mrs. Betty Barber
Mrs. Ernest M. Barber
Mrs. Malcolm G. Barboro
Mrs. J. N. Beley
Mr. Walter L. Berry
Mrs. W. Gorton Berry
Mrs. Arthur B. Birge
Mrs. Bill R. Bobbitt
Mrs. Millard M. Bosworth
Mrs. Armour C. Bowen, Jr.
Adele Brake, Cateress
Mrs. William T. Braun
Mrs. Carey G. Bringle
Mrs. John E. Brown
Mrs. Leo J. Buchignani
Mrs. Lemmon Buckingham
Mrs. R. P. Buckley
Mrs. Richard C. Bunting
Mrs. George S. Bush
Mrs. William E. Buxton
Mrs. D. A. Canale
Mrs. John P. K. Cavender
Mrs. William H. Chandler
Mrs. William C. Chaney
Miss Frances C. Church
Clara of the Hunt and
Polo Club, Memphis, TN
Mrs. Edward M. Cobb
Mrs. William D. Connor
Mrs. Edward W. Cook
Mrs. Everett R. Cook
Mrs. Jesse E. Cook
Mrs. Sam Cook

Miss Marjorie Cooke
Mrs. Pearl G. Cooper
Mrs. George A. Coors
Mrs. Daniel N. Copp
Mrs. Marion N. Crady
Mrs. Edward H. Crump
Mrs. R. Carl Dickerson, Jr.
Mrs. James K. Dobbs, Jr.
Mrs. Vaughan Dow
Mrs. Charles B. Dudley, Jr.
Mrs. George G. Early
Mrs. W. Jeter Eason
Miss Sadie Eilbott
Mrs. Henry Eisenbeis
Mr. Caswell P. Ellis
Mrs. A. H. Eskelund
Dr. C. Barton Etter
Mrs. Caruthers Ewing
Mrs. Sidney W. Farnsworth, Jr.
Mrs. Sidney W. Farnsworth, Sr.
Mrs. Stiles R. Fifield
Mrs. James H. Fisher
Mrs. Dore Fly
Mrs. W. L. Dean Ford
Mrs. Percy Galbreath
Mrs. W. D. Galbreath
Mrs. William D. Galbreath
Mrs. Jack Gates
Miss Frances Gibson
Mrs. Roy M. Gibson
Mrs. David T. Gildart, Jr.
Mrs. Paul T. Gillespie
Mrs. Jack S. Goltman
Mrs. Jack G. Gordon III
Mrs. Elizabeth Dantzler Grayson
Mrs. Henry H. Haizlip
Mrs. Edward A. Hall
Mrs. Emmett R. Hall
Mrs. Millard Hall
Mr. and Mrs. A. Arthur Halle
Mrs. James Harrison
Mrs. Ferd Heckle, Jr.
Mrs. Arch Henderson
Mrs. Adgate Ellis Hill
Mrs. Maryan E. Hill, Jr.
Mrs. Clarence Hinant
Mr. Hal W. Hirsheimer

Mrs. Tannen Hollenberg
Mrs. Andrew O. Holmes
Mrs. George Holmes
Mrs. Herbert Hood, Jr.
Mrs. Hal B. Howard
Mrs. John Huckabee
Mrs. Merrill Parrish Hudson
Mrs. E. Harrison Humphreys
Mrs. George W. Humphreys
Mrs. Robert Hussey
Mrs. James A. Huston
Mrs. Joseph Hyde
Mrs. M. A. Isaacs
Mrs. R. Frank Jackson, Jr.
Mrs. M. M. Jamieson
Mrs. Howard S. Jeck, Jr.
Mrs. Edwin Johnson
Miss Irene Johnson
Miss Stella Johnson
Mrs. Herbert P. Jordan
Mrs. Robert H. Jordan
Mrs. Wallace Jorgenson
Mrs. George Kendel
Mrs. John F. Kimbrough
Mrs. Charles M. Kortrecht
Mrs. E. Carl Krausnick
Mrs. W. E. Lamb
Mrs. Richard Leatherman
Mrs. William A. Leatherman
Mrs. Donald W. Lewis
Mrs. Putnam Livingston
Mrs. Henry Loeb, Jr.
Mrs. Joseph C. Lougheed
Mrs. J. W. MacQueen
Mrs. John D. Martin, Jr.
Mrs. John Maury, Jr.
Mrs. John M. Maury
Mrs. John M. Maury, Jr.
Mrs. Philip P. McCall
Mrs. Archibald McClure
Mrs. Donnell McCormack
Mrs. John McDonough
Mrs. Harold L. McGeorge
Mrs. Mary McKay
Mrs. Lewis K. McKee
Mrs. W. Lytle McKee
Mrs. Ed McKinley

Mrs. William M. McKinney
Miss Gloria McPhillips
Mrs. Erich Merrill
Mrs. George S. Miles
Mrs. Lovick P. Miles, Jr.
Mrs. Leslie Miller
Mrs. Sydney R. Miller, Jr.
Mrs. J. Pervis Milnor, Jr.
Mrs. Flora Mims
Mrs. G. Dugan Mitchell
Mrs. Charles W. Montgomery
Mrs. Hugh Montreath, Jr.
Mrs. Charles P. J. Mooney
Mrs. Harry S. Moore
Mrs. James W. Moore
Mrs. Gus Morgan
Mrs. Robertson G. Morrow
Mrs. William H. Morse
Mrs. St. Elmo Newton, Jr.
Mrs. William L. Nichol
Mrs. Frank M. Norfleet
Mrs. Charles P. Oates
Josie Oliver, Cateress
Mrs. Adele Orgill
Mrs. Edmund Orgill
Mrs. Allie Starke Patteson
Mrs. Hal Patton
Mrs. J. Hal Patton
Mrs. Solon A. Person
Mrs. Edwin B. Phillips
Mrs. George P. Phillips
Mrs. John Phillips III
Mrs. William G. Phillips, Jr.
Mrs. Frank Pidgeon, Jr.
Mrs. Charles L. Piplar
Mrs. Wallace C. Pollard
Mrs. Thomas R. Price
"Pump Room," Ambassador
East Hotel, Chicago, IL
Mrs. William L. Quinlen, Jr.
Mrs. Hubert K. Reese
Mrs. Cooper Y. Robinson
Miss Mary Robinson
Mrs. J. Warfield Rodgers
Mrs. Bliss Rogers
Mrs. Landon Rogers
Mrs. J. Tunkie Saunders

Mrs. M. Ames Saunders
Mrs. M. Ames Saunders, Jr.
Mrs. Paul E. Schroeder
Mrs. James E. Shannon
Miss Frances E. Shields
Mrs. C. D. Smith II
Mrs. Dayton Smith
Mrs. Stanford Y. Smith
Mrs. Walter Lane Smith
Mrs. William Leigh Smith
Mrs. Robert Smithwick
Mrs. Robert G. Snowden
Mrs. J. Spencer Speed
Mrs. Keith M. Spurrier, Jr.
Mrs. Maurice Edwin Stanley
Mrs. James E. Stark
Mrs. C. P. Stewart
Mrs. Marcus J. Stewart
Mrs. John A. Stout
Mrs. Joseph L. Tagg
Mrs. H. Duncan Taylor
Mrs. Robert L. Taylor
Mrs. Sadie Beck Taylor
Mrs. W. L. Taylor
Mrs. John H. Terry
Mrs. H. G. Thompson
Mrs. Lawrence K. Thompson, Jr.
Mrs. Phil Thornton, Jr.
Mrs. A. Barlow Treadwell
Mrs. Carrol C. Turner
Mrs. McKay Van Vleet
Mrs. Lilburne M. Vollmer
Mrs. St. John Waddell
Mrs. J. Richard Walker
Mrs. Dudley S. Weaver
Mrs. Henry Wetter
Mrs. Howard Willey, Jr.
Mrs. Willis H. Willey
Mrs. Frank L. Williams
Mrs. J. E. Williams, Jr.
Mrs. Edward G. Willingham
Mrs. Julian C. Wilson
Mrs. Louis E. Wittenberg
Mrs. James W. Wrape
Mrs. John Coulter Wycoff II
Mrs. Eugart Yerian
Mrs. L. C. B. Young

Party Potpourri

EDITORS

Mrs. Milton Lyman Knowlton, Jr.
Mrs. William Metcalf Prest

COMMITTEE

Mrs. John Apperson, Jr.
Mrs. John R. Bondurant
Mrs. Snowden Boyle, Jr.
Mrs. Ronald Byrnes
Mrs. William A. Coolidge, Jr.
Mrs. Floyd Humphreys Duncan
Mrs. Thomas Farnsworth, Jr.
Mrs. E. James House
Mrs. Allen Holt Hughes

Mrs. Kenneth O. King
Mrs. Charles McGee
Mrs. William Neely Mallory
Mrs. William G. Phillips III
Mrs. Richard Ranson
Mrs. James Guy Robbins
Mrs. Loyd C. Templeton
Mrs. Randolph Turner
Mrs. Spencer Wooten III

TYPISTS

Mrs. Frank A. Cianciolo
Mrs. Richard D'Alonzo
Miss Flora Maury
Mrs. Ralph Monger, Jr.
Mrs. John H. Shute, Jr.
Mrs. Edwin P. Voss

Party Potpourri Contributors

Mrs. Ben C. Adams, Jr.
Mrs. Newton Allen
Mrs. Robert G. Allen
Mrs. F. Pearson Allen, Jr.
Mrs. John Apperson, Jr.
Mr. Lawson Apperson
Mrs. Allen Applegate
Mrs. Robert Archer
Mrs. Donald G. Austin, Jr.
Mrs. Eric Babendreer
Mrs. Peter L. Ballenger
Mrs. John W. Barringer
Mrs. Frank G. Barton, Jr.
Mrs. John C. Barton
Mrs. E. Brady Bartusch
Mrs. H. K. Barwick
Mrs. Fred Beeson
Mrs. William M. Bell, Jr.
Mrs. Donald Berube, Jr.
Mrs. Charles Tiffany Bingham
Miss Lida Black
Mrs. William T. Black, Jr.
Mrs. Bill R. Bobbitt
Mrs. Robert Bonner
Mrs. Charles Boone
Mrs. Hyde Boone
Mrs. Hallam Boyd, Jr.
Mrs. Snowden Boyle, Jr.
Mrs. Denby Brandon, Jr.
Mrs. William J. Britton III
Mrs. James R. Brooks
Mrs. Annie F. Brougher
Mrs. C. Whitney Brown
Mrs. J. Hay Brown
Mrs. Marion Brown
Mrs. Robert C. Burleigh
Mrs. Robert C. Burleigh, Jr.
Mrs. Ronald Byrnes
Mrs. Bruce E. Campbell, Jr.
Mrs. Burch Caywood
Mr. and Mrs. H. Douglas Chism
Mrs. Arthur C. Clarke
Mrs. Everett R. Cook
Mrs. William A. Coolidge, Jr.

Mrs. Giles Coors, Jr.
Mrs. Dennis Coughlin
Mrs. Allen Cox, Jr.
Mrs. J. Lester Crain, Jr.
Mrs. Lawrence L. Crane, Jr.
Mrs. Wade Creekmore, Jr.
Mrs. Larry B. Creson, Jr.
Miss Jo Ann Cullum
Mrs. Jack Daly
Mrs. James M. Daly
Mrs. Alexander Dann, Jr.
Mrs. George R. Day
Mrs. William W. Deupree
Mrs. Richard Dixon
Mrs. Frank T. Donelson, Jr.
Mrs. Troy R. Douthit
Mrs. Vaughan Dow
Mrs. Charles B. Dudley
Mrs. Floyd Humphreys Duncan
Mrs. Kemper Durand
Mrs. Gary Falls
Mrs. Ernest W. Farrar
Mrs. John Finley, Jr.
Mrs. Daniel Fisher
Mrs. John T. Fisher
Mr. John J. Fitzmaurice
Mrs. William B. Fontaine
Mrs. Ned Mims French
Mrs. W. D. Galbreath
Mrs. William Galbreath
Miss Mildred Gates
Mrs. Chester Gelpi
Mrs. Everett B. Gibson
Mr. Edward Giobbi
Mrs. John D. Glass
Mrs. J. G. Gordon III
Mrs. Ralph Gore
Mrs. Claude E. Grimes
Mrs. C. Niles Grosvenor III
Grovel Road, St. Mary's
Episcopal Guild
Mrs. Harry B. Gunther
Mrs. Millard Hall
Mrs. Henry H. Hancock

Mrs. Gaither Hatcher
Mrs. Andrew Jackson Hays, Jr.
Mrs. Robert G. Heard, Jr.
Mrs. J. David Heuer
Miss Anna Marie Hill
Letitia Baldrige Hollensteiner
Mrs. Ralph Hon
Mrs. E. James House
Mrs. William Henry Houston III
Mrs. Allen Holt Hughes
Mrs. Cecil Humphreys
Mrs. Richard W. Hussey
Miss Margaret Hyde
Mrs. J. R. Hyde, Jr.
Mrs. J. B. Igleheart
Mrs. Frank Z. Jemison
Mrs. George B. Jett
Mrs. E. J. Johnson, Jr.
Mrs. Joseph H. Johnson
Mrs. Thomas F. Johnston
Mrs. Henry W. Jones, Jr.
Mrs. Leon Jones, Jr.
Mrs. Walk C. Jones, Jr.
Mrs. Herbert Jordan
Mrs. Herbert Jordan, Jr.
Mrs. Guy E. Joyner, Jr.
Mrs. Thomas Keesee, Jr.
Mrs. C. L. Kennedy
Mrs. Thomas Kimbrough
Mrs. John S. King, Jr.
Mrs. Milton Lyman Knowlton, Jr.
Mrs. Charles E. Kossmann
Mrs. Edward Labry
Mrs. R. Henry Lake
Mr. and Mrs. John Lary
Mrs. Harry W. Laughlin
Mrs. Edward J. Lawler
Mrs. Robert M. Leatherman
Mrs. George T. Lee
Mrs. Groom Leftwich
Mrs. Ted Lewis
Mrs. W. G. Logan
Mrs. W. G. Logan, Jr.
Mrs. Carruthers Love

Mrs. Charles Lowrance
Mrs. Robert Lowry
Miss Elizabeth Lynn
Mrs. Ross Lynn
Mrs. John E. Lyon
Mrs. B. Percy Magness, Jr.
Mrs. William Neely Mallory
Mrs. Raymond E. Manogue
Mrs. Vaughn Marshall
Dr. and Mrs. Benson Martin
Mrs. David B. Martin
Mrs. John M. Maury
Mrs. John M. Maury, Jr.
Mrs. James W. McClure, Jr.
Mrs. Barclay McFadden
Mrs. C. C. McGee
Mrs. Charles H. McGee
Memphis Dairy Council
Mrs. Rodgers Menzies
Mrs. Henry T. V. Miller, Jr.
Mrs. Howard S. Misner
Mrs. C. P. J. Mooney III
Mrs. James W. Moore
Mrs. J. T. Murff, Jr.
Mrs. Edward W. Newton
Mrs. Eugene R. Nobles, Jr.
Mrs. Lawrence L. Nobles, Jr.
Mrs. Herrick Norcross
Mrs. Robert E. Norcross
Mrs. Robert Norcross
Mrs. Charles P. Oates, Jr.
Mrs. Richard Ownbey
Mrs. J. Hal Patton
Mrs. John S. Phillips
Mrs. Eugene J. Pidgeon
Mrs. Charles L. Piplar
Mrs. James K. Polk
Mr. Robert R. Prest
Mr. and Mrs. William M. Prest
Mrs. T. Ralph Prichard
Mrs. Van Pritchartt, Jr.
Mrs. William Purdy
Mrs. James C. Rainer III
Red Apple Inn, Eden Isle, AR

Mrs. Charles D. Richardson
Mrs. Sydney Riddle
Mrs. F. Guy Robbins
Mrs. James Guy Robbins
Mrs. Mary J. Ryley
Mrs. J. Tunkie Saunders
Mrs. Harry B. Schmeisser, Jr.
Mrs. J. Fred Schoellkopf, Jr.
Mrs. Jack Shannon
Mrs. John H. Shute, Jr.
Mrs. W. Hamilton Smythe III
Mrs. Robert G. Snowden
Mrs. T. Grimes Snowden
Mrs. Philip Fox Southall
Mrs. William K. Stoddard
Mrs. Charles G. Swingle
Mrs. Fred Tarkington, Jr.
Mrs. S. Shepherd Tate
Mrs. Sherard Tatum, Jr.
Mrs. W. McDonald Thrasher
Mrs. John Hart Todd
Mrs. Thomas H. Todd, Jr.
Mrs. Thomas Todd
Mrs. Jerome Turner
Mrs. Randolph Turner
Mrs. Kimbrough Vollmer
Mrs. Edwin P. Voss
Mrs. Maury Wade, Jr.
Mrs. Robert P. Walters
Mrs. Roane Waring, Jr.
Mrs. Robert Donnel Warren
Mrs. Keith Lane Watson
Mrs. Alexander Wellford
Mrs. W. G. Wesche
Mrs. Ephraim B. Wilkinson, Jr.
Mrs. W. H. Willey, Jr.
Mrs. Byron Winsett
Mrs. Wallace Witmer, Jr.
Mrs. Fred C. Wolff
Mrs. Dale Woodall
Mrs. S. D. Wooten III
Mrs. James W. Wrape
Mrs. Hugh Wynne

EDITORS AND ORIGINATORS	COMMITTEE	ARTIST
B. Percy Magness, Jr.	Miss Minetry Apperson	Mrs. James W. Watson, Jr.
Robert D. Gooch, Jr.	Mrs. James H. Barton	
	Mrs. Kenneth E. Crocker	
	Mrs. J. Walker Hays III	
	Mrs. L. P. McVean	
	Mrs. Henry C. Pitts	
	Mrs. Harry G. Powell	
	Mrs. Bernard A. Rolfes, Jr.	

A Man's Taste Contributors

Tommy Adams, Jr.	Bullets Gillespie	Clyde Patton, Jr.
Pat Apperson	Trow Gillespie	Philip A. Perel
Bill Apple	Ed Giobbi	Henry C. Pitts (Bud)
William M. Apple	Dr. Ray Glotzbach	Henry C. Pitts, Jr.
Walter P. Armstrong, Jr.	Robert D. Gooch, Jr.	William D. Porter (Butch)
Bill Arthur	Robert Gooch	Harry G. Powell
Donald G. Austin, Jr.	Alan Mcl. Gordon	Robert Prest
James W. Baird	Henry Graeber	Robert Prest, Sr.
Ed Barnes	James P. Graeber	Jim Reeves
Jim Barton	Lewis Graeber, Jr.	Will Reid
Bob Bedford	Felix Greer	Dr. Richard J. Reynolds
Peyton Berry	John Grisanti	Haskins Ridens
William G. Boone, Jr.	Harry B. Gunther	Mark Robinson
Jim Bowen	William C. Harris, Jr.	James F. Ruffin
Cran R. Boyce III	Dr. A. Clinton Hewes, Jr.	Clarke Sanders
Winston Braun	Barry Hillyer	Reid Sanders
J. R. Brooks (Jim)	Andrew O. Holmes	Dr. Conley Hall Sanford
Gardner Brooksbank	Charles N. Hubbard, M.D.	Madison Ames Saunders, Jr.
J. Hay Brown III	Frank Huffman	Dr. Wilson Searight
J. Waldrup Brown, Sr.	Dr. Allen Hughes	Tait Seldon
Bev Buckingham	Tom Hunt	John Shute
Jon M. Buhler	Jim Hutto	John W. Slater, Jr.
Byron Burch	Frank M. Langford, Jr.	Charles F. Smith
William B. Burch	Bobby Lee	E. W. Smith, Jr.
Robert Canzoneri	George Leffler	Dr. Hugh Smith
Robert A. Carson	Percy Magness	John A. Stemmler
Mike Cody	Fletcher F. Maynard, Jr.	John St. John
Charles Custer	Bob McCarley	Harold C. Streibich
William M. Daniel	Phillip McNeill	George S. Sullivan, Jr.
Jim D. Davisson	Paul Mercer	David Swartzentruber
William K. Davisson	William S. Mitchell	Sherard Tatum
J. K. Dobbs, Jr.	Tom Monaghan	Lowell W. Taylor, Jr.
Mike Driscoll	LeRoy Montgomery	Roscoe Thompson
Jerald M. Duncan, M.D.	Clarence W. Moody	John H. Viser III
Jay Eberle	E. Walker Mulherin	Bill Wade
William D. Falvey	Lytle Nichol	Henri Wedell
W. Bowlyne Fisher, Ph.D	R. E. M. Nichol	Dr. Eph Wilkinson
J. W. Flowers	W. L. Nichol IV	Rick Winchester
Lew Frank	C. P. Oates, Jr.	Charles D. Winters
Marsh Gibson	Thomas F. O'Brien	Harvey Witherington

Nineteenth Century Architecture in Memphis and Shelby County, Tennessee

CO-CHAIRMEN

Helen Hays and Ginny Strubing

COMMITTEE

Buff Adams	Becky Deupree	Liza Kirk	Susan P. Robinson	Ainslie Todd
Deby Baker	Beth Elzemeyer	Mary Malone	Beanie Self	Jennifer Treadwell
Pam Bryce	Harriett Flinn	Linda Kay McCloy	Lou Slater	Sally Treadwell
Stephanie Cannon	Mary-Ann Gano	Martha McKellar	Linda G. Smith	Louise Tual
Nancy Chase	Marietta Haaga	Linda May	Robbie Smith	Cathy Turner
Penny Dart	Ann Hawkins	Maryan Mercer	Elise Stratton	Jenni Turner
Mary O. Davis	Jessica Heckle	Anne Miller	Ann Styron	Carol Watson
Blanche Deaderick	Mary Hewes	Snow Morgan	Mary G. Sullivan	Nora Witmer
Mary Deibel	Marilyn Hubbard	Robin Powell	Valerie Thompson	Lucy Woodson

Heart and Soul

CREATIVE DIRECTOR AND PHOTO STYLIST:
Nancy Wall Hopkins
DESIGNED BY: Mauck & Associates, Inc.
Graphic Communications
PHOTOGRAPHY: William Hopkins,
Hopkins & Associates
FOOD STYLIST: Kim Loughlin
FOOD EDITOR: Jill Johnson

Committees

COORDINATING BOARD

CO-EDITORS
Lisa Colcolough
Beth Ploch

EDITORIAL COORDINATOR
Helen Patterson

GRAPHIC DESIGN COORDINATOR
Virginia Curry

MARKETING COORDINATORS
Kelly Wells
Assistant, Lynn Koeneman

RECIPE COLLECTION AND INDEX
COORDINATOR
Lou Martin

TESTING COORDINATORS
Cynthia Cross
Kim Pitts

Chapter Chairs

APPETIZERS / BEVERAGES
Martha Hester

BARBECUE / GRILLING
Kim Blankenship
Jeanne Hollis
Nayla Nassar

BREADS / SAUCES / VEGETABLES
Harriet McGeorge

BRUNCHES / SALADS / SOUPS
Betsy Bell

DESSERTS
Kathy Adams

MEAT
Kim Blankenship

MENU / PASTA / SEAFOOD
Kathy Pitts

POULTRY
Susan Huffman

Committees

EDITORIAL COMMITTEE
Julie Barton
Cindy Flanzer
Mary Harvey Gurley
Kirk McClintock
Scott Sellers

GRAPHIC DESIGN COMMITTEE
Elisabeth Glassell
Julia Smythe

Marketing Committee Heads

ACCOUNT DEVELOPMENT
Karen Kearney

IN-LEAGUE PROMOTIONS
Terry Dillard
Sarah Walne

MEDIA
Ann Leatherman

SPECIAL EVENTS
Lynn Koeneman

MARKETING COMMITTEE
Sue Bartlett
Betsy Bell
Margaret Ann Brickey
Antoinette Cheney
Jennifer Goblirsch
Lisa Guyton
Jeannie Jones
Jennifer Jones
Becky Maury
Janie Mayfield
Susan Mays
Emily McKinney
Nancy Miller
Nayla Nassar
Debbie Patterson
Kathy Pitts
Jan Rochelle
Susan Schaefer
Allyson Stevenson
Mary Taliaferro
Holly Walters
Adele Wellford

Buff Adams
Connie Adams
Eileen Adams
Karla Adams
Kathy and Ben Adams
Lisa Adams
Sue Adams
Diane Adler
Laine Agee
Tricia Aiken
Ann Albertine
Ingrid Aldridge
Diana Allen
Jill Allen
Mrs. Richard Allen
Sally Alston
Susan Arney
Roberta Anderson
Dolly Angel
Merill Angelo
Wendy Ansbro
Lee Ansley
Minetry Apperson-Moore
Anne Dillard Arnold
Jennifer Atkins
Lisa Ayerst
Jeanne Ayres
Ruthie Baddour
Emily Bader
Debbie Bailey
Molly Bailey
Sharon Bailey
Margaret Barr
Gwynne Barton
Julie Barton
Steve Barzizza
Amy Baskin
Neely Battle
Ann Baxter
Bayou Bar and Grill
Perry Pidgeon Beasley
Terry and Jim Beaty
Betsy and Bill Bell
Lelia Bell
Jayne Berube
Ann Billings
Kathy Black
Kimberly and Earl Blankenship
Karen Blockman
Dudley Boren
Mrs. Kimbrough Boren
Pat Boren
Anne-Clifton Bowling
Martha Bradon
Martha Brahm
Sarah Brandon
Suzanne Brandon
Margaret Anne Brickey
Dr. and Mrs. Louis G. Britt
William J. Britton III
Wanda Brooks

Carolyn Brown
Lisa Brown
Rosalyn and Daniel Brown
Debbie Campbell
Mrs. John W. Campbell
Mary Campbell
Pam Campbell
Steve Campbell
Sherry Cannon
Colleen and Larry Capstick
Diane Cardwell
Les Carloss
June Carlson
Beth Carson
Leslie Carter
Linda and Scott Carter
Shain C. Carter
Shari Carter
Cat's Compact Discs
   & Cassettes
Cellular One
Ann Chaney
Nancy Chase
Antoinette Cheney
Arden Cheney
Christ United
Methodist Church
Lee Ann Clark
Sue Clark
Jennifer Cleary
Mrs. Baxter Lee Clement
Janet and Duke Clement
Eleanor Cobb
Leigh Cobb
Lu Lee Cobb
Nancy Coe
Lisa and John Colcolough
Ann Cole
Cissy Wagner Coleman
Kathryn Coleman
Christina Collier
Meg Collier
John Colmer
Nancy Cook
Renee Cooley
Mrs. Bailey Cowan
Alison Cox
Lucia Crenshaw
Marion Crenshaw
Stacy Crenshaw
Elise Crockett
Nancy Crosby
Cynthia and Mike Cross
Georgia Cross
Kathleen Cruzen
Suzanne Cunningham
Virginia and Ed Curry
Anne Curtis
Betsy Daniels
Mary Helen Darden
Ann Davis

Cindy Davis
Leslie Davis
Leona DeMere-Dwyer
Laura Dickinson
Patty Dietrich
Terry Dillard
Lesley and John Dillon
Lisa Discenza
Mrs. John Dobbs
Sue Don
Michael Donahue
Mr. and Mrs. Frank Donelson, Jr.
Judy Douglass
Suzanne Douglass
Jack Dowell
Amy Drennon
Peggy Drinkard
Susan Driscoll
Camille Duke
Leslie Dunavant
Lee Duncan
Tammy Duncan
Laura Echols
Laila Eckels
Judy Edmundson
Mary Edwards
Robin Edwards
Wendy Edwards
Missy Elder
Margaret Eldridge
Katie Eleazer
Beth Elzemeyer
Barbara Evangelisti
Dianne Dupree Evans
Ann Everett
Janet Everett
Claire Farmer
Fascinating Foods
Dot Fisher
Jan Flanagan
Cindy and Andy Flanzer
Jill Flournoy
Mr. and Mrs. Robert E. Flowers
Sarah Flowers
Carey Folk
Debbie Folk
Margaret Fox
Martha Culvahouse Fox
Lysbeth Francis
Elise Frick
Kate Friedman
Lynn Fulton
Catherine Swann Funk
Rachel Gabrielleschi
Christine Gaiennie
Rebecca E. Galyon
Sara Bess Galyon
Allen Garner
Nanette Garrett
Virginia Gaston
Susan Gates

Kathy Gatlin
Sloan Germann
Jennifer Ghess
Kim Gibson
Elizabeth Gillespie
Elisabeth Glassell
Jennifer Goblirsch
Patti Gonzales
Patti Gooch
Debbie Gould
Elenia Gray
Betty Green
Virginia Watson Griffee
Mary Harvey Gurley
Ann Gusmus
Catherine Gwaltney
Marietta and Fletcher Haaga
Julia Halford
Gina Hall
Llewellyn Hall
Sally Halle
Bonnie Hallsmen
Melinda Hamilton
Becky Harkins
Penny Harmon
Sallie Harris
Tama Harris
Bonnie Hartzman
Peggy Harwell
Lynn Hays
Margaret Headrick
Susan Hedgepeth
Mary Ben Heflin
Mrs. John Heflin, Jr.
Don Heidel
Theresa and Bill Heidrich
Edith Heller
Gaye and Haywood Henderson
Janie and Jim Henderson
Marilyn Hergenrader
Sidney Herman
Dawn Herwood
Becky Hester
Martha and Bob Hester
Dot Hicks
Jan Hicky
Mrs. L. D. Hill
Jane Hobson
Karen Hoff
Stephanie Hoffman
Jeanne and Richard Hollis
Sarah Holner
Janie Hopkins
Pat Horn
Susan and Bill Huffman
Lily Humphreys
Tricia Hunt
Catherine Hutchison
Katie Hutton
Cathy Hynes
Betty Ingram

Macon Ivy
J. L. Jalenak, Jr.
Robert Jamison
Lora Jobe
Rosalie Johnson
Jeannie Jones
Lexie Jones
Louise Epps Jones
Rosie Jones
Sharon Jones
Stephanie Jones
Valerie Jones
Beth Kakales
Karen Kearney
Ann Keesee
Lisa Kellett
Emily Kennedy
Mary Kenner
Eliza Kirk
Janet Knight
Mary Joy Knowlton
Lynn and Brad Koeneman
Mrs. Leslie Koinberg
M'Leigh Koziol
Meta Laabs
Ann and Dudley Langston
Frances Larkin
Gail and Wis Laughlin
Leigh Lawyer
Ann Leatherman
Karie Leatherman
Shannon Lenoir
Judy Lindy
Carolyn Loftin
Gail Loftin
Cindy Lone
Diane Long
Teresa Long
Judy Looney
Cindy Love
Mary Loveless
Katherine Lucas
Nita Lux
Carol MacGregor
Becky Maddux
Lisa Mallory
Margaret Mallory
Julie Maroda
Jessie Marshall
Lou and Jerry Martin
Carol and Paul Mathis
Sue and Paul Matthews
Anne Maury
Becky Maury
Susan Mays
Mamel McCain
Tracy McCalmont
Mrs. James McCann
Alice McCarthy
Kirk McClintock
Chris McClure

Caroline McCool
Leslie McCraw
Elizabeth McCuddy
Catherine McCuistion
Tonya Lauck McDonald
Harriet McGeorge
Mrs. Harold L. McGeorge, Jr.
Dr. Tom McInish
Martha McIntosh
Emily McKinney
Gretchen Perkins McLallen
Kathy McLallen
Beth McLaren
Tina McWhorter
Meat Board Test Kitchens
Amy Meyers
Ann Miller
Cindy Miller
Julie Mills
Janie Mims
Emily Minor
Lisa and Bo Mitchum
Didi Montgomery
Frances Montgomery
Betty Moore
Bond Moore
Brandon Morrison
Cindy and John Morrison
Gray Morrison
Nancy Morrow
Jamie Moskovitz
Ann Mueller
Camille and Bill Mueller
Linda Mundinger
Thomas Murray
Micki Muse
Tootie Muse
Larry Nagar
Nayla and George Nassar
Dorothy Neale
Lynn Nelson
Carroll Nenon
Marilyn Newton
Nancy R. Newton
Melissa Neyland
Lissa Noel
Joyce Turner Nussbaum
Mrs. Joseph O'Brien
Sharon O'Brien
Sara O'Dell
Herbie O'Mell
Opera Memphis
The Orpheum
Blythe Patton Orr
Caroline Orr
Sarah O'Ryan
Dolores Ostrowski
Carita and Alston Palmer
Laine Park
Jill Parker
Toni Parker

Gwen Parrish
Helen and Keith Parsons
Debbie and Sam Patterson
Helen and Richard Patterson
Jan Patterson
Jean Patterson
Kathy Daniel Patterson
Scott Patterson
Mrs. Hal Patton
Dorothy Pennypacker
Joan and Tommy Peters
Amanda Phillips
Jennifer Phillips
Paige Phillips
Sandy Phillips
Sisty Phillips
Weetie Phillips
Missie Pidgeon
Pam and Will Pierce
Pier 1 imports
Piggly Wiggly Eastgate
Kathy and John Pitts
Kim and Johnny Pitts
Beth and Tom Ploch
Mr. and Mrs. Herbert Ploch
Mary Ellen Plyler
Molly Polatty
Pat and Jack Pope
Poplar Tunes Records
Lisa Popwell
Dixie Power
Jean Price
Anne Pringle
Meredith Pritchartt
Prop Room, Chicago
Eileen Prose
Jennifer Pthoes
Anna-Grace Quinn
Julie Raines
Dr. Richard Ranta
Ellen Rardin
Dr. Robert Reeder
Meg Reid
Alice Reilly
Dr. and Mrs. Richard J. Reynolds
Mike Richards
Peggy Riggins
Janice Robbins
Jessica Robinson
Jan Miller Rochelle
Peg and Ron Ross
Melinda Angel Rothenberg
Debbie Rouse
Royal Worchester Porcelain
Ginger Rucks
Liz Rudolph
Ruetenik Gardens
Mary Ruleman
Gwen Rush
Ann Rutherford
Rita Rutherford

Jodie Sain
Chris Sanders
Patty Satterfield
Stephanie Satterfield
Nancy Sawyer
Susan Schaefer
Kristy Schaeffer
Linda Schmitz
Andrea Schoppet
Katie Schumacher
Peter Schutt
Lacy Scott
Joyce Sellers
Kathy Sellers
Scott and Grey Sellers
Amelia Shannon
Kathy Shannon
Laura Shappley
Juli Sharp
Ruthann Shelton
Sandy Sherman
Catherine Shirley
Jane Slatery
Sally Smart
Bernie Smith
Mary and Dan Smith
Jennifer Smith
Mrs. Louise Smith
Margaret Ivy Smith
Mary Smith
Miriam Smith
Rhoda Smith
Mr. and Mrs. Ham Smythe III
Julia and Ham Smythe
Jack Soden
Center for Southern Folklore
Beatrice Spiegel
Milner Stanton
Kathy St. John
Linda St. John
Margaret Steffner
Peggy Stephens
Prudy Stevenson
Kitty Stimson
Andrea Stratton
Margery Stratton
Kathy Stubblefield
Sharon Tagg
Catherine Talbot
Cindy Taylor
Linda Taylor
Ruthie Taylor
Deborah Terry
Mr. and Mrs. Clint Thomas
Jennifer and Steve Thomas
Joan Thomas
Libby Thomas
Verena Thomas
Anne Thompson
Anne Tinker
Julie Tipton

Mr. and Mrs. George Carroll Todd
Ginny Towner
Kathleen Towner
Nancy Utkov
Marilee Varner
Paula Slack Verbois
Kate Vergos
Beverly Wade
Gigi Wade
Ginger Wade
Vicki Wadlington
Beth Waldrup
Jana Walker
Margaret Walker
Stephanie Wall
Jill and Jon Wallace
Rivers Rhodes Wallace
Sarah Walne
Marianne Walter
Danette Watkins
Beverly Weels
Katie and Peter Weien
Adele Wellford
Beverly Wells
Kelly and Geordy Wells
Lynn Wells
Anne Wesberry
Paul Wesphal
Carole West
Cheryl West
Mrs. William West
Gina White
Lesley Whitehead
Russell Whitehead
Sandie Whittington
Lisa and Bob Wilder
Courtney Williams
Barbara and Lewis Williamson
Carolyn Brown Wills
Laura Wininger
Caroline Winters
Ann Witt
Craig Witt
Karen Witt
Mary Ruth Witt
Randolf Witt
Randy Witt
Samantha Witt
Stacey Witt
Stephanie Witt
Mary and Malcolm Wood
Denise Wright
Eddie Wright
WSMS
Beth Yerger
Carol Yochem
Irwin Zanone
Toni Zanone
Paul Zilch
Wurzburg, Inc.

INDEX

A Sterling Collection

THE BEST OF THE JUNIOR LEAGUE OF MEMPHIS

Name
_____

Street Address
_____

City _____ State _____ Zip _____

Telephone
_____

Your Order	Qty	Total
A Sterling Collection at $22.95 per book		$
Heart & Soul at $21.95 per book		$
The Memphis Cookbook at $10.95 per book		$
Tennessee residents add 8.25% sales tax on total book purchase		$
Postage and handling at $5.00 per book		$
Total		$

Method of Payment: [   ] Check payable to Junior League of Memphis

[   ] American Express   [   ] MasterCard   [   ] VISA

Account Number _____ Expiration Date _____

Signature _____

To order, mail or fax:
Junior League of Memphis
3475 Central Avenue
Memphis, Tennessee 38111
Telephone: (901) 452-2151
Fax: (901) 452-1470
Website: www.jlmemphis.org

Profits from the sale of these books will be returned to the
community through JLM projects.

Photocopies will be accepted.

order INFORMATION